The New York Times

FEROCIOUS CROSSWORDS

The New York Times

FEROCIOUS CROSSWORDS
150 Hard Puzzles

Edited by Will Shortz

ST. MARTIN'S GRIFFIN ✹ NEW YORK

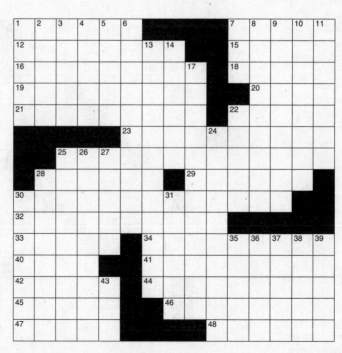

ACROSS

1 Like the reading on a thermometer
7 Molly who wrote "Bushwhacked"
12 Facility
15 Camp sight
16 Relations of Homer?
18 ___ river
19 Service for filmgoers
20 "I almost forgot . . . !"
21 Unwavering
22 Candlemas dessert
23 Private
25 "In a hurry, are we?"
28 Puts down, in a way
29 Forensic indicators of the presence of blood
30 Makes a fraidy-cat (out of)
32 Cause
33 Put two and two together
34 Modern marketing aid
40 Deborah who starred in "Tea and Sympathy"
41 Decorate
42 Give praise
44 Observatory doings
45 Strength of a chemical solution
46 Parts of mountaineering trips
47 Grippers
48 Having the most social anxiety

DOWN

1 Could be
2 Horse of the Year that won the 1949 Preakness and Belmont
3 "___ said many times . . ."
4 Soprano Albanese
5 Put in to start
6 Plant on after a wildfire, say
7 Post-O.R. post
8 Producing some clouds
9 Fit
10 Ones without a chance in the world
11 "Now listen!"
13 London locale of Prada, Dior, Gucci and Giorgio Armani
14 Wits
17 Gets ready for dinner
22 ___ de fraise
24 Olivia de Havilland film of 1949
25 Pilferers from ships and port warehouses
26 Alabaman who wrote the Best Novel of the Century, according to a 1999 Library Journal poll
27 Foreign title meaning "commander"
28 Part of Act IV where Marc Antony resolves to kill Cleopatra
30 "The first network for men" sloganeer, once
31 Overplayed?
35 Claudia ___, 1984 Olympic gold medalist in shot put
36 Tigres del ___, Dominican team that has won the Caribbean World Series ten times
37 "What have ___?"
38 Fall times: Abbr.
39 Meet away from prying eyes
43 ___-80 (classic computer)

by Raymond C. Young

2

ACROSS

1 Saucily titled best-selling diet book
12 Center starter?
15 It's featured in "A Night at the Opera"
16 Tickled user's response
17 Target of a school bully
18 ___-de-four (hemisphere-shaped vault)
19 3,280.84 ft.
20 Suspect's request: Abbr.
21 Internet site graphics
23 Chooses by divine election
25 Ice remover
26 Fig. on a 1970s dollar
27 Enamel strengthener
28 Has confiscated
31 Slip fillers
32 T preceder
33 Alliance
34 College bookstore stock
35 Château ___-Brion (Bordeaux wine)
36 Arizona senator Jon
37 Yes or no follower
38 Abundant sources
39 Lands in the Persian Gulf
41 John of Lancaster
42 Ben Jonson poem
43 N.F.L. salary limit
47 Like 1, but not I
48 Rest
49 Peggy of "The Dukes of Hazzard"
50 Not be generous with
51 They really ought to be kicked
54 Next to nothing?
55 Sign of stress?
56 An alien may take it: Abbr.
57 Is a hero

DOWN

1 University of Alaska Southeast campus site
2 Anne of fashion
3 ___ disco (European dance music)
4 Reactor overseer: Abbr.
5 Cry from a daredevil cyclist
6 1884 short story by Guy de Maupassant
7 St. ___ (Caribbean island, familiarly)
8 Wee, to a wee 'un
9 Foremost
10 Private dos?
11 They're straight
12 Yosemite Valley peak
13 Dumped
14 Harms
22 Manhattan's place
24 Every month has one
25 Ticket
27 Babes
28 Where Fredo Corleone gets shot
29 Passive-aggressive and the like
30 Common desiccant
31 Kentucky college
34 Body found high in the Andes
35 Where to hang, in slang
37 Steinbeck's birthplace
38 Apiece
40 No Yankee fan
41 Light into
43 Governor who helped found Ohio State University
44 Called out
45 UnitedHealth rival
46 Like plusher
48 Suffix with super
52 Explorer, e.g.
53 Dating letters

by Paula Gamache

ACROSS

1 Kind of year
6 Fed up with
13 It can be scary to go under this
14 Key
16 How some ashes are scattered
17 GQ figure
18 Detente
19 Dried out
20 Sound of contempt
21 Indication of feigned fright
22 They act on impulses
24 Like smooth-running engines
26 Black birds
27 Airport uniform abbr.
30 Mathematician famous for his incompleteness theorems
31 Pasta choice
32 One guarded in a soccer game
33 What you take when you do the right thing
36 Co-worker of Dilbert
37 Start of the Boy Scout Oath
38 Innovative chair designer
39 Innovative
40 Natural fluid containers
41 Backyard Jul. 4 event
42 Decision time
44 Fill-in
46 "Bummer"
49 Shortened word on a yellow street sign
50 It follows Shevat
51 "Win some, lose some"
53 Historic capital of Scotland
54 Concerning
55 "Outta sight!"
56 "Outta sight!"
57 ___ Landing (Philadelphia area)

DOWN

1 Pass superficially (over)
2 Free
3 Ditsy waitress player on "Mad About You"
4 Rough estimate
5 "Guilty," in a Latin legal phrase
6 Exchange of thoughts?
7 Burn up
8 Name of 11 ancient kings
9 Some collars
10 "White Flag" singer, 2003
11 Recovered from
12 Believed
14 Sign
15 Transition to a heliocentric model of the universe, e.g.
19 Late rocker Barrett
22 Auction
23 Draft
25 Nut cracker, perhaps
27 Negative sign
28 Requirement
29 They make connections
30 Fed
31 Sunburn preventer
32 Really take off
34 Winter coat?
35 Moon unit?
40 Minds
41 Drive nuts
42 Some sisters
43 ___ cat
45 Practices zymurgy
46 Toiletry brand introduced in 1977
47 Nail-biter's cry
48 Loud outburst
50 Long
52 Moon unit
53 Bribe

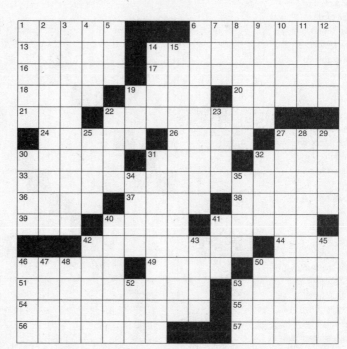

by Mike Nothnagel

4

ACROSS
1 Energize
10 Food fight noise
15 "Tom Jones" beat it for Best Picture of 1963
16 Singer Bryson
17 Cocky competitors might take them on
18 Star Steeler Stautner
19 Sends off again
20 Beards
21 Not do anything about
24 Basketmaker?
28 Touristy resort borough SE of Scranton, Pa.
32 Christmas story bad guy
33 Record holder
34 Writer of a five-volume Henry James biography
35 Curling setting
36 Young 'uns
37 Much unscripted fare
39 High hideaway
40 Acquisition before becoming a resident
41 Comparatively close
42 Fits behind the wheel?
44 1984 Cyndi Lauper hit
47 House style
52 Middle Eastern dish
53 Recording session starter
55 Stampless I.R.S. submission
56 Sultana-stuffed treat
57 Exercise
58 Showed

DOWN
1 Plymouth Reliant, for one
2 River at Rennes
3 Frames a collector might frame
4 "Citizen ___" (1992 autobiography)
5 Having turned
6 Monkey
7 Historically significant trial
8 Elementary school trio?
9 Univ. helpers
10 Small trunks
11 Achievement by 30-Down that had been previously unattained
12 Legal scholar Guinier
13 Rose's beau on Broadway
14 Web sites?
20 Take a bit of one's savings, say
22 Place of refinement
23 State second: Abbr.
24 Col. Potter on "M*A*S*H," to pals
25 Turned over
26 Mountain nymph
27 Title sport in a 1975 James Caan film
29 "Laborare est ___" ("to work is to pray")
30 Big name at the 1976 Olympics
31 1987 world figure skating champion
33 Having spokes
35 Leave in difficulty
38 Acknowledgment on a slip
39 Sterile
41 1994 U.S. Open winner
43 Sharp
44 Shoot out
45 Record holder
46 Designer Saab
48 View from Catania
49 Hands are under one: Abbr.
50 Steinbeck figure
51 Title
53 Many workers look forward to it: Abbr.
54 Golfer Woosnam

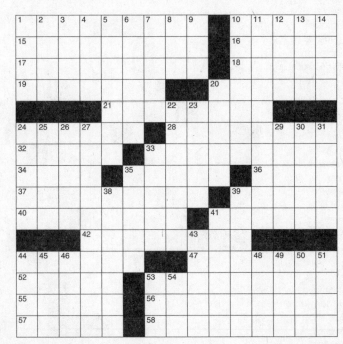

by Frederick J. Healy

ACROSS

1 Drawing power
10 Soigné
14 Suddenly
15 Stereo receiver button
16 Steely Dan hit of 1972
17 Villain in the Book of Esther
18 T formation participant
19 Cunning
21 ___ clue
24 Georgia ___ of "The Mary Tyler Moore Show"
25 Perishable fashion accessory
26 Certain sale item: Abbr.
28 Six-time All-Star third baseman of the 1970s Dodgers
29 Ancient fragrance
30 Molière comedy
33 Canadian equivalent of the Oscar
34 Filled treat
35 Properly filed
37 "Cooking With Astrology" author
38 "Moon Over Parador" star, 1988
40 "Buona ___"
41 You wouldn't sit for a spell in this
42 No-goodnik
43 Suffix with Darwin
44 "Divine" showbiz nickname
46 Motivational cries
49 Classic mystical book by Khalil Gibran
52 Brood : chicken :: parliament : ___
54 Asian title
55 Gulf of Taranto's locale
58 Echo, e.g., in Greek myth
59 Guided missile sections
60 ___ Atomic Dustbin (English rock band)
61 Have as an appetizer

DOWN

1 Not natural
2 Lengthwise
3 Skate
4 R.F.K. Stadium player, for short
5 ___ Carinae (hypergiant star)
6 Attire
7 Witless
8 Journal with an annual "Breakthrough of the Year" award
9 Where the wild things are?
10 Detective in "The Shanghai Cobra"
11 Pilgrims leave them
12 Not randomly arranged
13 Weigh
15 "The Amazing Race" host Keoghan
20 Thing on a ring
22 Earth, en español
23 Hard-to-break plates
27 18-wheeler
29 "Ode to Broken Things" poet
30 Beach house arrangement, perhaps
31 No longer gloomy
32 Rotary motions
33 Be a big success
34 Beta decay emission, sometimes
36 Subway Series locale, for short
39 Directorial demand
41 Thing with a life of its own?
44 TV star who said "Stop gabbin' and get me some oats!"
45 Prometheus Society alternative
47 Egypt's Mubarak
48 Honeybun
50 Potpie ingredients
51 Top-___ (leading)
53 Secure, in a way
56 & 57 Commercial entreaty

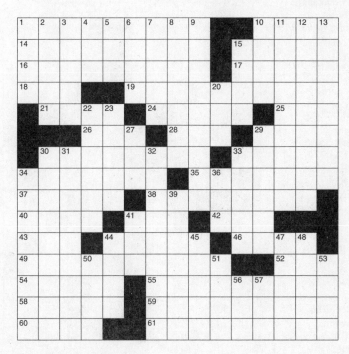

by Trip Payne

ACROSS

1 Mesoamericans of old
7 Mekong River sights
14 Warm up, as leftovers
15 Freak out
16 Small cavity, as around a cactus spine
17 Embassy issue?
18 Short cut
19 Look at a Playboy Club?
21 1993 rap hit with the repeated lyric "Bow wow wow yippy yo yippy yay"
22 Big name in sportswear
24 Concordat
26 Role in a Tchaikovsky ballet
27 Battlers, at times
29 Fiat headquarters
31 Part of many cultural venue names: Abbr.
32 Shrill
34 Long rides?
36 See 15-Down
40 Rise partly
41 Echelons
43 Gridiron stat: Abbr.
46 "Dead Souls" novelist
48 Platters' platters players
49 Indisposed
51 Gulf of ___, body of water next to Viet Nam
53 Bring down
54 Lit
56 Jim Beam and others
58 Univ. of ___, alma mater of Joe Namath and Bart Starr
59 Infer
61 Higher-priced
63 Put on the line, perhaps
64 Sportscaster with the catchphrase "Oh, my!"
65 Superlatively derogatory
66 Having one's feet up, say

DOWN

1 Mideast expert, maybe
2 Love all
3 Simon & Garfunkel hit after "Mrs. Robinson"
4 Affirmative action letters
5 ___ letters
6 Acclivitous
7 Adolphe with an instrument named after him
8 Not blasé
9 New York City transportation option
10 Hard-top
11 Sharp
12 Certain diet restriction
13 Influential one
15 Noted 36-Across passenger
20 Down
23 Actress Mazar and others
25 Rabbit food?
28 Christmas song favorite since 1949
30 Little terrors
33 Prefix with parasite
35 Letter finisher
37 Water towers?
38 Refuge
39 Father-and-son comedic actors
42 Comparatively bulky
43 Groups of plants
44 Entered
45 What a game plan leads to?
47 Romantic narrative
50 Helped, in a way, with "over"
52 Title role for Maria Callas in her only film
55 Mercury-Atlas 5 rider
57 Turned on
60 When repeated, an old-fashioned cry
62 ___ Lyman & His California Orchestra, popular 1920s–'40s band

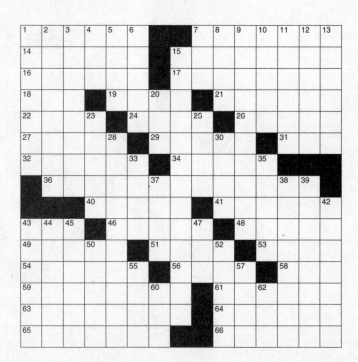

by David J. Kahn

ACROSS

1 War-torn Baghdad suburb
9 23-Across and others
15 One and only
16 Weather Channel topic
17 Fleet runner of myth
18 Key that doesn't include 58-Across
19 Up to
20 Ape
22 Habit
23 Shade shade
25 Biblical miracle setting
26 Powerful piece
27 Boarding spot
29 Call from home
31 1936 N.L. leader in slugging percentage
33 Brooklynese pronoun
34 Pilot's place
37 Part of Manhattan's Alphabet City
39 "Be honest"
41 Onetime Serbian capital
42 Show some spunk
44 Drops in a theater
45 Japanese model sold from 1970 to 2006
47 Meccan pilgrim
48 Some speakers
51 Abbr. before a date
53 Underhand?
54 Zip
55 Spotter's confirmation
57 Polit. label
58 It's almost a B, scorewise
60 Pilot's place

62 Apple application
63 Fancy haberdashery item
64 No longer in
65 Judge of films

DOWN

1 Henry Clay or William Jennings Bryan
2 It forbids religious tests for political office
3 Versatile actors may play them
4 Person found in a tree: Abbr.
5 Buck
6 Corinthian alternative
7 It might hold a couch potato's potato

8 Really hoped to get, with "for"
9 It can be drafted
10 ___ bark beetle
11 Stuck
12 11½" soldier
13 Online memo
14 Archaeologist David who found the lost Roman city of Kourion
21 Made some waves?
24 Word in some British place names
26 Put out
28 School exercises
30 Zoo de Madrid beasts
32 Shade of blue
34 Enter gently

35 Head of state known to his people as "Dear Leader"
36 "Of course"
38 Exclamations
40 Piehole
43 Swee' Pea's creator
45 Edmond Rostand hero
46 Calm
48 Composed
49 Dirección sailed by Columbus
50 British poet Tate
52 Track-and-field equipment
55 ___ dixit
56 1982 film title role for Bruce Boxleitner
59 Traffic stopper
61 School dept.

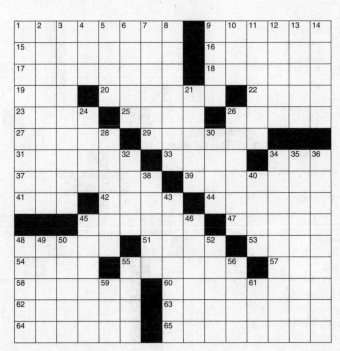

by David Quarfoot

8

ACROSS

1 Cash cache, often
10 No surprise outcomes
15 Happy
16 Liner threat, once
17 Well again
18 Spanish table wine
19 "Isaac's Storm" author Larson
20 Player of the Queen Mother in "The Queen," 2006
21 Determined to execute
22 Wanton type
24 Please, to Pachelbel
26 Shout across the Seine?
27 Green vehicle
29 They don't stay hot for very long
30 It's prohibited by the Telephone Consumer Protection Act of 1991
34 Vitamin A
36 Toughens
37 Kind of party
38 General equivalent
40 "New York City Rhythm" singer
41 Bills
42 "Turandot" composer Ferruccio ___
44 Sr.'s test
45 Dad's rival
46 Iranian filmmaker Kiarostami
51 Weasley family's owl, in Harry Potter books
53 Breaking sticks
55 Minnelli of Broadway
56 Biblical woman who renamed herself Mara
57 What kids might roll down
59 Old lab items akin to Bunsen burners
60 Darkroom equipment
61 Cold weather
62 Blues guitarist Vaughan

DOWN

1 They're seedy
2 Glass work
3 Ibid. relative
4 Crackpot
5 Hip-hop producer Gotti
6 "Vous ___ ici"
7 Peer group setting?
8 Peaked
9 Dwarf, maybe
10 Ill-prepared worker?
11 Drama honor
12 Potential canine saver
13 Personal manager
14 Playwright/painter Wyspianski
23 Direct
25 Mine shaft tool
28 Honeydew alternative
29 The Yasawa Islands are part of it
30 "The Thief's Journal" author
31 Review unfairly, maybe
32 Tops
33 Cheryl's "Charlie's Angels" role
35 ___ Raymonde, player of Alex Rousseau on "Lost"
39 Reels
40 Light white wine
43 Look askance
45 Rapture
47 Eight-time Grammy winner Mary J. ___
48 Patient one
49 Hyundai sedan
50 Fresh
52 It has an exclave on the Strait of Hormuz
54 Pomeranian or Dalmatian
58 Asian honorific

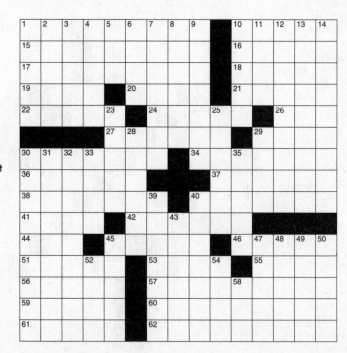

by Karen M. Tracey

ACROSS

1 Temper
8 Ape wrestlers
15 Be negative about
17 Hobbes in "Calvin and Hobbes"
18 Went to a lower level
19 Prefix with 6-Down
20 Body part above la bouche
21 Frames found in frames
22 Clubs: Abbr.
23 Señora's step
24 "A little ___ the mightiest Julius fell": Shak.
25 Actress Kimberly of "Close to Home"
26 Give away
27 Intimate
28 Tahini base
29 Well activity
32 Domesticates
33 Dramatic beginning
34 With 44-Down, Cajun dish with giblets
35 Polynomial components
36 Subject of some conspiracy theories
37 Prez's first name on "The West Wing"
40 Shot near the green
41 Little piggies?
42 Staff note
43 Ad follower
44 Playboy's plea?
45 She's dangerously fascinating
46 They're not easily overturned
49 Stereotypically smarmy sorts
50 Without much wind
51 Tickled the most?

DOWN

1 For one
2 Not at all sunny
3 Fit to be tried?
4 Id output
5 Mordant
6 Suffix with 19-Across
7 Going by
8 Fred of "The Munsters"
9 Hosts
10 Brand in a bathroom
11 Linguist Mario
12 Before being delivered
13 Unfrequented
14 Chief goals?
16 Smart
22 Exclusively
23 British meat pie
25 Actress Gray and others
26 ___-crowd (attendance booster)
27 Make like Pac-Man
28 They're bound to work
29 "Heads up!"
30 It stocks blocks
31 Less lax
32 Prepare for a shower, maybe
34 Foundations, often
36 Aggressively ambitious
37 Basso Hines
38 Hosts
39 "Who ___?"
41 August
42 Belarus's capital
44 See 34-Across
45 Longtime columnist who coined the term "beatnik"
47 Cloverleaf composition: Abbr.
48 Second-century year

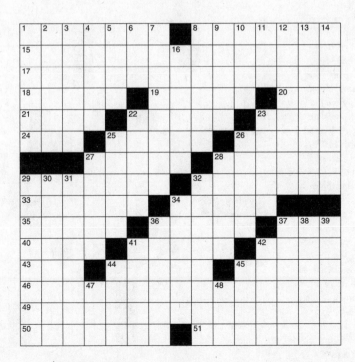

by Doug Peterson

ACROSS

1 "The County Chairman" playwright, 1903
4 Hershey brand
8 Tree
14 Spinners, for short
15 Southern university whose campus is a botanical garden
16 Interstice
17 Having the most pizazz
19 Cap and bells wearer
20 Convict
22 Meter readers?
23 Kind of batting stance
24 Nos.
25 Reddish-brown
26 Al-___
27 Big bang creator
28 Fifth qtrs.
29 Enforce the rules
31 Italian mine
32 Has as a foundation
33 "Rugrats" dad
36 Easter-related
37 "___ now the very witching time of night": Hamlet
38 Norm of "This Old House"
41 Coup d'___ (survey made with a glance)
42 Part of a moonscape
43 No longer under consideration
44 Tetris objectives
45 Like clayware
46 Seemingly silent types
49 Burns
50 "She's gonna blow!"
52 Ferris Bueller's girlfriend
53 Spoils
54 Where the utricle is
55 Like haunted houses, compared to ordinary houses
56 Good-looker
57 The Wildcats of the Big 12 Conf.

DOWN

1 Hoelike cutting tool
2 Neighbor of Somalia
3 Brewed drink
4 Checks
5 Two-time figure-skating Olympic gold medalist Protopopov
6 Snapped
7 Ecstatic
8 Option for wings
9 Smeltery input
10 Paraphrase, say
11 A jiffy
12 Decides
13 Least spotted
18 British P.M. when the U.S. Constitution was signed
21 Quality that's hard to express
22 Event for a king and queen
26 Father of Harmonia
27 Former Giant Robb
30 Gymnastics move
32 Butt
33 1979 film with sequels II to VI
34 Prophet of Thebes, struck blind by Athena when he accidentally saw her bathing
35 Drew on
36 Popular dish in an Asian cuisine
38 Guide
39 Zyzzyva, e.g.
40 Malignity
42 Protein-rich paste
44 Certain softball pitch
45 Amendment that prevents being subjected to double jeopardy
47 Oscar-winning French film director ___ Clément
48 Article in Hoy
51 Robert Morse Tony-winning role

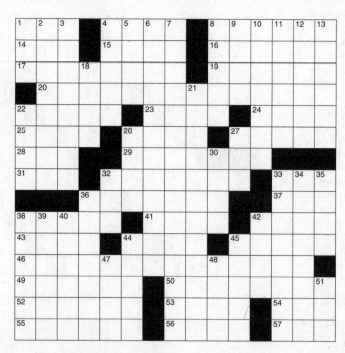

by Natan Last

ACROSS

1 Ways to get inside hip joints?
5 Results of compliments
14 Is not misused?
15 Invention convention
16 Bad mark
18 Opening on an environmentalist's agenda?
19 Wrangler rival
20 Pay stub data
22 Person after a lifestyle change, self-descriptively
23 How a goose acts
25 Charge
26 Lug
27 Modern vent outlet?
29 You may pass on these: Abbr.
30 Underachievers are not up to it
31 Old hippie hangout, with "the"
33 "Start doing your job!"
37 Restaurants are full of them
38 Singer Lennon and others
40 ___ shop
43 Where a tongue can be found
44 "No more!"
45 Rolls over, in a way
47 Probably will, circumstances permitting
48 Fragrant resin
49 Cornerback Sanders
51 Torch-lighting skater at the 1998 Winter Olympics
52 Africa's westernmost point
54 Woozy

56 Like some salesmen and preachers
57 Ryan of "Boston Public"
58 Brushes off
59 Club: Abbr.

DOWN

1 Laugh-producing game popular since 1958
2 What ethylene may be used for
3 Conspiring
4 Longtime Lakers commentator Lantz
5 Kind of resin
6 See stars?
7 Natives of Noble County, Okla.
8 Big ___
9 Short-term relationship
10 Alternate
11 Less apt to learn
12 Much-studied religious writings
13 May TV event
17 Ultra-obedient companions
21 Mugful, maybe
24 Measure that resulted in multilingual labeling on goods
25 They're hard to see through
27 Sect governed by the Universal House of Justice
28 Storyteller's pack
31 Web code
32 Attach
34 They're not positive
35 Turns over
36 Jersey workers
39 Pinch-hit

40 Abstract
41 Have a connection
42 Spare part?
44 Pitch preceder
46 Correct
47 It brings many people to church
49 Duel action?
50 "The Facts of Life" housemother ___ Garrett
53 Silent ___
55 1977 double-platinum album with the hits "Peg" and "Deacon Blues"

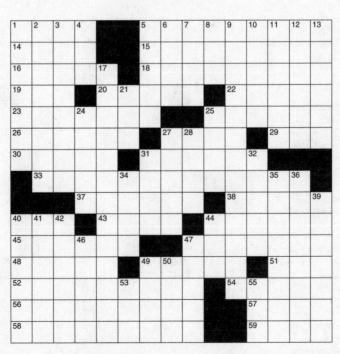

by Mike Nothnagel

ACROSS

1 It can really bite
8 Warrant
15 See 33-Down
16 Late afternoon, typically
17 Nothingness
18 Temporary
19 Former major-league pitcher ___ Seo
20 Home of Clarke College
22 Plymouth-to-London dir.
23 1847 tale of the South Seas
25 One of the losers in the War of the Pacific
26 Asian bowlful
28 Hot spots
30 Night table
32 Key word
33 Glut
34 Home of Waterloo: Abbr.
35 Growing problem?
38 Pick-up and drop-off point: Abbr.
40 French mathematician Cartan
41 Grain sorghum with stout, leafy stalks
45 Mush
47 It covers six time zones
48 Asked too much?
49 Sport
51 It's pulled by una locomotora
52 Plasma component
53 Foundation with ties
56 Dummy
57 It doesn't help much when it's cold
59 Where Mt. Suribachi is

61 Middle third of a famous motto
62 Puts down
63 Cicero, e.g.
64 Factor

DOWN

1 Latin American capital
2 Founding member of the Justice League
3 Prevent
4 Title robot in an Isaac Asimov short story
5 Lacking interest
6 Basic exercise routine
7 Fence-sitter's answer
8 Post codes?
9 Dish describer
10 Some prayers
11 Taxonomic suffix

12 Electrician
13 Standing out
14 Set right again
21 Built up
24 ___ wonder (athlete known for a single great play)
27 Hanna-Barbera character
29 Agent Gold on HBO's "Entourage"
31 Capo ___ capi (Bologna boss)
33 With 15-Across, sites for some corals
36 Come together
37 Kingston pop
38 Pinchpenny
39 Classic 1934 novel set in Prohibition-era New York City, with "The"
42 The moon has one

43 Madison Avenue types
44 Zipped by
45 Zip providers
46 Clever
47 Yarn variety
50 Bear
54 ". . . outrageous fortune, ___ . . .": Shak.
55 "Paradise Lost" illustrator
58 State with the lowest high point (345 feet): Abbr.
60 "The Gift of the Magi" hero

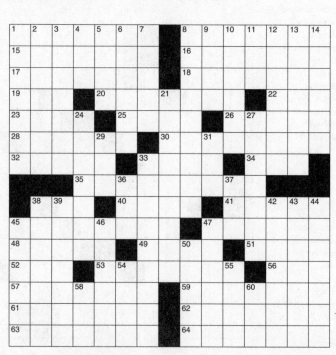

by Shannon Burns

ACROSS

1 Didn't take advantage of
9 Muscleheaded
15 He conducted the premiere performances of "Pagliacci" and "La Bohème"
17 Bands of holy men
18 Become one
19 Newspaper column separators
20 ___ Elliot, heroine of Jane Austen's "Persuasion"
21 Star of "Gigi" and "Lili"
22 Put on an unhappy face
23 Revival movement's leader?
24 Strand at the airport, maybe
25 Maker of Coolpix cameras
26 Stray animals don't have them
27 ___ Couple (yearbook voting category)
28 "Field of Dreams" actress Amy
31 1979 #1 hit for Robert John
32 More of the same
33 Like St. Basil's
34 Incite
35 Center
36 Yielding ground
39 Young cowboy in "Lonesome Dove"
40 Ships on the seafloor
41 Roofing choice
42 Compliant
44 Gives up responsibility
45 Sometime soon
47 One with a guitar and shades, stereotypically
48 Bathe in a glow
49 Most mawkish

DOWN

1 Game featuring Blinky, Pinky, Inky and Clyde
2 Photographer/ children's author Alda
3 Jelly seen on buffet tables
4 Kind of protector
5 Pennsylvania's Flagship City
6 Vet, e.g.
7 Stage actress who wrote "Respect for Acting"
8 Pilot light?
9 Treat badly
10 Albee's "Three ___ Women"
11 Vast
12 One that gets depressed during recitals
13 Awaiting burial
14 Files a minority opinion
16 Boxy Toyota product
21 Some emergency cases may be found in them
24 Steely Dan singer Donald
25 Some Degas paintings
26 1939 film taglined "Garbo laughs"
27 First African-born Literature Nobelist
28 "Is There Life Out There" singer
29 Titular mouse in a classic Daniel Keyes novel
30 1600 to 1800, on a boat
31 Big hit
33 Number to the left of a decimal point, maybe
35 Unlikely to rattle or squeak, say
36 Trifling
37 Political extremists
38 Roughly a third of the earth's land surface
40 Carthaginian statesman who opposed war with Rome
41 Rwandan people
43 Blue shade
44 Great literature's opposite
46 Possible work force reducer

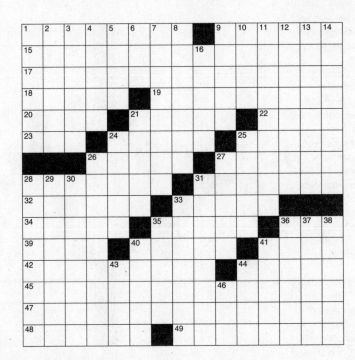

by Patrick Berry

14

ACROSS

1 Bristles
8 Post boxes?
15 Thinner option
16 Piece of silver, say
17 Lab tube
18 A lot of foreign intelligence intercepts
19 Relatively remote
20 Many-sided problems
21 Ready to be put to bed
22 "Rugrats" baby
23 Isn't O.K.
25 One of the Gandhis
26 Golden fish stocked in ornamental pools
27 Christening spot
28 Nottingham's river
29 Dirt
31 One protected by a collie
32 Patron of Paris
35 One making calls
38 Schubert's "Eine kleine Trauermusik," e.g.
39 Demand
43 Some apéritifs
45 Mother of Hyacinth, in myth
46 Hindu sage
47 Certain alkene
48 Incubator
49 Slew
50 Anti-ship missile that skims waves at nearly the speed of sound
52 Touch-related
53 Part of a special delivery?

54 Be quite enough for
55 Amscray
56 Hamlet, notably
57 Give a bad name
58 "On Your Toes" composer

DOWN

1 "The View," essentially
2 Home to Mount Chimborazo
3 Earthen casserole dish
4 Letting stand
5 Decayed
6 Put in up front
7 Skittish herd
8 Small, deep-fried pork cube
9 C_2H_4

10 Size up
11 Bait
12 Singer of "A Foggy Day" in "A Damsel in Distress"
13 Isn't very visible
14 Shooter that may be digital, for short
22 Caused to be scored, as a run
24 European Union member: Abbr.
26 Means of public protest
30 Was broad on the boards
33 Big Mac request
34 Real
35 Island entertainer
36 Kind of water

37 Nearest, to Nero
40 Lessen
41 One using a crib
42 They work the earth
44 Apply messily
49 __ Nurmi, nine-time track gold medalist in 1920s Olympics
51 Chowderhead
52 Peter or Paul, but not Mary
53 Picture producers

by Tony Orbach

ACROSS

1 Awfully accurate?
11 California wine center
15 Salade niçoise ingredients
16 "The company for women" sloganeer
17 Providers of exceptional service?
18 Neural network
19 With 50-Across, surmount
20 Turn out to be
21 Presidential middle name
22 Queen in a long-running comic strip
24 "What's ___?"
26 Pal
27 Disconcert
28 Strip alternative
30 Change from two to one
32 They might indicate hunger
33 "Centuries"
34 Where to find pop art?
37 Turns up
38 Start of some how-to titles
39 One who brings bad luck
40 Childish comeback
41 Some are manicured
42 NATO member: Abbr.
45 Boulogne-sur-___, France
46 Response of feigned innocence
48 Lose successfully
50 See 19-Across
52 Parry
54 Holder of many tracks
55 ___-Mints (Rolaids rival)
56 Singer of the 1967 hit "California Nights"
58 Incomplete picture?
59 Subject of the 2004 book "Dancing Revelations"
60 Jarrow's river
61 Outdoor toy that attaches to a garden hose

DOWN

1 Mil. V.I.P.
2 Eye component
3 Where I-25 and I-70 meet
4 Poet who won a Pulitzer for "The Dust Which Is God"
5 Prefix with directional
6 Shortening in the kitchen?
7 Level
8 Kinkajou's kin: Var.
9 1883 Maupassant novel
10 Dine, in Düsseldorf
11 Caper
12 Bit of kitchen wear
13 Execute exactly
14 Over, with "of"
23 Suffered a blow to one's pride
25 Magazine holder
29 Creation of 31-Down
31 See 29-Down
32 "Underboss" author Peter
33 Smythe of hockey
34 Cause of colonial unrest
35 "You don't say!"
36 Hide in the woods
37 It's out for a pout
39 Ruler of Scotland, 1567–1625
41 Hanks's "Apollo 13" role
42 "That's Amore" setting
43 Scented
44 Photo flaw
47 Papa Bear of the N.F.L.
49 Watch
51 What some people get caught on
53 Home of Davy Crockett: Abbr.
57 Title syllables in a 1961 Lee Dorsey hit

by Mike Nothnagel and David Quarfoot

ACROSS

1 Lard source
8 Service with a queue
15 G.P.S. receiver display
16 Explanatory tool
17 Uses a certain iron
18 Ousting
19 What flamingos often stand on
20 Reunion moniker
21 Vision de nuit
22 They travel by air
24 Part of some Muslim households
25 Ltr. recipient pinpointer
28 Candidate supporter, briefly
29 First to be admitted?: Abbr.
30 Frequent business traveler
33 Flow stopper
36 One who didn't say no?
38 Abbr. in some city names
39 They hang from the roof
40 Indications of good bowling
41 ___ Beach, Hawaii
42 What's left
43 Home to Al Jazeera
46 "Oh, right"
48 ___-Ude (Russian city on the Trans-Siberian Railroad)
49 Game intro?
50 Trust
54 An ace is a good one
56 Chin-wag
57 County west of Dublin
58 Some oilseeds
59 Subsequent
60 Things that wear well?

DOWN

1 Burkina ___
2 "East of Eden" twin
3 MTV segment?
4 South Dakota's ___ National Park
5 Robed ruler: Var.
6 Wear for rough outdoor activities
7 Some G.I. duties
8 Nostril
9 Chemical endings
10 Laddie's lid
11 Like some prints
12 Gallant
13 Donation declaration
14 Botanical nutrient conductor
20 Profanity
23 Atlanta commuting option
24 Afghan province or its capital
25 Mischievous
26 Sound of impatience
27 Some vacationers' acquisitions
29 One who might pick up toys
31 River formed by the junction of the Fulda and Werra
32 Amazed
33 Cordage material
34 Potent round
35 ___ Helens
37 Where you might get into a rut
40 Exotic estate
43 Faultfinder's concern?
44 Gridder Harper
45 Heads-down view
46 Like some bad goods: Abbr.
47 "___ sorry!"
49 Feelthy stuff
51 Space hog in a library
52 Israel's Weizman
53 Much ___
55 Sea bream, in a sushi bar
56 Birmingham-to-Montgomery dir.

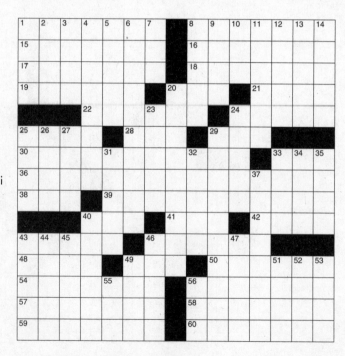

by Barry C. Silk

ACROSS

1 Product once advertised with the catchphrase "There's no step 3!"
5 Barely mention, as something one doesn't want to discuss
14 Putting regular gas in a diesel engine, e.g.
15 One abandoned at the altar?
16 Presently
17 In-house debugging
18 Person at the wheel?
20 Most useless
21 "Rich gifts wax poor when givers prove unkind" speaker
23 Snazzy
24 Region bordering Mount Olympus
26 Sound of a dropped scoop of ice cream
29 Certain chess piece, informally
30 Edward who created the Gashlycrumb Tinies
32 Coca-Cola creation
34 "Caribbean Blue" singer
35 Candle holders
36 Ford or Lincoln
37 "Notorious" setting
38 Dispel a curse?
39 Man
40 Unit of radioactivity
42 It protects car buyers
44 In the distance
46 #1 Beatles hit with the only known vocal contribution by Linda McCartney
47 Soft spread

51 Hang it up
52 1990 #1 rap hit that starts "Yo, V.I.P., let's kick it"
54 Mystical indicator
55 Bernard Malamud's debut novel
56 Ball boy?
57 One who refuses to shake hands, maybe
58 Poses

DOWN

1 Agitated
2 Like most 1950s recordings
3 Final Gene Wilder/Richard Pryor comedy
4 Neapolitan noblewoman
5 ___ volatile
6 Goes to bed, in Britspeak
7 Having a single purpose
8 Flowers named for their scent
9 Tendency toward chaos
10 "The Great God Brown" playwright
11 Classical art medium
12 Lifesavers, for short
13 Others
15 "___ Full of Grace" (2004 film)
19 Other
22 Pool owner's nuisance
25 Clodhopper
27 Continuously
28 Stop working
31 Push off
33 "Don't spread this around, but . . ."
35 Tightly embrace

36 Home for the Ojibwa and Cree
38 Split right before your eyes?
39 Go for a party, say
41 Wisconsin city that's home to S. C. Johnson & Son
43 Actress Streep
45 Picture writing, of a sort
47 Atoms
48 Comeback
49 Pullers of the chariot of Artemis
50 Practically unheard-of
53 Rule out

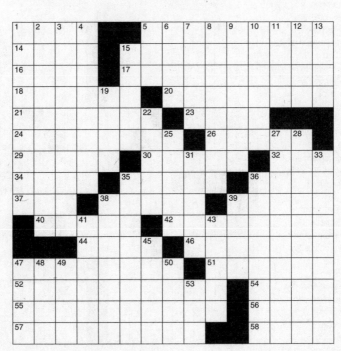

by Patrick Berry

18

ACROSS

1 Event in which teams may drink rounds during rounds
8 Comb
15 Minimal, with "of"
16 Broke out
17 Conditioning system
18 Dumpling dish
19 Defeats easily
20 Doesn't stick around
21 1920s birth control advocate Russell
22 Author of "Save Your Job, Save Our Country: Why Nafta Must Be Stopped — Now!"
24 Name on some euros
25 They may be found in sneakers
27 "___ vindice" (Confederacy motto)
28 Chairperson?
29 Big name in flight
31 Place on a game board?
33 A.L. home run champ of 1950 and '53
35 Mop holder?
38 Often-minimized thing
43 1966 Grammy winner for "If He Walked Into My Life"
44 Focus of some ball-handlers?
46 Spanish mistress
47 Samoan capital
48 Cuts into a pie, often
50 Field fare, briefly
51 Distribution slip
53 Ostensible composer of "The Abduction of Figaro" and "Oedipus Tex"
55 Summit goal
56 Bennett of the Ronettes
57 Worker doing a desk job?
58 Bright planet, sometimes
59 "First . . ."
60 Information technology subject

DOWN

1 Leader who claimed to have put a fatal curse on J.F.K.
2 Cousin of Ascii
3 Dances in waltz time
4 Some radio sources
5 "'___ Me?' I do not know you" (Emily Dickinson poem)
6 Get slippery, in a way
7 Zipped up
8 Boho-chic footwear
9 Big combo
10 Old marketplace surrounder
11 Saints, e.g.
12 Function whose domain is between -1 and 1
13 Not-so-new work crew
14 First pitcher to have defeated all 30 major-league teams
23 Having a better bottom?
26 Part of a certain kit
28 Wolf, e.g.
30 H.S. subject
32 Faster, maybe
34 "Danger!"
35 Enter for a spin
36 Bristly appendages
37 Words after "Whew!"
39 Least sensible
40 20th-century German leader's moniker
41 Part of a fin?
42 Load-bearing things?
43 Most intrepid
45 Man and others
48 Zagat contributor
49 Opinion opener
52 Italian province or its capital
54 Amts.

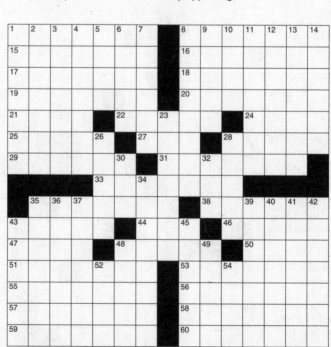

by Brendan Emmett Quigley

ACROSS

1. Climbing Mt. Everest, for Sir Edmund Hillary
12. 1937 Paul Muni drama
14. Art, metaphorically
16. History
17. Probe
18. Manfred ___ Earth Band
19. Roman well
20. Basic verse option
21. Whacked
22. Drum containers
23. Site of the siege of Candia
24. Feaster on frogs
25. Legato indicator
26. Coast Guard boat
27. It's hard to recall
29. Cowboys, but not Indians
32. Fitting decision?
33. Clued in, once
36. Stains
37. Delicate
38. Singer who is part owner of Forbes magazine
39. First name in fragrances
40. "In that area"
41. Cousin in a Balzac title
42. Cut across
44. Reminiscent of the 1890s
45. Census Bureau data
47. Only if it's worth the trade-off
48. London Zoo locale

DOWN

1. Remote access?
2. Stanford of Stanford University
3. Base runners?
4. Evidence that one is short
5. A foot has 305 of these: Abbr.
6. Like most medicine bottles
7. Things in rings
8. Big name in college guides
9. Old one, along the Oder
10. Holmes fought him
11. 50-50 proposition
12. Hand holding
13. Passing subject?
14. Artist Wyeth
15. Not lit
19. Princess Ozma's creator
22. Nine ___ (London district)
23. Bug zapper?
25. "Dear" ones
26. Under a quilt, say
27. Set off
28. "Blue II" painter, 1961
29. It's headquartered in the G.E. Building
30. Sacramento suburb
31. Global positioning system, e.g.
33. Bit of jazz improvisation
34. Bait
35. Meter makers
37. Certain inverse function
38. Get going
40. Honduras-to-Guatemala dirección
41. City bombed in the gulf war
43. Waste
44. Rockne protégé
46. Country singers England and Herndon

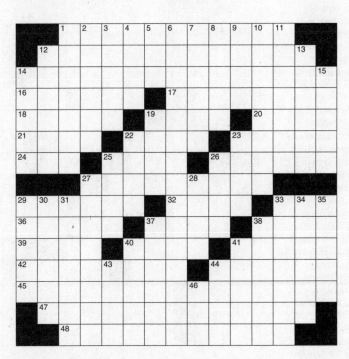

by Paula Gamache

ACROSS

1 Big flap on the road?
12 Yearbook div.
15 Song sung by Mehitabel in Broadway's "Shinbone Alley"
16 Treaty of Rome org.
17 Traitorous
18 First Fiesta Bowl winner: Abbr.
19 Since
20 Algorithm component
21 Forgoes a cab, say
23 Nickelodeon nut
24 Rijksmuseum subject
26 Ready to be driven
30 Poetry Out Loud contest org.
31 Vandals' target
32 Tennis's Ivanovic
33 Est., once
34 ___-Ball
35 Sketching
39 She's entertaining
41 Abba's "___ the Music Speak"
42 Subj. of the 2006 film "The Good Shepherd"
44 Identification aid in an obituary
45 Sponsoring publication of TV's "Project Runway"
46 Prefix with culture
47 The Danube flows through it
51 People in a rush
54 Host and winner of the 1966 World Cup: Abbr.
55 With 59-Across, it lasted from about 3500 to 1000 B.C.
56 Defeater of Schmeling in 1933
59 See 55-Across
60 Slogan ending
61 Dedicatee of "The Muppet Movie"
64 Flow checker
65 Dish with coddled egg
66 ___-Mère-Église (D-Day town)
67 Order of ants

DOWN

1 Prolific suspense novelist Woods
2 Soft, thin silk cloth
3 2006 Tony-nominated "Sweeney Todd" actress
4 1977 Steely Dan title track
5 They're often fried
6 Offended
7 Member of the 1960s Rams' Fearsome Foursome
8 Sports biggies
9 Insurance fig.
10 Cornelius Vanderbilt and Jay Gould
11 Cook, at times
12 Dangerous swimmer with an oarlike tail
13 Bathtub rings, e.g.
14 Deep-sixes
22 Card
25 Be in harmony
27 Bizarrely hellish
28 Aussie's place of higher learning
29 Mardi Gras, in the U.K.
35 Early-birds' opposites
36 Ride roughshod over
37 "Born to Be Blue" singer
38 Yield some
40 Lead-in to a sheepish excuse
43 Home to some fighters
48 Charles Darwin's ship H.M.S. ___
49 Ready to be driven
50 Steering committee's creation
52 Language in which "k" and "v" are the words for "to" and "in"
53 Kitchen gripper
57 It rises in the Cantabrian Mountains
58 Plaintiff's opposite: Abbr.
62 Beauty
63 Turncoat

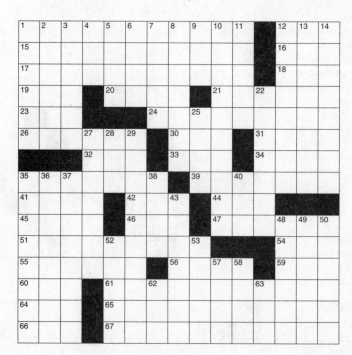

by Brad Wilber

ACROSS

1 Los Angeles's ___ Tower
7 They're seen around some cakes
15 Alaska's ___ Sound
16 Mom's partner?
17 What a toaster may hold
19 Un article défini
20 Modern greeting
21 Plays intensely, in jazz slang
22 It often follows something
24 Doesn't toss
26 Fictional upper class
27 One who doesn't chew the fat?
29 Find ___ for (match)
31 TV's Spike, once
32 Bygone explosive
34 Dungeons & Dragons race
36 "The White House," for "the presidency," e.g.
38 Abba's style
42 Rootless sort
44 Lombardia's capital
45 Game with sticks
48 Got on
50 Dog-___
51 It's mild and a bit nutty
53 Racket string material
55 Coll. elective program
56 Serenade, as the moon
58 Noted fifth-century invaders
60 Regrettable E.R. status
61 Refrain from eating pasta?
64 Where to find Nancy
65 Ready to receive visitors, say
66 Held
67 Beguiles

DOWN

1 One known for finger-pointing
2 "It's the truth"
3 M.I.T.'s class ring, familiarly
4 Long green box?
5 Informal demurral
6 Touch
7 Post-W.W. I conference site
8 Setting for some columns
9 It's issued to several stations, briefly
10 Caterpillar product
11 Caterpillar hairs
12 Raise, as a steering wheel
13 Long Branch Saloon visitor
14 Escorts after greeting
18 Earth personified
23 Bond girl player Shirley
25 Choose not to pick?
28 ___ bricks
30 Like some similarities
33 Preacher Beecher
35 Like the Julian calendar
37 Small, round sponge cake topped with fruit and whipped cream
39 Takeoffs
40 Direct
41 They may be received by free subscriptions
43 In up to one's neck
45 Interstellar matter
46 Some spuds
47 LaGuardia and others
49 "How then ___ he now see?": John 9:19
52 Twins' name at the 1984 Olympics
54 "I ___ Lover" (1979 John Cougar hit)
57 Bygone crown
59 Brain component
62 Gambler's place
63 Fort Worth sch.

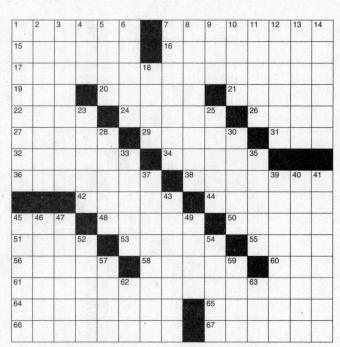

by Kevin G. Der

22

ACROSS

1 Judy Garland or Liza Minnelli
8 Sushi covering
15 It began in 1968, for tennis
16 Targetable
17 "Family Ties" family
18 Football coaching figures
19 Combustion product
20 Slice, say
22 An end to peace?
23 Behind
25 Bashkir's close cousin
26 Station
27 Weapon for Wonder Woman
29 TV shopper's option
30 Undertake
31 Dancer's guider, for short
33 Shallow
35 Big name in notebooks
37 Chips-in-a-can brand from Lay's
38 Silicon Valley city
42 Top of a slope?
46 Hill of law
47 Milieu for Katarina Witt
49 Old Testament patriarch
50 Romance, e.g.
51 Female demon
53 People's 1999 Sexiest Man Alive
54 City ESE of Utrecht
55 Botched salon job
57 OB, e.g.
58 Lagged
60 1970 western named for a fictional Texas city
62 Virtuoso
63 Ethnic conflict
64 Jacket option
65 Banderas's "The Mambo Kings" co-star, 1992

DOWN

1 Some four-wheelers
2 Popular costume party costume
3 "Groovy"
4 Undesirable result of making a pass?: Abbr.
5 High-ranking suits
6 ". . . then again, maybe I'm wrong"
7 Market for Microsoft
8 Bodybuilders' prides
9 "Scandalized Masks" painter, 1883
10 "But hark! __ comes gently to the door": Robert Burns
11 Weak
12 What a superscript in a text might refer one to
13 Chanel fragrance for men
14 Place for a trash can
21 Some four-wheelers, for short
24 Episcopal leader
26 Warning about people moving from side to side?
28 Speedy express
30 Wind
32 Piece of a candy bar?
34 "__ O.K."
36 Rodgers and Hammerstein refrain starter
38 Side
39 One way to do something stupid
40 Bit of cocoa?
41 Fool
43 55-Down with fiddles
44 Flipper
45 2003 sci-fi disaster film featuring a subterranean team of "terranauts"
48 Bimonthly magazine for environmentalists
51 Stimulating order
52 Met's lineup?
55 Blowout
56 Casual footwear, briefly
59 Bombed
61 Setting for an idyll

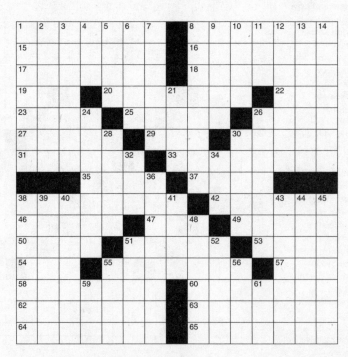

by David Quarfoot

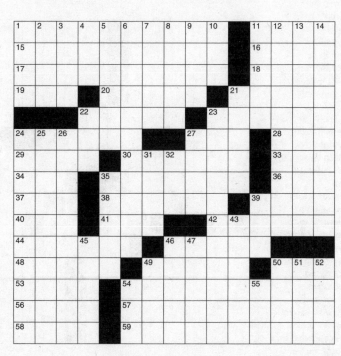

ACROSS

1 They have many sticking points
11 Falcons' grp.
15 1978 cult film with a mutant child
16 Gazetteer meas.
17 Sealing fans?
18 Oscar-nominated "My Man Godfrey" actor, 1936
19 One of four directions in 5-Down
20 Goes on
21 Mathematician ___ Henrik Abel
22 Brown and others
23 Hit the big time
24 Not too far away
27 Football Hall-of-Famer Huff
28 Where many pens are found
29 Corrida sticker
30 Pessimist in a Disney cartoon
33 Drop the ball
34 Letters between two names
35 One way to get through a wall
36 Severe
37 Checkers, e.g.
38 Uses as a bed
39 End of many a race
40 It involves many unknowns: Abbr.
41 Sched. maker, often
42 One using soft soap
44 "Michael Collins" title role player, 1996
46 Here and there
48 Fogs
49 Desk tray labels
50 Eye of the tigre?
53 At any point

54 Choice for intercontinental travel
56 Endow
57 Student activity
58 It is in Peru
59 Doll that was once a going thing

DOWN

1 Credit report damager, briefly
2 Prizes for top atletas
3 Curer
4 Tikkanen of hockey
5 It's no longer divided
6 Architectural subdiscipline
7 "___ Lady" (1971 hit song)
8 Meet preliminaries
9 Roadside stand units

10 Old sit-in org.
11 Lend-Lease Act provision
12 Zydeco instrument
13 Ease
14 Simplest, in math and logic
21 When doubled, what a rat does
22 Sound of disapproval
23 Home to San Quentin State Prison
24 Opening pair?
25 Tidy up the lawn, in a way
26 Marmalade ingredient
27 "I've been better"
31 Like some profs.
32 Cries for attention
35 "Stand and Deliver" Oscar nominee, 1988

39 Brewery fixture
43 Ban
45 Perfect Day maker
46 "___ of traitors!": Shak.
47 Gravy holders
49 Summer cooler
50 Taking care of business
51 Norwegian P.M. Stoltenberg
52 Immoderate indulgence
54 Where races are screened?: Abbr.
55 "They Like ___" (song from "Call Me Madam")

by Peter A. Collins

ACROSS

1 Yak
7 Nurses, say
15 Zebralike
16 Like anchors
17 Kept one's own counsel, online
18 Geographic feature depicted in the Armenian coat of arms
19 Some pointers
20 Big numismatic news
21 Steps away from
23 Forced, in a way
24 See 22-Down
25 "Obviously, Einstein!"
27 ___ legomenon (word or phrase used only once in a document or corpus)
29 Salt with the maximum proportion of element #53
35 Common soccer score
37 Star of "London After Midnight," 1927
38 1991 conflict between Slovenia and Yugoslavia
42 Western Australia, for example
43 Brawn
45 Compound with a double bond
46 Soft leather used in wallets, whose name derives from a place in California
51 Volkswagen Polo, for one
53 Shrub also known as Russian olive
55 One suspended in adolescence
56 Light mixer
57 Split personality?
58 As time expires, in a football game
59 Street lighting specialist?
60 Roller skate features
61 Claim of convenience, in ads or otherwise

DOWN

1 Jigger that jiggles?
2 Alternative to a water ski
3 Begin to blossom
4 Lance Armstrong foundation?
5 Hot month in Chile
6 Notable distinction for the planet Krypton
7 Where to go
8 Like some animal rights campaigns
9 Some DVRs
10 Legendary brothers in law
11 Sting
12 Spanish festival
13 Animal in Poe's "The Murders in the Rue Morgue"
14 Run-down
22 With 24-Across, number one position
26 Minute Maid drink brand
28 Earliest recorded Chinese dynasty
30 Quaker cereal
31 MTV reality show
32 Lifeless
33 Sets off
34 Parts of makeup kits
36 Flower of Pâques
39 Saw the light
40 Frogs and toads
41 One who stands for something
44 Composer of "Das Augenlicht," 1935
46 Tacitly acknowledge
47 First justice alphabetically in the history of the Supreme Court
48 First African-American golfer with 12 P.G.A. Tour wins
49 They go places
50 Plus
52 CD-burning software company that bought Napster
54 Neighbor of Ghana

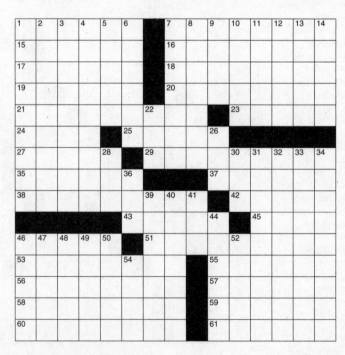

by Byron Walden

ACROSS

1 Pick up
8 Not as consequential
15 What seeds may be found in
16 A mouse may help you get there
17 Sprint competitor
18 Setting for TV's "Matlock"
19 Layer that scratches
20 Stadium snack
22 She, overseas
24 Time to burn?
25 Winter Olympics equipment
27 ___ Highway, old auto route from New York City to San Francisco
28 Overwhelms, with "down"
32 ___ Pacific Airways
34 Drag during the day?
37 Petroleum gases
39 Legalese adverb
40 Part of some complexes
42 Person lifting
43 "Symphony in Black" artist
44 Strike marks
46 Comics canine
47 Symbol of limpness
50 Symbols of authority
51 Where to order a cheesesteak "wit" or "witout"
56 Bully
57 Six bells, nautically
58 Reprimand lead-in
60 Patron saint of Palermo
61 Aid in picking things up
62 Make a point of
63 Brandy holder

DOWN

1 Where it's happening
2 Follows
3 W.W. II shelter
4 City area, briefly
5 "Last one ___ . . ."
6 Job-related moves, for short
7 Spectacle
8 Cousin of a flea market
9 Reading rhythm
10 Less error-prone
11 Its scores range from 120 to 180: Abbr.
12 Capital of Upper Austria
13 Major conclusion?
14 Coin on the Spanish Main
21 Ringleaders' nemeses
23 Be glued (to)
26 Not loco
28 His #13 was retired in 2000 by the Miami Dolphins
29 How much of genius is inspiration, according to Edison
30 Like typhoid bacteria, often
31 Gym shoes, e.g.
33 Referendum choice
35 Lukewarm reviews
36 Mountain ___ (Pepsi products)
38 Best substitute on the court
41 Bandar ___ Begawan, capital of Brunei
45 Some dips
47 Whippersnapper
48 "Silas Marner" girl
49 One of the Mercury Seven
51 Orch. section
52 Eager cry
53 Major start?
54 Tendon trouble
55 Subject of Nepalese legend
59 Mag founder of 1953

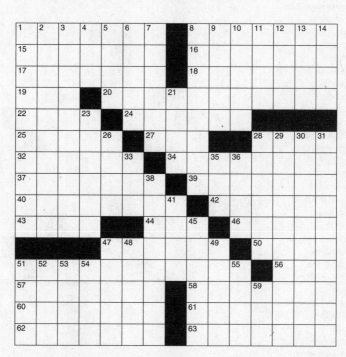

by Barry C. Silk

ACROSS

1 Scornful dismissals
7 Cause of temporary blindness
14 Symptom of nervous system impairment
15 Linebacker Brian banned from the 1987 Orange Bowl for steroid use
16 Sports stats specification
17 Current
18 They're often moved back in airports: Abbr.
19 It might help you dress in a shop
21 Ally's roommate on "Ally McBeal"
22 This, in Toulouse
23 Small wonder?
25 It begins near the end of winter: Abbr.
26 Associate of Thomas
28 Kind of rock
29 Mounts in a frame
30 Son and successor of Seti I
32 Relative of -ish
34 Very worried
39 Claptrap
40 Form of intimidation
41 Calls in the field
44 Warholian
46 "___ ask . . ."
47 Neighbor of Telescopium
48 Brand in the freezer section
50 ¹⁄₁₉₂ qt.
51 Point and click, e.g.
53 Cab opener?
54 Places
55 Series finale?
57 Affix, in a way
59 Caped combatant

60 Amusement park vehicle
61 Children's Bargain Town, today
62 Tuner's place

DOWN

1 Indy sights since 1911
2 Governor's guide
3 It's done in the slammer
4 Lines on planes
5 Youngest golfer ever to win a U.S.G.A. adult event (age 13)
6 Grandmother of Jacob
7 Seat of Shawnee County
8 Record finish?
9 In ___ (briefly)
10 Hounded

11 It's big in Rio
12 Swear
13 It may rain in these
15 Cinematic captain of Star Command
20 Start putting stuff away?
23 "___ him who believes in nothing": Victor Hugo
24 Words said when one's hand is shaky?
27 Old dynasty members
29 1965 march setting
31 It's heard on the Beatles' "Rubber Soul"
33 Runners' locations
35 Howled

36 Very wide, in a way
37 Result of getting even with someone?
38 Enter on the sly
41 Gov. Lester Maddox walked off his show in 1970
42 Reply to someone in denial
43 Fighting words?
45 Dupes
48 Rigel or Spica
49 1939 Wimbledon winner
52 Producers of some storage cells
54 The prodigal son is found in it
56 Part of many schools' addresses
58 Auction offering

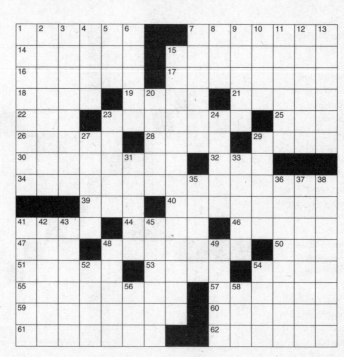

by Mike Nothnagel

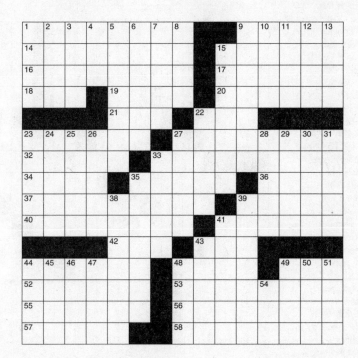

ACROSS

1 Abstainer's order
9 Ranger rival
14 Linden
15 Like some cubs
16 Accidental in the key of B or E
17 Olympic event since 1988
18 Call letters?
19 Retreats
20 Three-ingredient treats
21 Producer/director ___ MacNaughton of Monty Python
22 Peck parts: Abbr.
23 Beethoven's "Pastoral" Symphony is in it
27 Noted centenarian of 2000, familiarly
32 Chocolate snacks
33 Parent's ruse to hush noisy kids
34 Job preceder: Abbr.
35 Silence
36 Silk Road locale
37 Burger replacement
39 Key
40 One way to wax
41 Stands in line at an airport?
42 Member of an "ooky" sitcom family
43 Take in tentatively
44 Dash
48 Betray horror
49 Yamaha product, briefly
52 Title woman of a film that won the 1985 Camera d'Or
53 Dodger's dread?
55 Do borderline work?
56 Sleuth who "looked rather pleasantly like a blond satan"
57 Small pieces
58 Spellbinding "Batman" villainess played by Joan Collins

DOWN

1 Tynan player in "The Seduction of Joe Tynan"
2 Force
3 End of a loving trio
4 Huddled (with)
5 Places to make tracks
6 Unfulfilled duty
7 Rimes with "Blue"
8 Catch in pots
9 Band ensemble
10 1969 and 1974 Hart Trophy winner, familiarly
11 Number between drei and funf
12 About
13 Staying power
15 Largest tenant of Pittsburgh's tallest skyscraper
22 It often gets down
23 Réunion reunion attendee
24 German wine region
25 Poetic conjunction
26 2002 Denzel Washington drama
27 Pursuit
28 Contemporary of Agatha and Erle
29 Pair from a deck, maybe
30 Literally, "women's boat"
31 Board
33 Rare delivery
35 Guatemala's national bird
38 "Mmmm . . . Toasty!" sloganeer
39 It might get you backstage
41 Pecking order?
43 Miles of film
44 Old man
45 Modern home of ancient Medes
46 Feeding tubes?
47 Powerful D.C. lobby
48 Meat
49 When the Feast of Lots is observed
50 Periodic riser
51 Powerful engine
54 News inits.

by David Quarfoot

ACROSS

1. Not a very good drawing
11. Cache
15. A little red
16. Da capo ___ (Baroque piece)
17. Band with the 1982 platinum album "The Number of the Beast"
18. Fade
19. Honors
20. Thai relative
21. View from the back seat?
22. Wings
23. Certain code
25. Choreographer Lubovitch
26. Meas. of progress, at times
27. Labor secretary under the first George Bush
28. River past the ruins of Nineveh
30. Martin Luther's crime
32. Pluck
33. Get ready to take off
36. Singer whose 2002 song "Foolish" was #1 for 10 weeks
38. Runway topper
39. Cakes often made with ground nuts
41. Like some sires
43. Modern info holders
44. When Arbor Day is observed: Abbr.
47. Pound sound
48. Recent developments
50. Nebraska City's county
51. Cleaning target
53. Inclination
54. Central Florida Community College site
55. The other shoe, e.g.
56. Bean product?
58. Mordant
59. 10th-century exile from Iceland
60. Rosencrantz or Guildenstern
61. Upsetting types

DOWN

1. Joke indicator
2. Bygone New York daily, with "the"
3. Nonalcoholic beer brand
4. Twist things
5. Rolaids alternative
6. "An' singin there, an' dancin here, / Wi' great and ___": Burns
7. Like some chromium and arsenic
8. Base numbers, in math
9. Experiencing drunkenness
10. Charged
11. Cut
12. Test
13. Medium in a tube
14. It's hard to do this barefoot
23. Inner tubes, e.g.
24. Fountain requests
27. The Blue Demons of the N.C.A.A.'s Big East
29. Ranking nos.
30. "Pal Joey" lyricist
31. Standard
33. Burns overnight?
34. Two-part lake connected by the Strait of Tiquina
35. 1996 Emmy-winning role for Alan Rickman
37. Saves, e.g.
40. Unprotected, in a way
42. Put (on) gently
44. Connecting flight
45. Question answerer
46. Checks, as checks
49. Land in the Colosseum
50. Cousin of rust
52. Ancient denizen along the Caspian
54. ___ Rios Bay
57. Last in a series

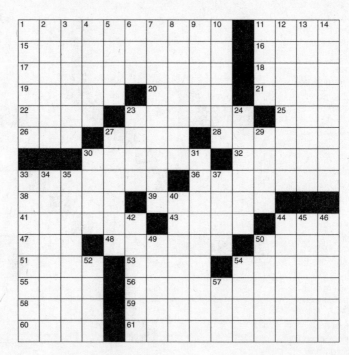

by Rich Norris

ACROSS

1 Is blessed with many assets, before "him" or "her"
16 Have cosmetic surgery, for example
17 Sources of government waste
18 Old Turkish title
19 Significant advancement
20 Excess
21 Awards for J. K. Rowling and P. L. Travers: Abbr.
23 Gulf of Aqaba city
24 Traps
25 Like an "eh," maybe
27 Something that shouldn't be left open
28 Three-time Masters winner Nick
29 Sensitivity
31 One of the Jackson 5
32 "___ votre permission"
33 Fix
34 Sounded smooth
37 1954 title role for Ava Gardner
41 Singer Jamie with the 2001 #1 country song "When I Think About Angels"
42 John
43 It's negative
44 D-Day sights: Abbr.
45 Heads of a tribe?
47 Turkish title
48 Onetime Bowie collaborator
49 Fired pitcher?
51 Void, in Vichy
52 Gross domestic product producer
55 Some bank offerings
56 At every point

DOWN

1 Connector in a song
2 Studies under a microscope
3 Most agile
4 Ham's place
5 Hardly hard questions
6 Roundish
7 Tops
8 Thug
9 Sometime ahead
10 Buzzards Bay, e.g.
11 Bags
12 Popular Volkswagen model
13 Carry out
14 "As You Like It" romantic
15 Leans against
22 Vast arid wastes
24 California city with a horticultural name
26 Carpenter's tool
28 Coca-Cola brand
30 But, to Brutus
31 See 38-Down
33 Progress in negotiations
34 Alternative to pasta
35 Straighten out
36 Double-check, as figures
37 Put in a bibliography, e.g.
38 Titles for Italian 31-Down
39 Words before "a Brain" and "an Animal" in book titles
40 Examine, in Exeter
42 Ohio city on Lake Erie
45 Nearing the hour
46 Book containing a prediction of the coming of the Messiah
49 Spring
50 Thomas ___, artist of the Hudson River School
53 Home of the Salmon River Mtns.
54 No score

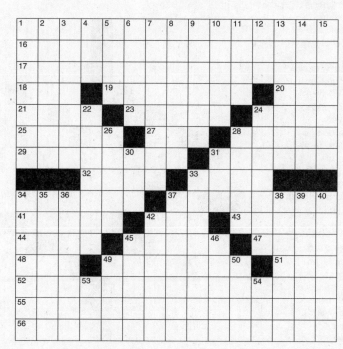

by Manny Nosowsky

ACROSS

1 Strip authority
8 Savanna bounders
15 Situation early in an inning
16 Target of some soccer kicks
17 Lipitor and such
18 State University of New York campus site
19 Like some glasses
20 1950s Dodgers pitcher ___ Labine
21 With 32-Down, end of an advertising pitch
22 Go-___ (certain motorized scooters)
23 Ink holder
24 French department that's home to the Chartreuse Mountains
26 G.I. hangout
27 Subject of a golf lesson
29 Pulitzer-winning historian Doris ___ Goodwin
30 Kennedyesque conquests
33 Player coached by Hank Stram
37 Mayor's introduction?
38 Wearer of a wraparound cloth called a lavalava
41 Like hoi polloi
42 With 14-Down, part of a U.S. political map
43 Customary start for Wimbledon singles finals
44 Finish, with "up"
45 Kegger cry
46 Bender
47 "___ sir . . ."
49 Tub handle?

51 A musician might pick it
53 TNT ingredient?
54 Bouts of madness
55 Kindergarten admonition
56 Sealed
57 Rested

DOWN

1 Like the grunge rock movement
2 Where Neptune can be found
3 Level
4 "America the Beautiful" poet Katharine Lee ___
5 Boo-boo
6 Gear impediment
7 M.O.
8 "Too rich for my blood"
9 Place for a comb

10 Top Médoc classification
11 Certain mail destination: Abbr.
12 More strung out
13 Not ahead
14 See 42-Across
20 Underwritten?
23 Recipe amount
25 Slovenian-born N.B.A. guard Vujacic
27 The Galloping Gourmet
28 "Watership Down" director Martin
29 Defend with focus, in football
31 Setting numbered in multiples of the square root of 2
32 See 21-Across
34 Admission of clumsiness

35 Polish
36 Palestinian fighters
38 Hospital patron
39 Stimulate
40 Big wheels
44 Winner of a record 82 P.G.A. Tour events
45 Ventriloquist's prop
48 Tennis's Nastase
49 ___ adagio (score direction)
50 Word with flute or horn
52 "Lucky Number Slevin" actress, 2006
53 Reciprocal action

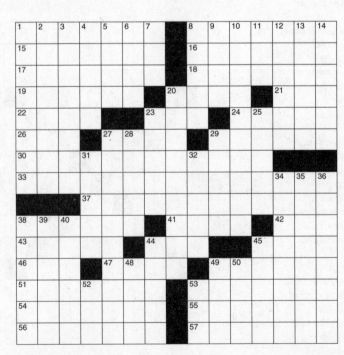

by Byron Walden

ACROSS

1 Films are shown in them
6 "This is how it's really done . . ."
15 Come to
16 Tried to buy
17 It's all for the Italians
18 Improving
19 Map line: Abbr.
20 Jazz singer Carmen
22 You can see right through it
23 Become balanced
25 Note taker?
27 Its closing duet is "O terra, addio"
28 "About Last Night . . ." co-star, 1986
31 Pay a visit to
33 Angel's garb
34 Domino with one spot
37 Lac contents
38 Florida island
40 Curse
41 Position
42 Common noun suffix
43 Blunder
45 "Please? Please? Please?"
47 Rival rival
48 What big eyes they have
51 Exam takers now, exam givers later
53 Café ___
54 Weekly World News newsmaker
56 Identify, informally
57 Site of Mackinac Island

60 Grammy-winning Baker
62 Begins to attack
63 Best by far
64 Retired
65 Sampling

DOWN

1 Certain rental arrangements
2 Spirits
3 Quit meddling
4 Put away one's groceries
5 Films can be shown in it
6 Pal
7 Main ingredient in tekka maki
8 Suffix with super
9 Cry of disgust
10 Former Japanese P.M. Shinzo ___
11 "That's easy"
12 Best
13 "Holy Sonnets" poet
14 Rear-___
21 Docks
24 Be off one's guard
25 "Indeed!"
26 "The Seven Year Itch" co-star
29 Ocean blue
30 High return
32 Moving
34 Americana symbols
35 Takeover
36 Bygone Montreal event

39 Cambodia's Lon ___
44 "___ Woman" (1972 #1 song)
45 "You ___ kidding!"
46 Theorized
48 Simmering
49 Freak out
50 Compare
52 Pass
54 Bust ___ (laugh hard)
55 It's handed down
58 Barkley was his V.P.
59 One might be involved in a hoax
61 Colt's fans?

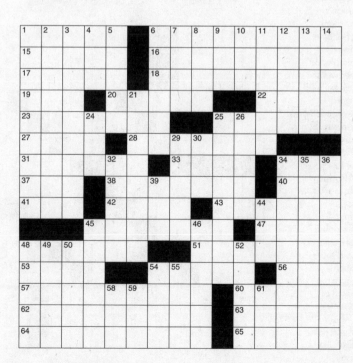

by Joe DiPietro

32

ACROSS

1 Lock combination?
5 "L'Orfeo" composer
15 It means everything
16 Compulsive shopper
17 Seeks change?
18 20th-century scandal
19 Poor devil
21 Court calls
22 List on a society calendar
23 Net sales
24 Product once advertised as "Ice-cold sunshine"
25 Bicycle pack
26 Birthplace of Sert and Miró
28 Bread
29 "A Clockwork Orange" instrument
30 "La Bohème" setting
31 "Casablanca" screenwriter Julius or Philip
35 Reason
36 Dawn observance
37 Like a raspberry bush stem
38 Folds
39 Giant perissodactyls
44 Lush sounds
45 Stooge
46 Like M, L or XL
47 Call upon
48 Spongelike cake
49 "I said that's enough!"
50 Mixture
53 Council of —, 1409
54 Visionary
55 Lassie creator Knight
56 Windy?
57 Check for letters

DOWN

1 Network seen in many homes, and not proudly
2 "The Last Don" sequel
3 Engaged
4 Boxing-related
5 Phototropic flier
6 It's next to nothing
7 "Love Jones" actress, 1997
8 City whose name is Siouan for "a good place to grow potatoes"
9 Engage in cabotinage
10 Drums
11 Heel
12 Western Sahara region
13 Flattering courtier who changed places with the tyrant Dionysius, in Greek legend
14 Blade holder
20 Only starting pitcher since 1971 to win a league M.V.P. award
24 Cousin of a kinkajou
25 Hamlet
27 "Such Good Friends" novelist Gould
28 Writer of the story upon which "All About Eve" is based
30 "Treasure Island" character
31 What "!" provides
32 Defensive structure
33 Person not easily budged
34 Makes ends meet?
35 Something well-placed?
37 It could end up in a fiasco
39 Powerful
40 Big maker of tires
41 Neoclassic style
42 Dark purplish blue
43 Whole
45 Dickens's "merry old gentleman"
48 Make a bundle
49 Cut to bits
51 Relief provider, maybe
52 Roar

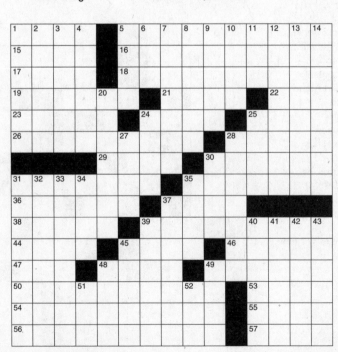

by Bob Klahn

ACROSS

1 Tournament organizer's concern
9 Cheerleaders' doings
15 Hombre-to-be
16 Bring out
17 Accurate
18 Simple inflorescence, as in a lily of the valley
19 Outlook
20 Zero-star movies
22 "___ Kommissar" (1983 pop hit)
23 Much often follows it
24 Future star athlete who debuted with the Rangers in 1989
25 Food described in Exodus
27 Start to salivate?
28 Dr. Seuss book, with "The"
29 He was succeeded by his archdeacon Hilarius
30 With 36-Across, shortsighted
33 Disappear, in a way
35 Run out
36 See 30-Across
38 Editorial cartoonist Hulme
39 Work out
40 She played Fantine in "Les Misérables," 1998
43 Piece of cake in school
45 Programming command
46 "T. J. Hooker" actor Adrian
47 Its logo is a goateed man in an apron

48 Two strikes?
50 In on
51 Plug
53 Landmark on the Chicago shoreline
55 Fill up with gas
56 Rushing home?
57 Some natural history museum attractions
58 Its dome was designed by Michelangelo

DOWN

1 No Oscar contender
2 Encounters
3 Is temporarily
4 Raps
5 ___ Sea (arm of the Arctic Ocean)
6 Thing that keeps track of the beat?: Abbr.

7 Long-running Art and Chip Sansom comic strip
8 In a manner of speaking
9 Dinar earner
10 Tissue material
11 Need to get hitched: Abbr.
12 Some are sweetened
13 Mountain, e.g.
14 Inflammation reducer
21 Fictional secret agent
24 Sequel title starter
26 ___ number (set theory concept)
28 Dirty
30 Iloilo's island
31 Helen Keller's "The World ___ In"

32 Response facilitator: Abbr.
33 Urged persistently
34 Come home more often than?
36 Views through a keyhole
37 Gunpowder alternatives
40 Masked official
41 Streaker with a tail
42 Trims
44 It's never right
46 "Shut your pie hole!"
49 Goons
50 1995–2001 House Judiciary Committee chairman
52 Irene's Roman counterpart
54 Kind of lounge

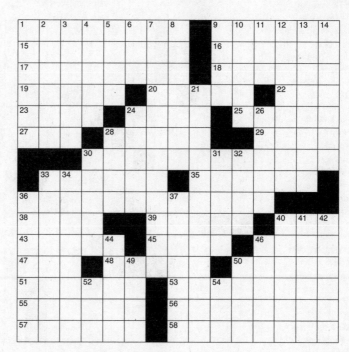

by Mike Nothnagel

ACROSS

1 Pound sign letters
5 Play for which Julie Harris won the 1952 Tony for Best Actress
15 Galley output
16 Title housewife in an Oscar-winning film
17 Burdens on some shoulders
18 Something damned with faint praise, in British lingo
19 Navigation abbreviation
20 Desktop accessory
21 Married woman abroad
22 Drones
24 Call
27 Old-style call to arms
28 Kind of skeleton or symmetry
29 Like Olympic races
30 Rhapsodize
34 Ending like -like
35 Torpedoes
36 Syst. of unspoken words
37 Song title followed by the lyric "Lovers say that in France"
40 Gunsmith Remington
42 Croaking flier
43 Cousin of the sandpiper
44 Titular author of two books of the Bible
47 Swedish soprano noted for her Wagnerian roles
48 Rent
49 Synthetic
50 Crispy Twister sandwich offerer
51 Like King Kong in New York City
55 Gila River native
56 Its currency unit is the ariary
57 Time of Ta'anit Esther
58 O. Henry specialty
59 Hyphenated figs.

DOWN

1 Techie's drawing
2 Cell's lack
3 Indicators of intelligence?
4 Sounds of feigned sympathy
5 Response to "Don't panic"
6 Green dragon and skunk cabbage
7 Letters on a new car sticker
8 Overseer of some practices: Abbr.
9 Summons: Abbr.
10 Hydrocarbon suffix
11 "Lose" at the office
12 Winner of six U.S. Opens
13 Splendid
14 Get into it, so to speak
20 Give a glowing review
23 More than upset
24 Replacer of the Humble brand in the early 1970s
25 Defeats narrowly
26 Process of nature by which all things change
28 One of a pair of biblical brothers
30 Max who wrote "Politics as a Vocation"
31 Some airplane runners
32 Douglas is its capital
33 High-occupancy vehicles?
35 Center of industry
38 Small, furry African climber
39 Gathered dust
40 Whimper
41 Timecard abbr.
43 Some like them hot
44 Jazz Age dance
45 Like much music
46 Home of "The Garden of Earthly Delights"
47 Plague
49 Buds
52 Rep.
53 Cavernous opening
54 Telepathy, e.g.
55 Announcement carriers, for short

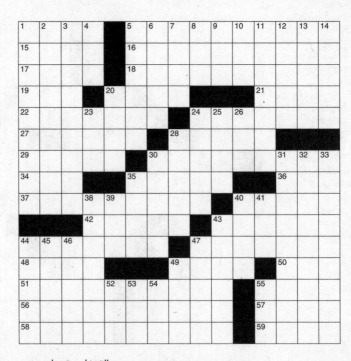

by Brad Wilber

ACROSS

1 Contest with many missions
10 Showing shock
15 Cousin of a Rob Roy
16 1972 top 10 hit that's seven minutes long
17 Heads
18 Purification process, briefly
19 Pays
20 Charge
22 Jagged
23 "And their lies caused them ___": Amos 2:4
24 1960s Elvis-style singer ___ Donner
25 Beach Boys title girl
27 Kid's query
28 "See It Now" producer of 1950s TV
31 Record listings?
33 Couple seen in a restaurant
34 Ice relative
35 Some fishermen
36 Sonata that might not sound good
37 Turn over
38 Leatherworking dyes
40 Philosopher Mo-___
41 Some Bosnians
42 Capital just south of the Equator
47 Famous finger-pointer's declaration
49 Torpedo
50 "Well, golly"

51 Declare "I will go no further than this"
53 ___ Wafers
54 Became a participant
55 George ___, longtime Cleveland Orchestra conductor
56 Unrevivable

DOWN

1 Gooey goody
2 One of a lot of workers?
3 Wind: Prefix
4 Rock on a stage
5 Bay Stater or Garden Stater
6 Some are rural: Abbr.
7 Took sides?
8 Egg holders
9 Came after
10 Tree with catkins
11 Iona College athlete
12 "Sheesh!," south of the border
13 One whose work may be catchy
14 "What's My Line?" participant
21 Bronchoscopist's view
23 Garage jobs
26 City where Chocolate Avenue crosses Cocoa Avenue
27 Magazine figure, for short
28 Kraft brand

29 Great Seal image
30 "I Wish" rapper ___-Lo
32 Kazan Cathedral locale
33 Paper parts
34 I.R.S. data: Abbr.
36 Still "well," but not beyond
39 Undermines
41 Diamond datum
43 Anarchic
44 Ammonia derivative
45 "Lost" actress Raymonde
46 Without a break
48 1994 Jodie Foster title role
49 "Jubilee Trail" novelist Bristow
52 ___ Z

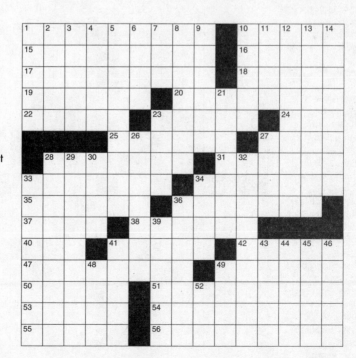

by Barry C. Silk

ACROSS

1 On the other side
8 Painter ___ del Sarto
14 Interestingly folded sheet
15 Guru residences
16 Nectar collectors
17 Soup vegetables
18 Friction reducer
19 Put together
21 Certain spread
22 Richard's love in "Bleak House"
23 Storm
24 Full of activity
25 Uses a chaise longue
28 Film with the Oscar-nominated song "Papa, Can You Hear Me?"
30 PC key
31 Still O.K. financially
33 Cunning in a practical way
35 Some Ivy Leaguers
37 Computer command
38 Recuperative drinks
42 Right-leaning, you might say
46 Anita Baker's "Same ___ Love"
47 Anthologized, e.g.
49 Bargain
50 Morgan ___ (King Arthur's half-sister)
52 American ___ (Southwest plant)
54 Virtuoso
55 Not-so-strong oath
56 Ante, say
57 Bond component
58 Two, in a way
60 "Mutiny on the Bounty" locale
62 Heads
63 Painter tutored by Titian
64 Ill-tempered
65 Like many Bedouins

DOWN

1 Fashion world exclamation
2 Vain about
3 Game played on a sloping field
4 Arch type
5 For example
6 Hinder
7 Consternate
8 Old symbols of royalty
9 Goal-oriented grp.
10 Needs a washer, possibly
11 Gatling gun sound
12 How one might stare into space
13 Maintains
15 Knuckles under
20 Passes the time?
24 Tips
26 ___ Classical Library, 500+ volume series begun in 1911
27 Amount expressed in K
29 Half-human "Star Trek: T.N.G." character
32 Slate alternative
34 Conseil d'___
36 "Wine, Women and Song" composer
38 Doesn't deviate from
39 Henry II's wife
40 "Fa la la la la la la la la," e.g.
41 Stinger?
43 Dead Sea Scrolls material
44 "Where Have All the Leaders Gone?" author
45 Where William (the Refrigerator) Perry played college football
48 Cat burglars' no-nos
51 Hock
53 ___ Gay
56 "___ makes suffering contagious": Nietzsche
57 First razor with a pivoting head
59 Poetic contraction
61 "What a nightmare!"

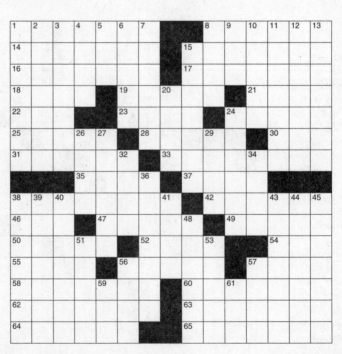

by Patrick Berry

ACROSS

1 Terrifying tales
12 Org. that called '60s strikes
15 One might have a stunt double
16 Egyptian ___ (cat breed)
17 Bit of ballistic evidence
18 Market figure, briefly
19 Weber per square meter
20 Certain fund-raiser
21 Organization originally called the Jolly Corks
22 Philanthropic focus
24 Buddy-buddy
25 Where many lives are expended
29 Bat shapers
30 Computer connection
31 Some cameras
35 The 10 in 10/20: Abbr.
36 The lower 70s, say
39 Ricky Nelson's "___ Late"
40 Builder of a hanging nest
41 Home of Utah Valley State College
42 Kir ingredient
44 Some believers
46 Projecting bit of architecture
47 Jib used to give a boat more speed
50 Coloring
51 Designer Kenneth
52 Rush
57 "Oklahoma!" bad guy
58 It often includes surround sound
60 Suffix of some cyclic compounds
61 One who may do a wire transfer
62 A multiple of CLI
63 Chips and such

DOWN

1 Shakespeare's own?
2 Feel eager
3 Plural suffix with urban
4 Moon marking
5 "Doonesbury" journalist Hedley
6 Not at all recent: Abbr.
7 Something to project
8 "Such a tragedy"
9 Poisons
10 Actress Morelli of "The Leopard," 1963
11 Div.
12 Predawn period
13 Potential reputation ruiner
14 Secondary arrangements
21 Fill up on
23 Trappers with pots
24 Simon & Garfunkel's "El Condor ___"
25 Yellowish-orange spread
26 Rummage
27 It tells you where else to look
28 One passing notes?
29 1960s TV western
32 British record giant
33 You might take stock in it: Abbr.
34 Certain character sketch
37 It's not light work
38 French pronoun
43 Word in a 27-Down
45 Park with great care, e.g.
47 TV marine
48 Provide a seat for
49 Like lace
51 Mixer option
53 Cousin of a guinea pig
54 Axiom ender
55 Alternative to cedar
56 Flying piscivores
58 Not squaresville
59 Crowd-thrilling hits: Abbr.

by Jim Page

38

ACROSS
1 Ledger no.
5 Painter Fouquet
9 Dance of African origin
14 Suspensions
16 Aquafina alternative
17 Antarctic environmental concern
18 It might be jewel-encrusted
19 Family in 1980s news
20 Falafel seasoners
22 It's hit with a pinky
24 Be a part of, as a film
25 Nixon adviser Nofziger
26 Blessing
29 Like some vino
32 Nixon creation of 1970: Abbr.
34 "The Cosby Show" actress Alexander
35 Rudy's coach in the 1993 football film "Rudy"
36 Preferred seating, for many
38 Top suit?
39 Decongestant brand
41 Mogul
42 Oenological category
43 Source of some big waves
45 John __
47 Stop up, in a way
48 Gulf states
53 Kept charging shots, say
55 Back together, for now
56 "The Red Tent" author Diamant
57 Indie rock band whose name is Spanish for "I have it"
59 Finger
60 Bump in the road?
61 Not nodding
62 Lake craft
63 Spare in a boot

DOWN
1 Venetian balladeer's topic
2 Gull
3 Dalmatian, e.g.
4 Citrus tree
5 16th-century founder of Scottish Presbyterianism
6 Jagged-edged
7 Bother
8 Caledonian contradictions
9 Bit of securing hardware
10 One whose idea may be taking off
11 1980s TV show or 2006 film
12 In the raw
13 Santa ___ (meteorological phenomena)
15 Pathetic
21 "Israfel" writer's monogram
23 Classic game with 13 categories
27 Professional helper, for short
28 Part of French Indochina until 1949
29 Freshness
30 Work on it began in Rome in 1817
31 Hebrew or Phoenician
33 Really warped
36 More than happy
37 Stock
40 It's just north of Nauru
42 Assaying aid
44 Booking letters
46 Make an impressive delivery
49 Meat grinder
50 Commodore competitor
51 Peak southeast of Bern
52 Boredom indicator
53 Hard to find in Latin?
54 Longtime West Virginia senator
58 War on Poverty agcy.

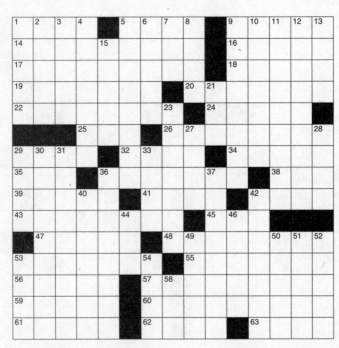

by Karen M. Tracey

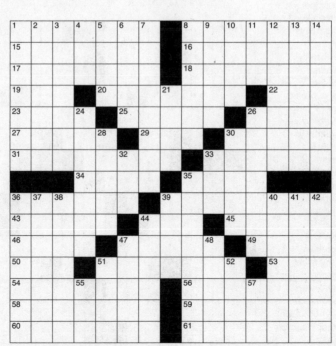

39

ACROSS

1 Steam room alternative
8 "Yo!"
15 Dodge
16 His last novel was "Chloe Marr," 1946
17 Cellar's opposite
18 Technicolor
19 See 34-Across
20 Most clowns
22 Word of approval
23 Emerson said intellect annuls it
25 "The West Wing" actor
26 Jazzman Saunders
27 He called the U.S. vice presidency a "most insignificant office"
29 Marzo to marzo, e.g.
30 Sculpt
31 Like some griddles
33 Read syntactically
34 With 19-Across, domain of civics, in brief
35 Multifaceted things
36 Noisy complaint
39 Alternative to Friendster or MySpace
43 Bit
44 Military grp.
45 Old sticker
46 Bank guard?
47 Places to develop one's chops?
49 Bundle of nerves
50 It can be double-sided
51 Tasty triangles
53 Back-of-airline magazine feature
54 Gather
56 Water-skiing need
58 Quiet
59 Merchant whose customers click
60 Blogger, e.g.
61 Cause of some blushing

DOWN

1 Elated person after Super Bowl III
2 Tree of the laurel family
3 Santiago skipper
4 Constitution lead-in
5 Flies
6 Flies
7 More than friendliness
8 Signal, in a way
9 Some crime scene evidence
10 Many former senators and governors: Abbr.
11 Yes or no follower
12 Assassins
13 Frazzle
14 Like many blooms
21 One may be sent in an e-mail
24 Typography measure
26 Chocolate treat
28 She wrote of Topsy
30 Transport over sand?
32 Nature
33 Muscle mag topic
35 Parts of some Bach suites
36 Crush holder that's crushable
37 Visionary
38 Not neat
39 Island that Truman wants to go to in "The Truman Show"
40 Range of some fitness tests
41 Pump numbers
42 Big fish, maybe
44 "The Mickey Mouse Club" regular __ Tracey
47 Opposite of agitato
48 Truth from long ago?
51 She co-starred in "Gangs of New York," 2002
52 Dominion
55 Designer born in Guangzhou, China
57 Chinese author __ Yutang

by Kevin G. Der

ACROSS

1 Places such as Anatevka in "Fiddler on the Roof"
8 Helper after a crash
14 Big syrup maker
15 Designer of a stained-glass window in the U.N. building
16 Together
17 Holy Roman Emperor, 855–75
18 Shot
19 Architectural starting point
21 Jacket locales: Abbr.
22 Dreaded victimizer of Charlie Brown
26 Old activist org. revived in 2006
27 As a companion
28 Newsman Roger
30 Turning point?
31 Smart
32 Moves briskly and easily
36 Star of the 1970s detective drama "Harry O"
37 ___ Hargreaves, first woman to complete a solo climb of Everest, 1995
38 ___ hold on
39 "McSorley's Bar" painter
40 Great depression?
41 One of the Bobbsey twins
44 Torch song subject
47 Int. generators
48 Site of a much-visited mausoleum
49 World of Warcraft participant, e.g.
50 Cardinals' wear
53 Elegant fabric

55 Caused to disappear over time
56 Grateful person's reply
57 Want to know
58 Jumper's cables?

DOWN

1 Swindlers, in slang
2 One of two sides of a story?
3 Political essays
4 Popular perfume
5 1979 novel, 1983 film and 2002–07 TV series
6 Place for woolgathering?
7 Signs
8 Go-go dancer's tip holder
9 Fontaine contents
10 Film special effects, for short

11 Distant stars?
12 Motto of a 1950s grass-roots movement
13 "We'll give a long cheer for ___ men" ("Down the Field" lyric)
15 Chuck wagon bell sound
20 Prompt delivery
23 Not natural
24 Of a university's relationship with its surroundings
25 They're stranded in the body
29 ___ St. James, first woman to be named the Indy 500 Rookie of the Year, 1992
31 "Relâche" composer
32 Functioned as

33 Intimate
34 Terrifying thing to be thrown into
35 Rimsky-Korsakov's "The Tale of ___ Saltan"
36 Not much at all
38 Four and four, say
40 Crime syndicate sobriquet
41 Dieter's request, perhaps
42 Photographer who was the inspiration for "Funny Face"
43 Shape-shifting Greek god
45 Land of Wahhabis
46 Unexpectedly potent
47 Holder of bird food?
51 Bamboozled
52 It's inspired
54 Main ingredient in taramasalata

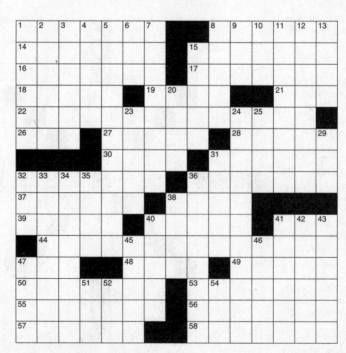

by Mike Nothnagel

ACROSS

1 Blister
7 Dr. Seuss story setting
15 "Anyway, after that . . ."
16 Parting words
17 Fop in "The Wind in the Willows"
18 Memorable "Marathon Man" query
19 Réunion, for one
20 One of a French literary trio
22 National Do Not Call Registry org.
23 1987 Costner role
25 Like a wet blanket
26 Cross
27 Untagged
29 Bush league?
30 Reddish-brown gems
31 "If you shoot at mimes, should you use a silencer?," e.g.
33 Plane part
34 Celebratory cry
35 Literally, "art of softness"
39 Animation bit
40 Popular teen hangout, once
41 Drives away
44 Item on a vine
45 Doesn't spoil
46 Fifth state to ratify the Constitution: Abbr.
47 Study aid?
49 Where you can find hammers and anvils
50 Beginning and end of 20-Across's motto
51 Philosopher who coined the phrase "the best of all possible worlds"

53 Muscle strengthened by a pulldown exercise, in brief
54 1989 film set in an inner-city high school
56 Cheese type
58 Like some airport purchases
59 Charm
60 Spirits
61 Boot

DOWN

1 It was shipwrecked in 1964 somewhere in the South Pacific
2 Crime family name
3 Bore witness (to)
4 Le Duc ___ (Nobel Peace Prize refuser)
5 Bucket of bolts
6 ___ a high note
7 Have in prospect
8 "Quiet!"
9 Constellation with the star Betelgeuse
10 Kerry and McCain, e.g.
11 "Grey's Anatomy" hookups
12 Good-for-nothin'
13 Stolen
14 Builds up
21 Doctor often seen on writers' bookshelves
24 Element used to make semiconductors
26 Potential buyer's question
28 Destroyers of many castles
30 Three-time Emmy-winning game show host
32 Zero

33 Mac
35 Title girl in a 1958 hit by the Playmates
36 Historic mission
37 Crime family
38 Popular boxing venue
40 Military construction crew
41 Burns
42 Lie low
43 Like postmidnight TV shows
44 Furniture cover
47 Art class
48 Played out
51 Converted housing
52 Man-to-man alternative
55 U.N.'s home
57 Word with weather or world

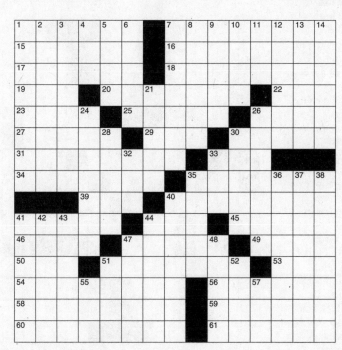

by Patrick John Duggan

ACROSS

1 One taking a shot
8 Worthless stuff
13 Exposed
15 Mideast royal name
16 What some patches provide
17 Second in court?: Abbr.
18 Like a family man
20 First volume heading starter
21 "To you, Antonio, ___ the most": Shak.
22 Old Testament book: Abbr.
23 Pitch between columns
28 Ending for some gases
29 More likely to be fresh
30 Second
32 Cy Young had a record 815
34 One of the Blues Brothers
35 "Just watch me!"
36 Sticker
37 Counterpart of "pls"
38 What most couples try to have together
43 Slow runner in the woods
44 Erase
45 '60s theater
46 Be like Clark Kent
52 Long gone
53 Got ready to pounce
54 Went (off)
55 Deli sandwich material
56 Went off
57 Girl with a future?

DOWN

1 One taking a shot
2 Certain Christian
3 Funds may be in it
4 Restaurant business bigwig
5 Coll. entrance hurdle, once
6 Real estate agent on "Desperate Housewives"
7 Split
8 Split
9 Gamble
10 Repeated musical phrase
11 Brought down
12 Horror movie character
14 More innocent
15 It's stuffed with dough
19 Super finish?
24 Kind of song
25 Area of interest to Archimedes
26 In a daze
27 Zoologist's foot
31 Makings of a suit
32 Beer brand since 1842
33 One with a duty
34 Prefix with calyx or thalamus
35 Song from Bernstein's "Wonderful Town"
36 Not be upright
39 Tzimmes
40 Not going anywhere?
41 They have family units
42 Polishes
47 Illustrator of "Paradise Lost" and "The Divine Comedy"
48 Gulf of San ___ (Caribbean Sea inlet)
49 West African capital
50 Ovidian infinitive
51 "There was an old man . . ." poet

by Charles Barasch

ACROSS

1 Elaborate procedure
10 Creep
14 Soapmaking compound
15 Playful trickster
16 Living end
17 In with
18 Where to find lifesavers, for short
19 "The Wandering Heir" novelist, 1872
20 Settles
21 "The Big Lebowski" director
22 River in Hades
24 Occupies
27 Not view innocently
30 Something to take in court
31 Orsk is on it
33 Rabbit punch landing site
34 Shape-shifting giant of myth
35 "Just in Time" composer
36 Call in the game Battleship
37 "Without ___" (Grateful Dead album)
38 Four-legged film star of the '30s
39 Let out
40 The classical elements, e.g.
42 Luxor Temple sight
44 Bouncing off the walls
46 Animal some believe to be the source of the unicorn myth
47 Big bang creator
49 Keys
51 Org. that can't be lax about LAX?
54 "The Fog of War" director Morris
55 Old comedian known for his unique piano-playing style
57 Squalid
58 "Oh well"
59 Disclosure on eHarmony
60 "My parents are gonna kill me!"

DOWN

1 Something to put on before trying?
2 He played one of TV's Sopranos
3 Goes right
4 Fire starter?
5 Peter who wrote "The Last Testament of Oscar Wilde"
6 Eastern royals
7 Sealab inhabitants
8 Invented things
9 Old bomb
10 Follower of Sha Na Na at Woodstock
11 Clears
12 Flames shoot in it
13 They're tapped
15 Belt
21 Question while eying someone else's plate
23 Publication with an annual "Green Issue"
24 Pit
25 Be a whipping boy
26 "___ Forget" (Harbach/Kern tune)
28 Sneak ___
29 Lean
30 Plane wing part
32 Process of molecular synthesis
35 She had a 1993 hit with "No Ordinary Love"
39 Eschew aid
41 Well
43 Assembles
45 Golden Globe-nominated actress for "The Opposite of Sex," 1998
47 Leaves home?
48 One before four
50 Jets used to be seen there
51 Top pick, slangily
52 Scena segment
53 Dumped
56 Unbalanced

by Natan Last

44

ACROSS
1 Porky
10 Socs.
15 "Whatever"
16 "The Wreck of the Mary ___" (1959 film)
17 Where habits are picked up?
18 Near the hip
19 Seat
20 "That's good enough"
21 Get down
24 "The Novel of the Future" author
25 First Earl of Chatham
29 Proceeding
32 Ready to get engaged?
34 Exchange for something very valuable
35 Vertical piece in a door frame
36 Grp. issuing IDs
37 Tennis star Petrova
38 Like some adult hippos
40 Product with a rotating ball
41 Curious to a fault
43 Text messaging command
44 Meatball
45 Lyric stand-in, perhaps
47 Clammy?
50 Flight passengers often work on them
55 Not independently
56 Not too much of a stretch
58 Jenny Craig testimonial starter
59 Read the riot act
60 Heavenly discovery of 1801
61 "Sure looks that way"

DOWN
1 Obnoxious sort
2 In unison
3 1956 Olympic skiing sensation ___ Sailer
4 Saint ___ Bay, Jamaica
5 Retaining instructions
6 Spread statistic
7 Top arrangement?
8 Bank deposit, of sorts
9 Some appliances
10 Passage to get 8-Down
11 Bears do it
12 Tool for sewing canvas
13 Certain atomic X-ray emission
14 Tick source
20 "Splendor in the Grass" Oscar winner
22 Day when courts are not in session
23 "Amarantine" Grammy winner
25 After the Pentateuchal period
26 Between seating sections
27 Attic, often
28 Like many a backsplash
30 It's 8 for O
31 Recovers
33 Lurch
36 Sportsman of the Year co-winner of 1998
39 Cot spot
40 One of three French auto-making brothers
42 Chichewa and English are its two official languages
46 Sites of some religious statues
48 Massachusetts motto starter
49 Court hangers
51 "The washday miracle" sloganeer, once
52 One found in the woods
53 Extremely desirable
54 Fixes
56 Oscar show airer?
57 Mekong Buddhist

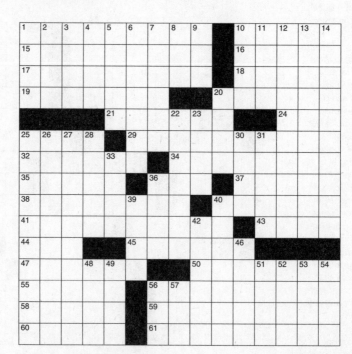

by Robert H. Wolfe

ACROSS

1 R.B.I. or E.R.A., e.g.
5 Return addressee?
8 Zeroes
14 Boston specialty
16 Saint whose name means "good"
17 Mean crossword clue writer's challenge to solvers?
19 Meal source
20 Something about Mary?
21 People who aren't positive?
22 Gets passed down, perhaps
27 Potential pass target
28 Flight data recorder?: Abbr.
29 Fortune 500 company whose toll-free number ends with 23522
30 Major work in grad sch.
32 Commuting choices: Abbr.
34 Molly of early stage and screen
37 Movie line spoken by Renée Zellweger after "Just shut up"
41 "Scandalized Masks" painter, 1883
42 Wall St. deal
43 What you might wind up with
44 They often cross
47 Considered groovy
49 Land in the Thames
50 Sunrise, say
54 Cover-letter letters
55 1970s tennis star Ramirez
56 Nitwit
57 Event starting on 08/08/08 at 08:08:08 p.m.

63 Inspire
64 Contingency funds
65 Specially trained soldier
66 Replies of comprehension
67 Psalm starter

DOWN

1 What a scene is seen in
2 Cold evidence?
3 Unimpeachable
4 Eastern music
5 Wall St. deal
6 Very desirous person's sacrifice?
7 Psalm ender
8 Split
9 Graded item
10 Posed
11 Heinous war crime

12 Compound added to natural gas to give it an odor
13 Flip
15 Interior designer's creation
18 Parts of gastrointestinal tracts
22 Turn red, maybe
23 Word with card or catalog
24 Olden ointment
25 Fictional river of verse
26 Three-time skiing world champion Hermann
31 Spit, e.g.
33 Chlorure de sodium
35 ___ acid
36 Best Actor nominee of 1991 and 1998

38 Like Manhattan's East Village
39 Fahd's successor in Saudi Arabia
40 Duty for a docent
45 Oscar-winning "Titanic" score composer James
46 Heroin, slangily
48 Texas senator succeeded by Cornyn
50 Keep out
51 End of ___
52 1980s–'90s New York governor
53 Neighbor of Helsinki
58 Kind of band
59 British verb ending
60 Field divs.
61 One driving a bus.?
62 "Charley's Aunt" star Chaplin

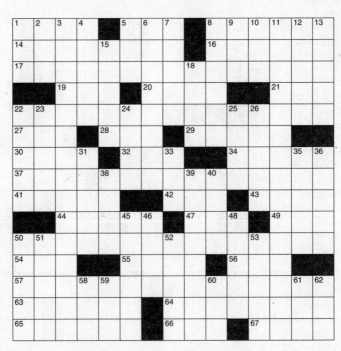

by Ashish Vengsarkar

ACROSS

1 Subject for a Venetian boat song
6 Deflation indication
10 Fleece
14 Tanglewood Music Festival town
15 Coast Guard noncoms
16 Cager Kukoc
17 Track cover-up?
19 Southern university
20 Nancy's home
21 Diploma word
22 Hangover
24 Radiation unit
27 Its players bow
28 Like siblings
29 Tanglewood concert hall dedicatee
31 Quality of glucose and fructose
35 Sorted, sort of
37 1887 play on which a 1900 opera is based
38 Solicited
40 Behind
41 ___ cap
42 Foreign denial
44 Ways around: Abbr.
45 1929 globe circumnavigator
49 "Jazz in Silhouette" composer
50 Earmark
53 Menu choice
54 Summer cooler
56 Eight-state coast-to-coast rte.
57 It's a square
58 Hewlett-Packard competitor
59 Slander, e.g.
60 Uitlander foe
61 Shelters

DOWN

1 Zany comic Ritz and others
2 Act like a baby
3 ___ cat
4 Cooper's role in "The Fountainhead," 1949
5 Big production
6 Some sufferers of personality disorders
7 Red gemstones
8 Tabitha formerly of MTV News
9 Former boomer
10 Audible small appliance
11 Some opinion offerers
12 Part of a Crookes tube
13 One in a rush?
18 Coll. entrance hurdle, once
21 High water?
23 Drs.' reading since 1883
24 March grp.?
25 Poisoned husband in "Mourning Becomes Electra"
26 Many a Hawaiian tourist
30 Any one of the concentric circles in a ripple, in physics
32 1957 film with the 1963 sequel "Savage Sam"
33 Bluebonnet
34 Gorges
36 Ab ___ (absent)
39 Go into a cabin
43 Repeated word in Mark 15:34 that means "my God"
45 Attire for a trip around the world?
46 Total
47 Sunning spot
48 Child tenders
51 Atomic
52 Kyoto Protocol concern: Abbr.
54 Like Brahms's Piano Trio No. 1
55 Disney deer

by Karen M. Tracey

ACROSS

1 Shakespeare's Sir Toby ___
6 Italian architect Rossi
10 Hot rod?
14 Riotous
16 Part of the view in "A Room With a View"
17 Organization concerned with good breeding
18 Early career trajectory
19 First-aid expert, briefly
20 Vengeful Quaker of literature
21 Pal, in Pau
22 Highest-scoring Scrabble word that doesn't use A, E, I, O or U
25 Cryogenic refrigerant
28 Objects
30 Health facility
31 Sony BMG record label
32 They have people eating in a lot
37 1972 #1 hit for the Staple Singers
38 Sentence fragments often beginning with "wh-" words
39 Nos. pressed after getting through
40 Neuter pronoun
41 "A Fine Romance" composer
42 Dorothy Lamour's trademark garment
44 "You should really know better!"
48 Org. that gives out Jazz Masters Awards
49 Something to do in a virtual room
52 Satyajit Ray's "The ___ Trilogy"
53 Cereal box nos.

54 Piñata material
57 Baseball team owner Moreno
58 Pitcher?
59 Force divided by acceleration
60 Kids to watch out for
61 1950s sitcom family name

DOWN

1 Exercise room lineup
2 "Politics is the ___ of the imagination": Ian McEwan
3 Walter who created Woody Woodpecker
4 "Reliable Sources" broadcaster
5 Shade
6 Roguish
7 "Run ___ Run" (1998 thriller)
8 Smear (on)

9 Divining device, in sci-fi
10 Opera impresario Caldwell
11 Election year events
12 Two-faced
13 Sock part
15 QB's talent
23 Big Three locale
24 Unit of explosive force
25 Dress uniform adornments
26 Golden Horde members
27 Moves carefully
29 First name shared by both founders of Apple
30 Son of Sarek
32 Street contacts?
33 Ripley who wrote the "Gone With the Wind" sequel "Scarlett"

34 Abuses
35 Dollar bill symbol
36 Dull sound
43 Travelers' stopping points
45 Come to the point?
46 Used up
47 Literary character whose last words are "The horror! The horror!"
49 Learn a lot, say
50 Album after "Beatles VI"
51 Acts like
53 Run into
54 Series of violent episodes?
55 Product sold in spray cans
56 Period

by Patrick Berry

ACROSS

1 Modern coinage meaning intuition without regard to facts
11 Pop group that inspired a 2001 Broadway musical
15 Can still get
16 Some strays
17 Better
18 YouTube offering
19 1867 book subtitled "Kritik der politischen Ökonomie"
20 River forming the eastern border of Charlemagne's empire
21 Kansan or Coloradan
23 Cautious gamblers
28 Movie set?
29 Form a league
31 Saul Bellow's March
32 Life choices
33 Like many a parked vehicle
35 City near Boston
36 Nudists
38 Less of an illusion
40 Left out
41 Flight field
43 "The King and I" film director
44 Displaying
52 Others, to Octavian
53 Best-selling 2003 Khaled Hosseini novel, with "The"
54 Old character
55 By a certain measure
56 Modern storage units, briefly
57 Subjective side-by-side comparisons

DOWN

1 "A Child Is Born" trumpeter Jones
2 Arthur C. Clarke's "Rendezvous With ___"
3 Runs through
4 Cheap commodity?
5 Dynasty before the Shang
6 Co. that bought Applebee's in 2007
7 Seaweed wrapped around sushi
8 Proponent of strong governmental control
9 Character in Twain's "The Mysterious Stranger"
10 ___ Maris (title of the Virgin Mary)
11 Underline
12 Attacked with fierceness and anger
13 Boodlers' acts
14 Smeared
22 Tick, e.g.
23 Connected (to)
24 What schools have
25 One of the Wayans brothers
26 Trip
27 Literally, "scraped"
29 It might not indicate true worth
30 It's the same in Paris
32 Thing that'll deter someone from taking a ride
34 "___ right?"
37 Diplomat and Adventurer
39 Live dangerously, maybe
42 Kind of doll
45 Took a turn
46 Micmac relative
47 Where to find the Wienerwald: Abbr.
48 N.F.L. offensive guard Chris
49 Cozy retreats
50 Cozy retreat
51 Hurdles for some srs.

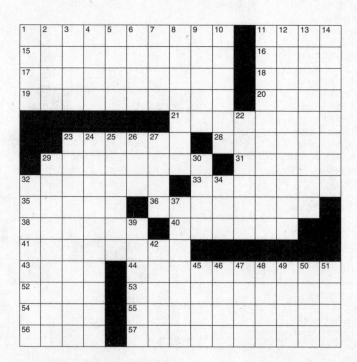

by Brendan Emmett Quigley

ACROSS

1 Flurries
7 How you might meet someone
14 Head of an alley?
15 1.0
16 Not forsaking
17 Without warning
18 Sticking point
19 Old-time comic Ed
21 Gravlax ingredient
22 Kind of column
23 A National Cartoonists Society award is named for him
25 Short cut?
27 City on the Trans-Canada Highway
30 Nashville-based awards org.
31 So much, on a score
32 Carter's second secretary of state
34 Like dirty rice
37 Farm unit?
39 Championship cricket matches
40 Left unceremoniously?
42 Two-time gold medal skier of the 1998 Olympics
44 Using devices
45 1990 Grammy winner for her album "Days of Open Hand"
50 Crew team?
52 State bordering Lower Saxony
53 Film role for Russell in 1993 and Costner in 1994
54 One might be in a cast
56 Course for the dead?
57 Exciting experience, in slang
58 Chair
60 Like
62 Comic's creation
63 Their tails do not wag
64 Where Covent Garden is
65 Craft often utilizing rubber bands

DOWN

1 Bench warmer
2 Still in development
3 Came back together
4 "I haven't got all day!"
5 Part of an even exchange
6 Traps, perhaps
7 Title role in a 1986 Woody Allen film
8 Loser to Audrey for the 1953 Best Actress Oscar
9 Far from family-friendly
10 Hardly hardy
11 A 15-Down might have control over them
12 Provision for holding certain jobs
13 Word next to a check box
15 Underground movement leader?
20 Dirt spreader
24 Butt
26 Gretna Green rebuffs
28 Miami team, informally
29 Classless one?
33 Be in the can
34 "___ fini!"
35 Helplessly?
36 Teens' escapades
38 Member of the aster family
41 "Ya think?!"
43 Ballpark
46 Made more exciting
47 Like some runs
48 Strongly realistic
49 Put side by side
51 Get the lead out?
55 It might be baked for an appetizer
58 Overwhelm, with "down"
59 "King Kong" role
61 Carp variety

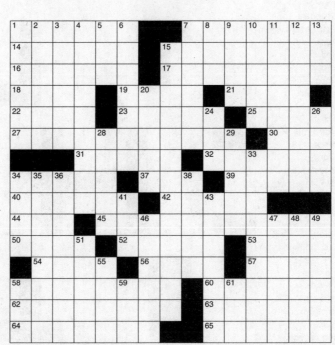

by Mike Nothnagel

50

ACROSS

1 Midwest farmers work later on it: Abbr.
4 Line on an appl. form
8 Group whose logo has a clock set at 11:00
12 E. S. ___, game company that popularized Yahtzee and Scribbage
14 "___ having fun yet?"
15 Collect, as benefits
16 Like "Beowulf," in brief
17 Fuss, in a way
18 Six-Day War battleground
19 "The nerve!"
21 Its drops may be alarming, with "the"
22 One may have many runners
25 It contains M.S.G.
26 John Lennon's adopted middle name
27 ___ Center, second-tallest building in Chicago
28 Filler for a gun
30 Line on an appl. form
31 Planet system in several "Star Trek" episodes
34 "Let's go!"
35 Santa ___, Calif.
36 Girl who's the "you" in the lyric "I'll see you in my dreams"
37 See 41-Across
40 Printed over
41 37-Across's birthplace
42 Cartoon character who fathered octuplets

43 Old N.Y.S.E. ticker symbol that's now just "T"
44 Something given at a meeting
50 Numerical prefix
51 Not make it
52 Pioneering agriculturist Jethro
54 La ___, capital of Buenos Aires province
55 ___ Oder (German river)
56 German-occupied capital in W.W. II
57 Psychologist Havelock
58 "Bill & ___ Bogus Journey," 1991 comedy
59 Love ___
60 Skin-and-bones
61 Rummy

DOWN

1 Hook's place
2 O, often
3 Fourth-quarter strategies
4 Washes
5 Gets more interesting, say
6 Not get over
7 Actress O'Connor of TV's "Xena"
8 100 nanojoules
9 Front-of-magazine pieces
10 Buzz producer
11 Produce
13 Moles go behind them
14 Copier
20 Portable shelter
23 Ending of many a chase
24 Can opener?

28 Delta Tau ___ ("Animal House" house)
29 Voice
32 Its end is often observed
33 Iberia : Spain :: ___ : Chile
37 Title role for Greta Garbo
38 Swedish home of Scandinavia's oldest university
39 Enter suddenly
44 Crash pad?
45 Locked, as a lavatory
46 Encourage
47 Weather may affect them: Abbr.
48 Beat
49 Late 1940s event, in headlines
53 Load

by Tyler Lewis Hinman

ACROSS

1 Luau lighting
10 Do the dishes?
15 Singer who plays herself in "D.C. Cab"
16 "Any fool can make ___, and every fool will mind it": Thoreau
17 "Tone it down!"
18 Conglomerate parts
19 Carbon compound
20 Gernreich who invented the monokini
21 Conviction
22 Legendary abductee
23 "Per Ardua ad ___" (Royal Air Force motto)
24 Some are minor
28 Love
30 Six-time Rose Bowl winner: Abbr.
31 Future star
32 Bellies up to
34 Schedule maker: Abbr.
35 Bankrupt
36 With 46-Across, program pitched by Queen Latifah
37 Activity near a 1-Across
38 Workup locales: Abbr.
39 Wasn't gentle with
40 Crew leader
41 Archaic verb ending
42 Schedule maker: Abbr.
43 It may be found in one's chest
44 Lofty
46 See 36-Across
49 Less specious
50 Mechanical
51 Nailed
55 Son of Gloucester in "King Lear"
56 Norman Rockwell specialty
58 Repetition mark, in music
59 Stops being funny, say
60 Billet-doux suggestion
61 San Bernardino suburb

DOWN

1 Trend
2 Unyielding
3 Drawing game
4 Not just at home: Abbr.
5 Your, in Tours
6 Canyon tones
7 "The Phantom of the Opera" suitor
8 Neanderthal
9 With respectful humility
10 Loungewear
11 Spring arrival
12 Get all sentimental
13 Big sticker?
14 Where to act on a gut feeling?
22 "___ Cardboard Lover" (Norma Shearer film)
24 What a potential player must pass
25 Summons, e.g.
26 Sight in Lancaster County, Pa.
27 Footballer Ford
29 "Le Comte ___" (Rossini opera)
32 Ticker with headlines
33 Charlotte-to-Raleigh dir.
36 Be discordant
37 Post ___
39 Pining pantomime persona
40 Give up on, in slang
43 Radio code word after 47-Down
45 Is cockeyed
47 Radio code word before 43-Down
48 Squad stars
51 When Maggie calls herself "a cat on a hot tin roof"
52 "Let It Snow" lyricist
53 Cherokee Strip city
54 Francis ___, signer of the Articles of Confederation
57 Montreal, e.g.: Abbr.

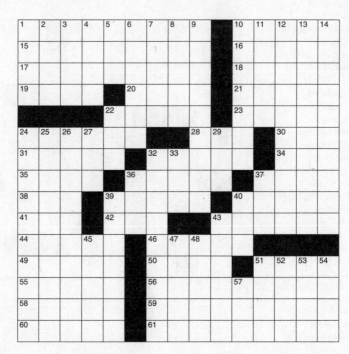

by Brad Wilber

52

ACROSS

1 Holder of many a sandwich
10 They come with strings attached
15 Piquant base for a sandwich
16 Heart of ancient Athens
17 2005 reality show hosted by Fabio
18 They come with strings attached
19 Steam-driven devices that pump water from mines
21 Letter getter: Abbr.
22 "Lost" actor Somerhalder
23 Track numbers
24 Video from a kidnappee's family, e.g.
25 Coming right back at you?
29 Save
31 Playwright Peter of "Equus"
33 Cramped quarters
34 "Where's my serpent of old ___?": "Antony and Cleopatra"
35 "Gilgamesh," e.g.
36 Dinette settings
39 Heart failures?
43 Doesn't need more seasoning
45 Pelvic bone
46 Eponymous oilman Halliburton
47 Not kosher
49 Janissary commander
50 Chemical suffix
51 Item called a geyser in Britain
55 Change at the top?
57 Ingredient in a mojito highball
58 Gull
59 Goes yellow, say
60 Malcolm X eulogist Davis
61 Will work?

DOWN

1 Corps of corpses
2 Gettable
3 Ruthless type
4 1785 invention of England's Edmund Cartwright
5 "All Eyez ___" (1996 Tupac Shakur album)
6 Start of some blended juice names
7 What a beatnik beats
8 Auks, puffins and related birds
9 Owen ___, rebel in Shakespeare's "King Henry IV"
10 Makes bales, say
11 Long ___
12 The "I" of Elizabeth I?
13 Changeable
14 Steps lively
20 Houdini's stock in trade
24 Unit that's larger than 19 trillion miles
26 Prominent
27 San Diego-to-Seattle rte.
28 "Dance of the Sugar Plum Fairy" instrument
30 100 aurar
32 Uses in desperation
36 Corroded
37 Storage rooms
38 Anthony Hopkins role in "Shadowlands"
40 "Deo ___"
41 Southern historical novelist Price
42 With fashion sense
44 Not lag
48 Beau-___ (French in-law)
51 More than stirred
52 Flush, for one
53 Manx relative
54 A bushel and a peck?: Abbr.
56 Century starter in the papacy of Gregory I

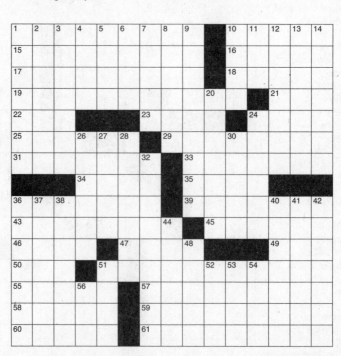

by Byron Walden

53

ACROSS

1 Designer known for his "American look"
6 Cruel one
10 It might include hot dogs and baked beans
14 Freeload
15 Wile E. Coyote or the Road Runner
16 "Three Places in New England" composer
17 Go-getter
18 Org. offering college scholarships
19 "Bye-bye!"
20 1916 work by 28-Across
23 Thurman of "Dangerous Liaisons"
24 Greenwich Village campus inits.
25 Blue
28 Subject of this puzzle
34 Writer LeShan
35 When doubled, a book by Gauguin
36 Locale for some Gauguin art
37 Defeat
40 Middle of a patriotic cheer
42 "We didn't do it!"
43 Like some designs
45 Trauma sites, for short
47 Sport ___
48 Title subject of a 28-Across work
52 Cupcake
53 ___-Magnon
54 N.R.C. predecessor
55 Sobriquet for 28-Across
61 Items for Rambos
64 Ames Research Center org.
65 Broadcaster
66 ___ vaccine

67 Anita who sang "Is You Is or Is You Ain't My Baby"
68 Where Hercules slew the lion
69 Mimics mockingly
70 Sugar amts.
71 May gift recipients

DOWN

1 Austen's Woodhouse
2 Tower
3 It is "resistless in battle," wrote Sophocles
4 Spring river breakup
5 Small fry
6 Barbara Kingsolver's "___ América"
7 Slip
8 Spiral pasta
9 Make secret, in a way
10 Ball catcher
11 "Die Meistersinger" heroine
12 Volleyball need
13 Start of a patriotic cheer
21 Sammy the lyricist
22 Sontag who wrote "In America"
25 Get into uniform
26 Shrewd
27 Ceremonial sites
28 Like some delis
29 Teeth: Prefix
30 Supreme Court justice Stone
31 Chit
32 Beamed intensely
33 "Well, looky here!"
38 Fraternal patriotic org.
39 Former CBS chief

41 Poetica opening
44 Be afraid to
46 Opposite of legato: Abbr.
49 Tent dwellers, maybe
50 Put back on display, in a way
51 More gross
55 Clucking sounds
56 Without dawdling
57 They may be caught on a beach
58 "Garfield" waitress
59 Want
60 Pâté de fois ___
61 End of a patriotic cheer
62 Get rid of
63 Nouvelle-Calédonie, e.g.

by John Underwood

ACROSS

1 Spanish 101 conjugation part
6 Further
10 Staunch
14 Greek port
15 Opal alternative
17 Lemony Snicket's count and one of Snoopy's brothers
18 Supposed tools of the devil
19 Serbian provincial capital on the Danube
21 Supermarket suppliers
22 Pulitzer-winning critic Richard
23 Dawdling
24 1999 comedy featuring aliens called Thermians
27 "Glengarry Glen Ross" Tony winner Schreiber
28 Zimbalist's violin teacher
29 One of the Obama girls
34 Pope during the reign of Charlemagne
36 Stole
38 Clipper trio
39 Hua succeeded him
41 "Morning Dance" band Spyro ___
42 Duo first seen in "Puss Gets the Boot," 1940
45 Portable power tool
49 Much-repeated part of binary code
50 Father figures?
51 Earlike organ
54 Morning cry
56 Puffy hat wearer
57 Less than upstanding
58 A stroke might indicate it
59 "Right"
60 Shared-bath accommodations, briefly
61 Opel model

DOWN

1 Monopoly subj.
2 Stand-out performance
3 Big name in insurance
4 Court evidence, at times
5 Domestic chicken breed
6 In
7 City near Ben-Gurion airport
8 Perseveres
9 Father-and-daughter actors
10 Possible result of a gunshot
11 Fool in "Pagliacci"
12 Bitter-___
13 Unpleasant
16 Acupuncture alternative
20 Nordic
23 Exactly
24 Rock type
25 2000 musical that won four Tonys
26 One who asks a lot?
30 Modern dwellers in ancient Numidia
31 Zoom
32 Foreign address
33 Diurnally
35 On both sides of
37 Invasive Japanese import
40 Oxcart driver's shout
43 Honors for top scorers?
44 Leaping desert rodent
45 Italian apology
46 Rhône-___ (French region)
47 1970s Big Apple mayor
48 Keebler's chief elf
51 Acct. numbers
52 "A Book of Nonsense" author, 1846
53 First name in humor
55 Prefix with tour

by Karen M. Tracey

ACROSS

1 It can be used to get your balance
8 It's flaky and nutty
15 Fine trappings
16 Modem, e.g.
17 Activity in which stakes may be laid
18 Suspect eliminator, often
19 Hatch ___
20 Big name in Web-based correspondence
22 Old televangelism letters
23 Ice
24 Appropriate
25 Play to ___
26 Early Japanese P.M. Hirobumi ___
27 Old sitcom couple's surname
28 Reads online
29 Comparable to a pin?
31 Buoys
33 Ranked
35 Square
36 So-called "Texas White House," once
40 Natives of Umm Qasr
44 Minor's opposite
45 Back ___
47 Stay-at-home worker?
48 Beep, say
49 Date preceder
50 Gifford's replacement as Philbin's co-host
51 Barrister's deg.
52 Cloudiness
53 Charming person?
54 Very hot
56 Ascii alternative
58 Argue
59 Degree divisions
60 Holds out
61 Doctor's order

DOWN

1 Peaceful place
2 Ones left holding the bag?
3 Hollywood icon since 1924
4 Stuffed and roasted entree
5 Put down
6 Abbr. after Sen. Richard Lugar's name
7 It has a sticking point
8 Impress, and then some
9 Tony winner between "A Chorus Line" and "Ain't Misbehavin'"
10 Heat meas.
11 Studio site
12 Having a knack for
13 Shadow
14 Natural
21 Tiny bit
24 Not likely to be dissuaded from
25 Microwave option
27 Safin who won the 2005 Australian Open
28 Word on a prescription label
30 ___ Wheeler, 1964–70 chairman of the Joint Chiefs of Staff
32 Whence the song "The Lady's Got Potential"
34 He said "I am free of all prejudice. I hate everyone equally"
36 "Mécanique Céleste" astronomer
37 Barnes & Noble acquired it in 1987
38 It might include a washboard
39 Ring after exchanging rings?
41 Extravagant romantic
42 Bars
43 Least copious
46 Fritz the Cat's creator
49 Singer profiled in "Sweet Dreams," 1985
50 Come and go
52 Great Trek figure
53 Kind of leg
55 Heat meas.
57 When German pigs fly?

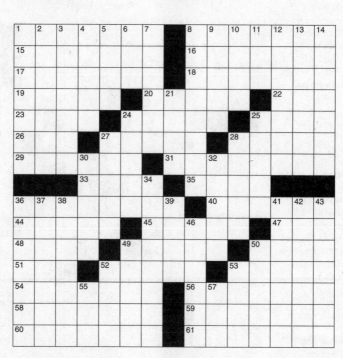

by Barry C. Silk

ACROSS

1 911 pest, e.g.
12 V.P. between Wallace and Barkley
15 D. H. Lawrence novel made into a 1969 film
16 Time for Tours tourists?
17 Many a first course
18 Dull finish?
19 Hit with a heavy blow
20 Had sum problems
22 30-day winter month
25 Flip
26 1999 Clorox acquisition
29 "A penny saved is a penny earned," e.g.
31 Fed. accident investigator
32 Makes a big hit
34 Home of the Museum of International Folk Art
36 Quinn who played Annie in film
37 Land at a Spanish airport?
38 Be down, apparently
40 Clown
41 Idaho motto starter
42 Least likely to crack
44 Parisian possessive
45 Ones with shovellike forefeet
47 What a virtuous woman is worth more than, according to Proverbs 31:10
49 Aromatic herbal quaff
51 ___ Dove (the constellation Columba)

55 Follow closely (along)
56 Restaurant parties, often
59 Archaic ending
60 Fruit with a pit, to a Brit
61 Got into the swing, say
62 Clandestine classroom communicators

DOWN

1 100-lb. units
2 Study, e.g.
3 Childish retort
4 Flight destinations
5 Desk features
6 Enemy of the Moors, with "the"
7 True, at times: Abbr.
8 Cud chewers

9 Alluring adolescents
10 NASA spacewalks
11 "Yet do thy cheeks look ___ Titan's face": Shak.
12 Track edges
13 Unpressured
14 Comforters on kids' beds
21 "The Count of Monte Cristo" hero
23 "Uncle Vanya" wife and others
24 What directors sit on: Abbr.
26 Play halters
27 Any one of Handel's Op. 2 pieces
28 Longtime flame?
30 Mashed potato alternative

33 Sri Lanka exports
35 They're hooked up to some TV's
39 Be more than reluctant to
40 American Heart Mo.
43 Shade
46 French city that shares its name with a car
48 Bars that gradually get smaller
50 It can stop the show
52 Exactly, after "to"
53 Catch, in a way
54 Bygone grp. of 15
57 "To Helen" writer's inits.
58 Salt std., e.g.

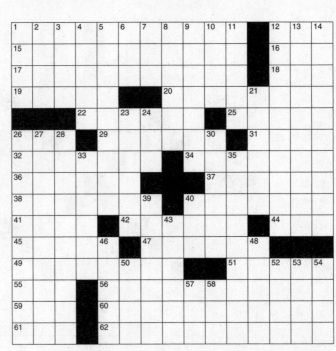

by Myles Callum

ACROSS

1 Steps up
10 Treasured instrument
15 Strike out
16 Goes down
17 Polka heard frequently on "The Benny Hill Show"
18 Part of a chronicle
19 Frustrate
20 1950s political slogan
22 A, B or C, often: Abbr.
23 Part of a telephone worker's routine
24 Baseball's Vizquel
27 Hunter of literature
28 Part of CORE
31 Marks off
36 Doesn't puff idly
38 Subject of the biography "All or Nothing at All"
39 Develops anacusis
41 Spurs
42 Pollster Roper
43 ___ the Great (detective of kids' books)
44 One end of a canal
48 Chemical ending
50 Frequent area of auto damage
51 Symbols
55 Lord's realm
56 Boeing employee
58 "He seemed like such ___ boy"
59 Chance
60 When to see la luna
61 Votaries

DOWN

1 Country rocker Joe and others
2 You might run for it
3 Forming clumps
4 Parts of some services
5 Admit
6 "I understand now"
7 Set-___
8 Like spam
9 Masters topics
10 Realization
11 "Un bar aux Folies-Bergère" artist
12 "Maybe" musical
13 Durable woods
14 Dot on a map, maybe
21 How a snake may be caught?
24 Before being retitled: Abbr.
25 War preceder
26 Flu symptom
29 Bearer of catkins
30 Actress Sobieski
32 Make attractive
33 Words with shame or boy
34 Order at a horse show
35 Levelheaded
37 TV witch
40 A bad way to be left
44 "The Rights ___"
45 Heavens: Prefix
46 Nervine, for one
47 Methuselah's father
48 ___ least
49 Like some stocks
52 Brio
53 Cartoonist Walker
54 Criteria: Abbr.
57 Geom. figure

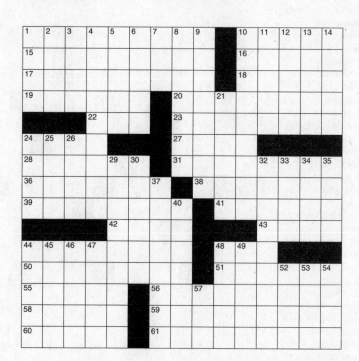

by Eric Berlin

58

ACROSS

1 Top in a certain contest
10 1988 Olympics superheavyweight gold medalist
15 Reply on a ship
16 Transcontinental railroad city
17 Tanzanian tourist destination
18 It has a cap in the kitchen
19 Hesitate in speaking
20 One of two N.T. books
21 Coastal feature
23 Tell
24 ___ Bank (U.S. loan guarantor)
26 Wire: Abbr.
28 Wrong
29 Expired
31 "I think," succinctly
32 Georgetown athlete
33 Soil
34 Artist on the cover of a 1969 Life magazine
36 "___ Her Go" (Frankie Laine hit)
38 W.W. II city on the Vire
39 Brest friends?
43 TV producer Don
47 Prefix with -stat
48 Puck
49 Key of Brahms's Fourth
50 C.D., e.g.: Abbr.
51 "Peter ___ Greatest Hits" (1974 release)
53 Tot minder
54 Afg. neighbor
55 Catch in a pot
56 While, briefly
58 It may be AM or FM: Abbr.
59 Crony of Tony on "The Sopranos"
61 One of the five major circles of latitude
64 Up to
65 Become disconnected
66 Coasts, say
67 Hot-blooded ones

DOWN

1 They have loads of work to do
2 Task to focus on
3 Extreme ends
4 Inventor's inits.
5 See 27-Down
6 With 22-Down, disgruntled remark about a failed partnership?
7 Alpine feeder
8 Score abbr.
9 Ancient vessels
10 Glen Gray's "Casa ___ Stomp"
11 Rock genre
12 Center for strategic planning
13 "Right on, brother!"
14 Oppressive measure that helped spark the French Revolution
22 See 6-Down
25 French Impressionist Berthe
27 With 5-Down, match, in a way
28 Add
30 Ralph Bunche's alma mater
35 Basic: Abbr.
37 Delays
39 Ones doing push-ups?
40 1959 Neil Sedaka hit
41 Windsor, e.g.
42 A season: Abbr.
44 Bothered
45 Annuity scheme
46 Spells
52 10th-century emperor known as "the Great"
55 Hosp. procedures
57 "Trionfo di Afrodite" composer
60 Poll abbr.
62 Alphabet trio
63 Height in feet of the Statue of Liberty, expressed in Roman numerals

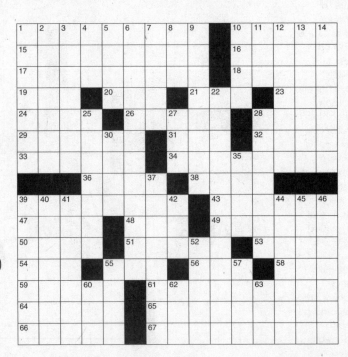

by Bob Peoples

ACROSS

1 Bristly
7 Sports anchor's offering
12 Henry Clay's estate in Lexington, Ky.
14 1997 Michael Douglas film
16 Unexplained phenomena
18 Quai d'Orsay setting
19 Possible sentence in the slammer
20 Unfriendly
21 Whom Pocahontas married
23 U.K. award
24 "__ and Louis" (1956 duet album)
26 It doesn't stay in for long
30 Like silhouettes, typically
32 Subject to debate
33 1950s–'90s singer called "The High Priestess of Soul"
34 Ones forging
36 Congregation location
37 Finish a hole
39 There are no plans for this
43 18-Across feeder
44 "Of course!"
45 Footballer Haynes
47 Former state: Abbr.
48 Some misses
52 On the other hand
54 Classic 1894 swashbuckler, with "The"
56 Bound
57 Satisfied customer's request
58 Send another invitation
59 Sharp

DOWN

1 Relatively smart
2 George's mother on "Seinfeld" and others
3 HBO showing of 1975
4 1937 Oscar role for Luise Rainer
5 Less likely to lose it
6 College dept.
7 Torn
8 Kellogg's brand
9 Epic achievement?
10 Blob
11 Put down
13 Let down
14 Carroll creatures
15 Scoot
17 Some PC image files
22 Conjectures
25 Two-time A.L. home run champ Tony
27 Exempt
28 "__ can't be!"
29 Stevie Wonder's "__ Have You"
31 Something often fallen out of
34 Supporter
35 Falls off
38 Threefold
39 The "blood" in bloodstone
40 Brian of "Juarez," 1939
41 Full
42 Bridge piece
46 Close cutter
49 Cub bearers, in Spain
50 Swing alternative
51 Glass finish
53 "The Cotton Club" star
55 Put paper into

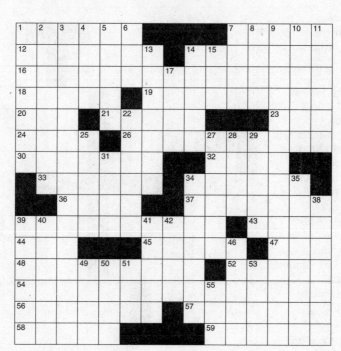

by Charles Barasch

ACROSS

1 Facility with many schools
9 One using the metric system?
13 Way over the line
15 Less likely to reconcile
16 Further stirring
17 Very small serving
18 Jude, e.g.
19 Toys, for tots
21 Mine shaft borer
22 Put a ceiling on
23 Telemarketing need: Abbr.
24 Eponymous Scottish inventor
25 High-rise, e.g.
27 Habitations
29 Don Juan
30 Saturnine
31 Some sprouts
32 Ski resort sights
36 Soft, transversely ribbed fabric
39 Unfeminine
40 ___ of Court
41 Where tests are often given: Abbr.
42 Angus rejection
43 Medical school course
46 Supplement
48 Daring adventurer
50 See 20-Down
51 Advanced point
53 Defeater of Holyfield and Tyson
54 Decorate
55 Eremitic
56 Sullies

DOWN

1 Captain's command
2 Feckless
3 Landing place
4 Miss in a derby?
5 Step on it
6 Not merely like
7 Chafes (at)
8 Pronoun for Pliny
9 Givers of unfriendly hugs
10 Like some poisoning
11 Go back
12 Valets, at times
14 Director's cry
15 Clueless
20 With 50-Across, acted
26 Sharer of both parents
27 Spider producer
28 Torches
30 Hunter's lure
33 Lessens the force of
34 Tony's player on "NYPD Blue"
35 Pasta variety
36 Galician galas
37 It's on the other end of the Albert Canal from Liège
38 How decisions shouldn't be made
44 "Charlie ___ Secret" (1935 film)
45 "On a similar note," e.g.
47 Jazz singer Anderson
49 Ones with talent?
52 "I ___ shepherd of those sheep": Millay

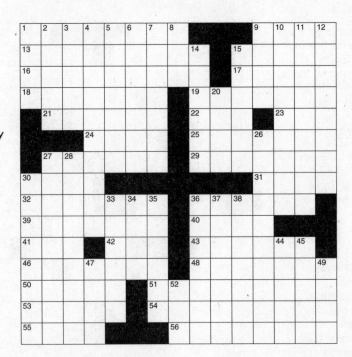

by Robert H. Wolfe

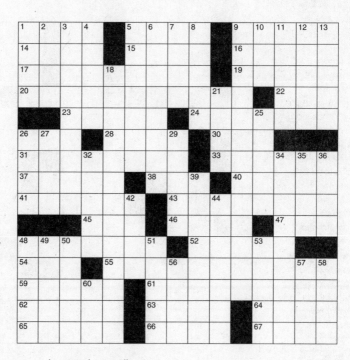

ACROSS

1 Kind of blocker
5 Clay defeater
9 Standard jacket feature
14 Conference intro
15 26 on a table
16 Girl's name meaning "born again"
17 Dangerously
19 8½-pound statue
20 Comment of abandon
22 ___ Bad Wolf of comic books
23 Cement layer
24 "Hey, just a second!"
26 W. Coast airport
28 ___ horn
30 It works as a translator
31 Tragic figure of literature
33 Splash guard
37 1960s TV dog
38 Head
40 Like some myths
41 "No more"
43 High-waisted to the extreme
45 Psych 101 topic
46 Poet/cartoonist Silverstein
47 Affliction
48 "Who knows?!"
52 Pioneering 1940s computer
54 Business card abbr.
55 Modern phone display
59 ___-Car
61 Event souvenirs
62 Island shared by two countries
63 Eastern queen
64 Study of figures: Abbr.

65 Spirited
66 Partner of letters
67 Business page inits.

DOWN

1 Lay up
2 Phnom ___
3 ___ Springs, Fla.
4 Former Los Angeles and New York Philharmonic conductor
5 It admits very little light
6 Like the Mikado and Nanki-Poo
7 Shetland Islands sight
8 They're often found under desks
9 Difficult means of communication
10 Article in a French magazine
11 Poseidon, to Athena
12 Show over
13 Star of "Always Leave Them Laughing," 1949
18 "Too much to go into now"
21 Early "What's My Line?" panelist
25 Red River city
26 Game in which jacks are the highest trumps
27 Seek at random, with "for"
29 Grad student's hurdle
32 Welcome

34 Star of a former self-titled sitcom
35 Onetime distributor of free maps
36 Nerve network
39 Very strong
42 Hemisphere
44 Creation
48 Common sugar source
49 No longer working for the Company
50 Smithereens
51 Part of a crowd, maybe
53 "It's ___" ("Maybe it's meant to be")
56 Do 80, say
57 Sporty cars
58 Salinger dedicatee
60 Directory data: Abbr.

by Patrick Merrell

ACROSS

1 Sensational news format
10 In line with
15 End of a challenge
16 Was a star?
17 "The Prisoner of Zenda" setting
18 Seat of generative power
19 Those, in San José
20 "___ say it is good to fall": Whitman, "Song of Myself"
22 ___ for peace
23 Place to sleep
24 Is ready for the task
27 DVD viewing option
28 Census designation
31 Common tater
34 Subject of the 2006 documentary "Toots"
35 Japanese ___, bonsai plant
37 Entertainer who owns Big Dog Productions
38 Derelict
39 Hanky-panky
41 Calliope filler
44 Place for a pin
46 Bikini-to-Fiji dir.
49 Lesser star designation in a constellation
50 Query to the Lord in Matthew
51 Symbol of gracefulness
52 Study aid?
54 Flimflammery
57 Schoolroom feature
58 It's brilliant in handicrafts

59 Succulents for salves
60 Bond dealers?

DOWN

1 With 5-Down, run-down
2 Words with light or blow
3 Originator of the phrase "truth is stranger than fiction"
4 "Family Guy" mom
5 See 1-Down
6 Ballerina Rubinstein, for whom Ravel wrote "Boléro"
7 As a 16-year-old actor, youngest nonroyal with an individual portrait in Britain's National Portrait Gallery

8 First step in division?
9 Italian entrees
10 Not flat
11 Cable option
12 Vitriolic
13 Lassitude
14 Tamper with, as an odometer
21 Big ___
24 Festivity
25 Ancient rival of Assyria
26 Webers per square meter
27 Last king of Egypt
28 Seat, quickly
29 P
30 N.B.A. scoring leader, 1974–76
32 A.C.C. school

33 One who remains nameless
36 ___ Style Awards
40 Neighbor of Mo.
42 Commandeers
43 "Baby ___ You" (1962 hit)
44 Popular block game
45 It has a certain ring to it
46 Cop
47 More sound
48 Corps personnel: Abbr.
51 Pole classification
53 U.K. honor
55 ___ American
56 School fig.

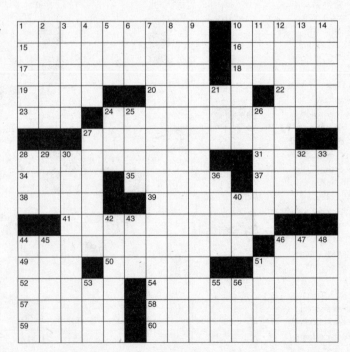

by Byron Walden

ACROSS

1 Waylay
7 Object of ailurophobia
10 Penny : pound :: ___ : krone
13 Bug's midsection
14 "Hollywood Homicide" actress, 2003
15 Box to check on a form
16 TV show that earned Jane Wyman a Golden Globe
18 Protestant denom.
19 Handy thing to know?: Abbr.
20 Like some church matters
21 List heading
22 Try
24 Band components
26 Polo of "Meet the Fockers"
27 Archaeological handle
28 Out of this world
29 The Oscars, e.g.
31 What two zeroes after a dot may mean
33 1978–80 F.B.I. sting that forced a U.S. senator to resign
35 Big bills
36 Green shade
37 First name in architecture
38 One not pure of heart
39 Boss for agents Youngfellow and Rossi
41 Object of a scout's search
45 Alcohol-laced cookie
47 Blue prints?
48 Play bit

49 "Willow Song" opera
51 Cost
52 Here, over there
53 Common and cheap
55 French pronoun
56 Certain asst.
57 Snap out of it
58 Bygone flier
59 Animal with a white rump
60 Destroys

DOWN

1 Equally quick
2 Pure
3 Arrest
4 Dungeons & Dragons beast
5 Adaptable aircraft
6 Sandwich filler

7 End-of-season event
8 It divides people
9 "We know drama" sloganeer
10 Rocker with the 1981 triple-platinum album "Diary of a Madman"
11 Signs back in
12 Some "60 Minutes" pieces
14 Ocean threats
17 Dessert garnish
21 Dangers for paragliders
23 Hoo-ha
25 Ornamentation
30 "What ___!"
32 It's to the left of a dot
33 Misers' feelings
34 Plant supervisor?

36 Words of contentment
40 Other side
42 Floors
43 France's F.B.I., formerly
44 Some assistants
46 Tyrolean refrain
50 Must, say
53 Peer Gynt's mother
54 Medical suffix

by Eric Berlin

64

ACROSS

1 Rapper with an MTV show . . . whose name sounds like a word meaning "show"
7 Total
15 Defiant dare
16 Weigh
17 What some bars provide
18 Any of the teens, say
19 Ducky
20 Madrilenian madams
21 Maker of many sprays
22 Woodbine or twinberry
25 Special favor providers
28 With 8-Down, "Happy Trails" songwriter
29 Steps on a scale
31 Jolly exclamation
33 Manuel de Falla opera "La ___ Breve"
35 Cow's first stomach
36 Items in many a still life
38 Cuff link companions
40 "Since Marie Has Left ___" (Sinatra song)
41 They make charts
43 Start to date?
44 Poultry preparation tool
46 Fabric features
48 Setting at 0 degrees long.
49 Singer who wrote the poetry collection "The Lords and the New Creatures"
52 Terminal abbr.
53 Electrolysis particle
54 Pioneer in the development of nuclear power
58 Baja California port
60 "Oryx and Crake" novelist, 2003
61 One once again
62 Modernize, as a factory
63 What a lot may have a lot of
64 Intricate

DOWN

1 Marvel Comics comic
2 "The Phantom" star Billy
3 Big name in furniture
4 Slip
5 "Nothing for me, thanks"
6 Writer Josephine
7 Lured
8 See 28-Across
9 Freeboot
10 Something that has long needed settling
11 Him, in Le Havre
12 "Chitty Chitty Bang Bang" author
13 Showers of purchases
14 Not allowed to go
20 Finger-lickin' good
23 Place for a flock
24 He had a 1941 hit with "Drum Boogie"
25 They offer hot links
26 Her "Don't Know Why" was 2002's Record of the Year
27 Initial public offering, e.g.
30 Atlas feature
32 Two bells, in the Navy
34 Make
37 Like the Danish language
39 Some surfers' choices, briefly
42 Forays
45 Liszt wrote only one
47 Cushion
50 Amendment
51 Hardly an old pro at
52 Its flag has a vicuña on it
55 Etymologist's concern
56 Kind of point
57 One way to sit
59 Last
60 Sanctuary

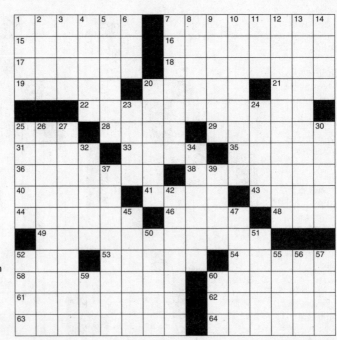

by Karen M. Tracey

65

ACROSS

1 He appointed the first chairman of the A.E.C.
4 Secretive places
14 Simple choice
16 What a standard deviation measures
17 Oscar-nominated actress for "Leaving Las Vegas"
18 Like some fears
19 Hint
21 City at the confluence of the Lehigh and Delaware rivers
22 Team member
24 Without a break
28 Christmas at St. Peter's
30 First lady before Eleanor
31 2000 best seller on social epidemics
37 Climax at Daytona
38 Title boy in a nursery rhyme
39 Ability to let a pitch go by
41 Historic beginning?
42 Budget item
43 Doesn't follow the party line
47 Pension supplements
51 Make good progress
53 Yellow bloomer
54 Artful gossip
58 Crackerjack
59 Common elevator stop
60 Hedge fun?
61 Communist collectives
62 Bit

DOWN

1 Precipitate
2 1987 BP acquisition
3 Jack's place
4 Program introduced by R.W.R.
5 Person of intelligence?
6 Begin, say
7 Body shops?
8 Row
9 Singer/film composer Jon
10 In harmony
11 "Henry & June" role
12 Big inits. in camping
13 Broadcast from Rockefeller Ctr.
15 "Go easy"
20 Office communications
23 How some stock is bought
25 Go straight
26 Kind of section
27 Person in a class of one
29 Part of a ship
31 Cookbook amts.
32 Compassion
33 Hall-of-Fame Viking Carl
34 Tales of derring-do
35 Baseball, in slang
36 Dental routine
40 Cicero or Publius
44 Feed for a fee, as cattle
45 Fictional matchmaker
46 Things
48 Be a bad winner
49 Where you may have a yen for shopping
50 1994 Sandra Bullock film
52 Start of a Christmas chorus
54 Possibilities
55 Picked peeve
56 Mme. of La Mancha
57 Traffic at Union Sta.

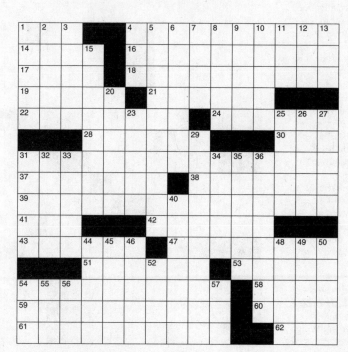

by Randolph Ross

66

ACROSS

1 Real name of a Disney title character
6 Small drawing?
10 15-ml unit
14 Broadcasting
15 Falls into decline
17 With the help of
18 Providers of tip-offs?
19 Laurel and Hardy film with the line "Well, here's another nice mess you've gotten me into!"
21 Middle-earth resident
22 Gene ___, 1932 U.S. and British Open champ
23 Nikola Tesla, for one
25 Information for the record
30 Becomes an issue
32 Total
33 Rock group whose members all assumed the same last name, with "the"
35 Flip alternative
37 Eclipses, to some
38 At the back
39 Headmaster's faculty
42 "I must have missed the ___"
45 Concern for a hostess
47 Part of a certain college course
48 Desserts from the South
53 Wild-haired stock character
54 One of the Traveling Wilburys
55 Prepared to strike, perhaps
56 Coat hangers-on
57 Bristle (with)
58 Outfit
59 Lets fly

DOWN

1 Pickles
2 It's often underfoot
3 "Big iron," in hacker slang
4 Plastic containers
5 Greek city that remained neutral during the Persian Wars
6 Grocery stores
7 What many Latter-day Saints are
8 Architectural element often decorated with bas-reliefs
9 Computer desktop icon
10 Radio's "___ American Life"
11 Ill will
12 Amphilochus, in Greek myth
13 Sound from a test cheater, say
16 Divisions of a mark
20 Made-up
24 Unbroken mount
26 Witching hour follower
27 Laundry that's often food-stained
28 "Strange Magic" band, for short
29 Designing
31 Demand
33 Retinal cell
34 Any of the Three Musketeers
35 Narrow-bladed weapons
36 "___ we all?"
38 Said the same
40 ___ AC (pharmacy purchase)
41 "Truthful words are not beautiful; beautiful words are not truthful" espouser
43 Female bacchanalian
44 Take hold of, in a way
46 Follows a course
48 Scuzz
49 Flag
50 Warhol actress Sedgwick
51 Birthplace of Herod the Great
52 One of Carter's charges, on TV

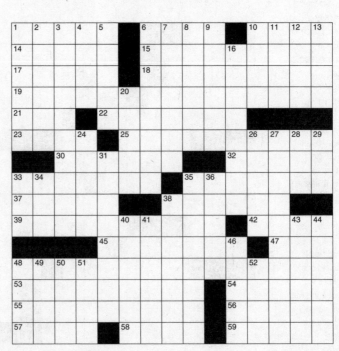

by Patrick Berry

ACROSS

1 "Same here"
6 Journey part
9 A.A.A. offering
13 Backless furniture
15 Let go
16 Martini & Rossi product
17 Punish arbitrarily
18 It has its highs and lows in math
20 Longtime TV host with a 1997 Lifetime Achievement Emmy
22 Something gotten on principal
23 Alternate name indicator
26 Feeling of excited anticipation
29 Pal
30 Antique dealers' destinations
31 Washington capital?
33 Make a sacrifice, perhaps
34 Treason
42 Affairs
43 Producer of many fragrances
45 Hirer's request: Abbr.
46 "Sense and Sensibility" sister
47 Microscopic code carrier
51 It was on the 37-Down of Johnny Unitas and Lenny Wilkens
54 Heavy metal
55 Like the ocean
56 Rembrandt van ___
57 Complaints, informally
58 Head-turner

59 Navigation abbreviation
60 Crib parts

DOWN

1 Exile of note
2 Winery in Sonoma County
3 Pennsylvania and others: Abbr.
4 Variety of swallow
5 Holy smoke?
6 World Series team manager of 1977, 1978, 1981 and 1988
7 Pressing
8 River through Rochester
9 Gum holders
10 33-time Walker Cup winner

11 "Road Rules" airer
12 Quiche, e.g.
14 Some dormitory purchases
19 The sculptures "Rigoletto" and "La Tosca," e.g.
21 Check for a place to stay
23 Drive at, with "to"
24 Really into
25 Seconds: Abbr.
26 Experts sit on them
27 Strands, somehow
28 Bit
29 Some infiltrators
32 Informal states?
35 "American Buffalo" playwright
36 Bullies, often
37 See 51-Across

38 French philosopher Gilson
39 Tien ___ mountains in central Asia
40 "Romance de Barrio" and others
41 Poet Thayer and others
44 Skinny?
47 Stuff in a locker
48 Reporter Skeeter of Harry Potter novels
49 Jour's opposite
50 Gremlins and Hornets
51 Be off one's guard
52 Brightness measures
53 Some college Greeks

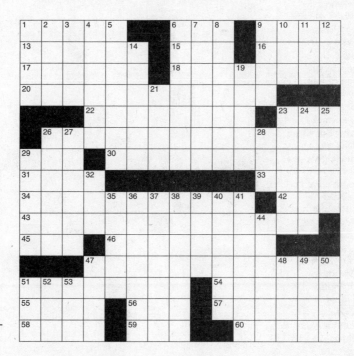

by Eric Berlin

ACROSS

1 Racetrack habitué
9 They have many cuts, typically
15 Masters of verse
16 "The Night Listener" novelist
17 Bars on bases
18 Olympic skating champion between Kristi and Tara
19 Operator of 17-Across, for short
20 An old secretary might sit in one
22 Swings
24 Plays out
25 Sites for fights
26 Smidgen
27 It's sometimes mined
28 Sophia Loren/Paul Newman comedy, 1965
29 Con game
31 "Who ___?!"
32 Result of running off?
35 One of four in mythology: Abbr.
38 Pomade alternative
39 Some Russians until the Emancipation Manifesto of 1861
43 Conference member
45 Tolstoy's "Voyna i ___"
46 Paris Opera debut of 1928
47 "Hair of the dog" alternative
49 Packhorse or mule
50 Seniors
52 Flash
53 Brought honor to
54 Allow
56 Surround
57 Roast ingredient?
58 Critic with an opposable thumb?
59 Dead center?

DOWN

1 Potential result of a conflict of interest
2 Magazine of the National Space Society
3 Winked at
4 Like 2-Down: Abbr.
5 Line delivered before lines are delivered
6 Actress Graff and others
7 Habitation obligations
8 Lucy-___ Museum in Jamestown, N.Y.
9 Become
10 Aviation entrepreneur Sir Freddie ___
11 Smacked
12 Looming in the distance
13 Ricoh rival
14 Criticizes impatiently
21 Preserves fruit
23 Cameo choice
26 One working on a canvas?
29 Actor Alfred of stage and screen
30 Hydrotherapy option
33 Prompt
34 Small protest
35 Arrange alternately
36 What a politician often avoids saying
37 French astronomer who wrote the seminal "Celestial Mechanics"
40 Strong Greek wine
41 Spoilage slower
42 Potter's field?
44 Mutual fund category
46 Fast food
48 Her "Don't You Know" was a #1 R&B hit
49 "I ___ reason not to"
51 Grab, slangily
55 N.Y.C. educ. inst. since 1926

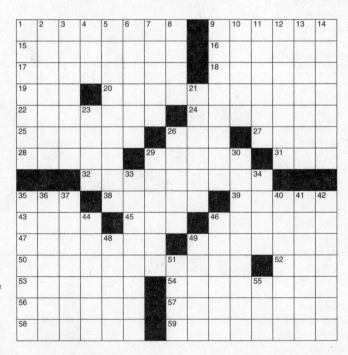

by John Farmer

ACROSS

1 Moguls on a ski run
6 Gimcrack
14 And others, in the Forum
16 Snacked
17 When duelists duel, sometimes
18 Points on bell curves
19 Family name preceder
20 Vikings, e.g.
22 "Gotcha!"
23 Stoker of literature
25 Buildings on the English countryside
26 ___-humanité
27 "Star Wars" character, informally
29 Kind of power
30 Begat
31 Really succeeds
34 Spans
38 Be fed up to here (with)
39 Some religious artwork
42 Squall
43 Like some straws
44 ___ Galerie (Manhattan art museum)
45 Christmas entree
47 Means (of)
48 Chronometric std.
49 Hoydens
51 Architect born in Guangzhou
52 Sweet wine
54 Pitcher Don of the 1950s–'60s Cubs
56 Parenthetical information
57 Whet again
58 "Acoustic guitar" or "push lawn mower," e.g.
59 Revolver

DOWN

1 Some retro chairs
2 Hogwash plus
3 Femme fatale
4 Org. for Mahmoud Abbas
5 Priory of ___, group in "The Da Vinci Code"
6 "So?!"
7 Be in charge
8 Head lights?
9 Teacher, in dialect
10 Ring org.
11 Kind of education
12 Military command
13 Interconnected
15 Dope
21 "Enough joking around!"
24 Light, white wine
26 Not hear a single word?
28 Four Holy Roman emperors
30 Course in the behavioral science dept.
32 Military training acad.
33 Parlor piece, for short?
35 Stealthily, maybe
36 Broadway opening
37 Lookout
39 Relative of Sven, possibly
40 Reserved
41 Kickoff
45 Were friendly
46 Appraiser
49 Food with cheese topping
50 Ton
53 It must be tired to work
55 "That's enough!"

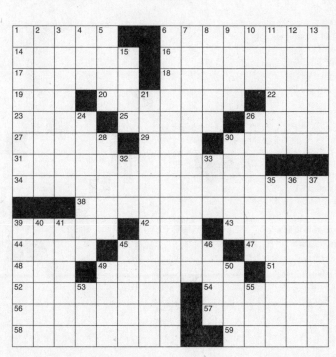

by Manny Nosowsky

ACROSS

1 Stock report heading
11 Early astronomer for whom a lunar crater is named
15 "Pretty fishy, if you ask me"
16 Work unit
17 Persevere
18 It's surrounded by agua
19 ___ course (plans)
20 Grandma Moses' first name
21 Group that included the L.A. Express
22 Game opener
23 Cave, in poetry
24 Utah senator who co-sponsored a 1930 tariff act
25 Bastille Day party site
28 Shade of green
30 The Rams of the Atlantic 10 Conf.
31 Dartboard wood
32 Fedora feature
34 Complicate
38 Like curling stones
39 Some come with twists
41 Pier grp.
42 Suffix with lact-
43 Literally, "disciple"
44 Huns, e.g.
48 Shakespearean title
50 Archaic adverb
52 Want ad abbr.
53 Prefix with Aryan
54 Cagney player in the "Cagney & Lacey" pilot film
55 Black on the screen
57 Detroit's ___ Arena
58 Drink mentioned in Rupert Holmes's song "Escape"
60 Blues guitarist Taylor
61 "This isn't a good time"
62 ___ Hilario, Brazilian-born N.B.A. star
63 Survey participants

DOWN

1 Question from far away, perhaps
2 Bony
3 Forger
4 Shadows, briefly
5 ___-Mints chewable antacid
6 Second-century year
7 Steppes settler
8 They're pressed into service
9 Boastful
10 Singer Jones
11 Kind of pipe
12 "___ Waltz," which begins "Hush-a-bye, ma baby, slumbertime is comin' soon"
13 Gung-ho
14 Immediacy of data processing
23 John F. Kennedy or George H. W. Bush
24 Parts of perianths
26 Harvard Science Center architect
27 ___ Midgen, fellow student of Harry Potter
29 It's catching
33 ___ B'rith
34 E-mail attachment?
35 Steady correspondence
36 Wonder-ful place?
37 "Ditto"
40 Contracts
45 Fill up with gas
46 Have-not
47 Finding things?
49 Hanger?
51 Show impatience, in a way
54 Exchange ripostes
55 2006 World Cup city
56 "___-in His Lamp" (Bugs Bunny classic)
59 Major suit

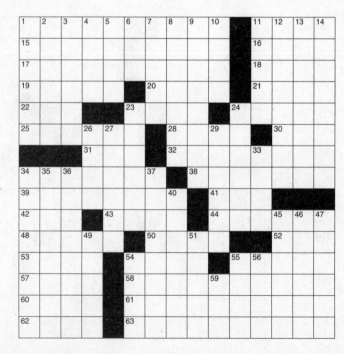

by Rich Norris

ACROSS

1. With 60-Across, much-heard sound bite of 1988
11. "The Human Stain" novelist
15. Singer of the Top 10 hit "Walk on Water"
16. Emperor for only three months
17. Unpleasant cause of being woken up
18. Start of a break-in?
19. Part of a party line
20. Pale purple shade
21. Slight
22. Obsolete
23. Draw alternative
24. One of Canada's two main polit. parties
25. Do-do link
26. "Miracle on 34th Street" director
28. Range of some robe wearers
29. "We definitely should"
31. Service cover-up?
33. Top prize at las Olimpiadas
34. Drainpipe discovery
35. Circuit City alternative
39. Flouts
43. Scuffling
44. Exercise
46. Org. established by Nixon
47. Hill, in Hebrew
48. Some dolls
49. Cover
50. Language closely related to Montagnais
52. With no imperfections
53. Pop label
54. 1999 Jodie Foster title role
55. Cardinal, e.g.
57. Fermentation locations
58. Being supportive
59. Actress Sommer
60. See 1-Across

DOWN

1. Athlete's downtime
2. "With Reagan" memoir writer
3. 1821 elegy to commemorate Keats
4. Like some banks
5. An athlete might swim in it
6. First name in exotica music
7. Teases
8. Bored with life, say
9. Olivine variety
10. Jazz singer Sylvia
11. Range
12. It was first performed at Whitehall Palace in 1604
13. Posh place to stay in Piccadilly, familiarly
14. Hood moniker
23. Start
26. Dweller on the Morava River
27. Greek sea god
28. Broadway opening
30. Dole's successor in the Senate
32. Grp. founded by a former high-school principal in 1958
35. Robin's place
36. Never cut off
37. Knuckle head?
38. "Starpeace" performer
39. Brand available in "fire" and "ice"
40. Pitch
41. Serial number?
42. Hospital supply
45. Miller's "S.N.L." "Weekend Update" successor
49. Part of v.v.
51. Opposite of aggravate
52. Fund-raising suffix
53. Slug, say
56. Place of worship

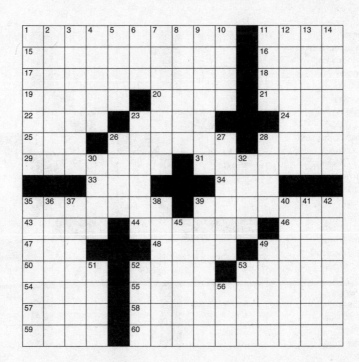

by David Quarfoot

72

ACROSS

1. Mistake at the hospital?
5. See 22-Down
10. Freddy Krueger and others
14. Modern library offering
15. Continental locales
16. Dollars for quarters
17. Sell short
19. Head out on the range
20. ___ Valley
21. Musician with the first record formally certified as a million-seller
26. Not
28. Baby brother, often
29. Gym amenity
31. Jacquerie
35. Doctor
36. One who shakes in a kitchen, maybe
37. Veins
38. Canada's Battle of Fort ___, 1866
39. Card game with a bank
40. Like Oedipus' marriage
45. A barber may shave this
48. Like human skin
49. Hamstrings
54. Four-in-a-row U.S. Open winner
55. Mulling
56. Duties
57. Crepe paper feature
58. More than ready
59. Some lobsters

DOWN

1. Famed host near Broadway
2. "___ in the Money" (1933 hit)
3. Graphic ___
4. Confidential warning
5. Tiny distance unit
6. At three or nine o'clock
7. With 24-Down, like 10-Across and others
8. Pari-mutuel machine
9. Lets go
10. Deep-fry alternative
11. Hope chest contents
12. Mary ___, Shakespeare's mother
13. Kind of bank
18. Land on the Med.
19. Scheming
21. '00s, now
22. With 5-Across, phrase of clarification
23. Been intimate (with)
24. See 7-Down
25. G.E. employee
27. Tyler or Jackson
29. Starter, often
30. Marc Antony's love
31. Junkie
32. Senior, in French names
33. S.C. Johnson spray
34. "Mm-hmm, mm-hmm"
39. Put coins in
40. Life
41. Severely outscore, slangily
42. It's just one thing after another
43. Godfrey's woman in "My Man Godfrey"
44. Embeds
46. "Green ___"
47. Object of an April Fools joke
49. ___ Drago, "Rocky IV" villain
50. Dict. label
51. Doctor
52. Comment at the poker table
53. Cookie holders
54. Fraternity letter

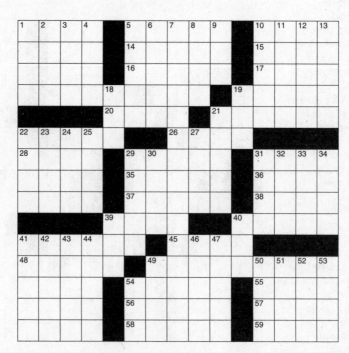

by John Duschatko

ACROSS

1 Recently
7 Data recorders
15 Loud warning signal
16 One of the Zappas
17 Really regret
18 Like some damages
19 Without skimping
20 What a resignee calls it
21 Russian peace
22 One of a matched set
23 W can be a vowel in it
24 Color close to cranberry
25 Be outstanding?
26 Book of Kells, e.g.
27 Something to wrangle with
28 Perchance
30 Sub
32 Store
34 Reeling feeling
38 Interior decorator's concern
40 Choose not to take
41 Molly of classic radio
44 Parts of 24-Down
46 Bird with giant talons
47 Bring in
48 Not go on
49 Chinese export
50 Super Bowl played at Dolphin Stadium
51 Can't refuse
52 Work of Passion
53 "This is the last straw!"
55 Lacking liveliness
56 School in culture
57 Best degrees
58 Order of roses
59 Player of Lincoln in "Abe Lincoln in Illinois," 1940

DOWN

1 "People Will Say We're in Love" musical
2 Result of provocative posters?
3 Marine suckers
4 They're more than full turns
5 Annual prize since 1947
6 Creature in "The Two Towers"
7 Hospital containers
8 Ruler for 72 years
9 The 4 in 4/6, e.g.
10 León liqueur
11 Fiend
12 Bad blood
13 High school course
14 Like some recordings
20 Letters seen by a proof reader?
23 Schneider's "The Dukes of Hazzard" co-star
24 They cover the bottom
26 Olympics craft
27 Turkish bread
29 Atlas and others
31 Mobile home
33 Not enlarged or shrunken
35 Side in a 1967 war
36 Blast
37 Quotidianly
39 Level
41 1970 and 1986 World Cup host
42 Hoops Hall-of-Famer Murphy
43 Sorrow
45 Initially the same?
48 European port founded by the Phoenicians
49 Dumps, so to speak
51 Sign of virtue
52 Sobriquet for singer John Phillips
54 Shaded
55 Petite pooch, for short

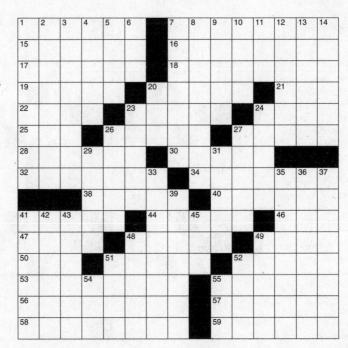

by Will Nediger

ACROSS

1 Defame
8 It may be hard to resist
15 Opining
17 Composer of a set of variations on "God Save the King"
18 Like some wines
19 Send
20 ___ prof.
21 "The Situation Room" airer
23 Musical circles?
25 Some TV programs are shown on it: Abbr.
28 Bowl bonuses, briefly
30 ___ lo tanto (therefore, in Spain)
31 With 13-Down, they go off with a bang
34 "Happy birthday" wish
38 Ideally
39 "You know where I live"
40 Test administration locations: Abbr.
41 The Lake of Thun is a widening of its course
42 Worrisome letters to send
43 Prefix with thermal
44 Company leader: Abbr.
45 VCR standard
47 Sly
50 1950s White House name
54 Lot
58 Spectacle
61 Home-coming time?
62 Actual
63 Long Island community northeast of Mineola

DOWN

1 95 for Am or 100 for Fm: Abbr.
2 Many Iranian believers
3 Go with
4 Atlas shelfmate: Abbr.
5 "Gunga Din" distributor
6 Alternative to a berating
7 Keto-___ tautomerism (organic chemistry topic)
8 Just right
9 Cause of deep division
10 Station info: Abbr.
11 Skeletal parts
12 Important pieces in échecs
13 See 31-Across
14 Salon job, informally
16 Campus figure?: Abbr.
22 Muzzle attachment
24 Clean laundry that hasn't yet been ironed
25 Castigate
26 Title for un profesor
27 Plantation head?
29 As of now
30 Results of some peacekeeping efforts
31 Good dog for livestock droving
32 "Starry Night Over the Rhone" setting
33 Name of either of the only two emperors of Brazil
35 Capable, facetiously
36 Calendario unit
37 Calendar abbr.
44 Alexander of debates
46 Bygone royalty
47 Like wine
48 Quotable review
49 Sign seen in front of some bars
51 Classically named Martian crater visited by the Opportunity rover
52 Producer: Abbr.
53 Slips in pots
55 1961 earth orbiter
56 Take ___ from
57 Forward
59 Quick shot?
60 Unit of conductance

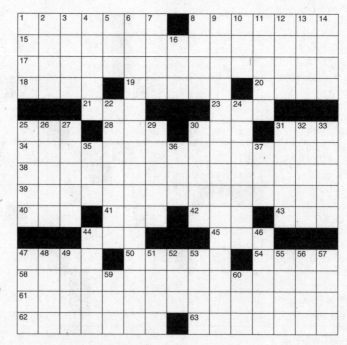

by Michael Shteyman

ACROSS

1 Four Noble Truths formulator
7 It might wind up in the kitchen
15 Hebrew for "one who wrestles with God"
16 Country where Taki-Taki is spoken
17 Appeared
18 Dove
19 Red square
21 Clears
22 Archetypical 1940s worker
23 Have an effect on
24 Wordsworth's "___ to Duty"
25 Showing fatigue
26 Kind of pen
27 Handles clumsily, as a pail
31 Went up and up and up
32 Took a powder
33 Launch sites
34 Pick
37 Stuck in traffic, say
40 Unmake tracks
41 Blackguard
42 Monthly originally published by EC Comics
44 Feast
45 The letter O doesn't have one
47 Device that may include an anemometer
48 Philosophical comment on people's differences
51 Gradually adopted
52 Available
53 Balloonist
54 Many a revolutionary
55 1989 film set at Eastside High
56 Still

DOWN

1 Eatery
2 Unix system numbers
3 Top of the holiday season?
4 Muffles
5 No-goodnik
6 Black ___ (winterberry plant)
7 Señores' other halves
8 Veronica ___, 2003 title role for Cate Blanchett
9 Any number from 1 to 12
10 Impressionists exaggerate them
11 Overjoyed
12 Subject of a 2006 biography subtitled "A Legend Like Lightning"
13 Mideast land
14 Entered anew
20 Blew away
26 Gin fizz ingredient
28 This is no time for playing games
29 Fruit used to flavor liqueur
30 "In ___ Shoes" (2005 film)
31 1940s–'50s pitcher Maglie
33 Gathering storm
34 Like some complex feelings?
35 Request starter of old
36 Trumpet blast
37 Star of the 1930s musical "Jumbo"
38 Spring
39 Moves gently up and down
41 Element in photoelectric cells
43 Xerophyte's home
45 Midsize
46 Nature trail sights
47 It has openings for a knight
49 Casino game with tickets
50 Heal

by Patrick Berry

76

ACROSS

1 Dessert preference
8 Pontiac, for one
14 They're clean
16 Took its toll?
17 Proof provider
18 Encroachment
19 Spa employee, generally speaking
20 So-so series
21 Benjamin's love in "The Graduate"
22 Medication administration stipulation
24 Not wanting more
25 Changes color, maybe
26 ___ Cruces (Andean peak)
27 They'd like to take things back
31 Back of front?
32 Some relieved people
33 Very beginning?
34 Dresses down
36 Grammy winner Winans
37 Enfants attend them
38 Stripes
39 Went at
42 Toxic condition
43 Slight noticeable effect
44 Hitchhike
46 Not gauche
47 Diva's problem
48 Best in
49 Need for a quiet report?
50 Declines
51 Things are often returned to them

DOWN

1 Like some poetic feet
2 Neighborhood
3 Producers of some shorts: Var.
4 Kids' concoctions
5 Belgian port
6 Inventive Vermont blacksmith of the 19th century
7 It's spoken in Stornoway
8 Classic novel with the heroine Alexandra Bergson
9 Novel price, way back when
10 Maximally sharp
11 Tons
12 Move through traffic, say
13 Like bonuses
15 Rulers
23 Tears
25 Delight
27 Gilda's father, in opera
28 Beginning on
29 Device for converting alternating current into direct current
30 Experiences dizziness
32 Sinatra or Capra
35 Places to put some bags
36 "Fanfare for the Common Man" composer
38 Petty officers' inferiors
39 Nejd natives
40 Single component
41 Stick alternative
42 Nipped
45 Auspices: Var.

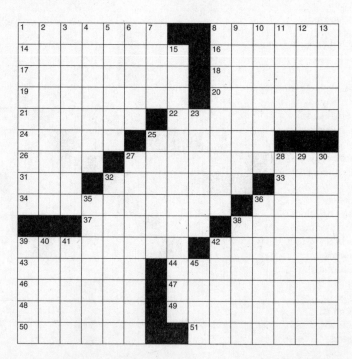

by Sherry O. Blackard

ACROSS

1 One who doesn't want to grow up, in a jingle
11 Dramatists' degs.
15 Versatile combatant
16 Set down
17 Popular '90s workout video
18 Cause for an "Excuse me!"
19 Matin's opposite
20 Interpretation of a dog's growl
22 E.U. mem.
23 Larry or Louise on "Bewitched"
24 Modern communication
26 Harmonia's antithesis
27 Make one
28 Show
29 Turnoffs, e.g.: Abbr.
30 "___ chance!"
31 Like some limits
32 Where hangings are witnessed: Abbr.
33 Bogart's only horror film title role, 1939
34 Sore spot
37 Move on a court or a diamond
40 Western setting: Abbr.
43 Scylla or Charybdis
44 Starting point?
45 "And the ___ raths outgrabe" ("Jabberwocky" line)
46 a, b, c, d, e, etc.
48 Capital on Upolu island
49 Dude
50 Yankee Clipper company

51 Old Fords
52 Golden Age writer
54 Home of Southern University
57 Pendant
58 Church section
59 Dark times, in literature
60 Berlioz opera based on Virgil's "Aeneid"

DOWN

1 Wedding reception figure
2 Participating in a group
3 Insistent affirmation
4 Three-ingredient treats
5 W.W. II inits.
6 Young ___

7 Audited
8 Presidential abode
9 Song on the Beatles' "Let It Be"
10 "Time Out of Mind" Grammy winner
11 Queen of folklore
12 Seasonal safeguard
13 Broadcasting unit?
14 Gateman?
21 Exile
24 Optometria concern
25 Meat
30 Wrap for a nursery plant
32 World leader who resigned in 1974
33 Gets into
34 Bars from a store

35 Birthplace of René Coty
36 Old Army meal
37 Muffin, for one
38 Conceives
39 Monopoly avenue
40 Chart maker
41 Dash
42 Some TV spots
45 "Le Morte d'Arthur" author
47 Intrigue
53 Stat for infielders
55 Big A.T.M. maker
56 Zoo critter

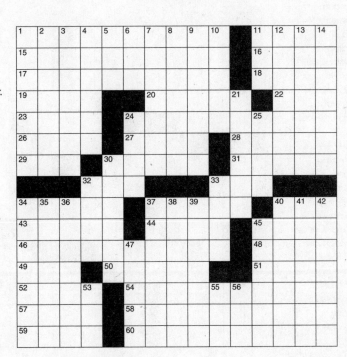

by David Quarfoot

ACROSS

1 Sputtered
10 "Go ahead!"
15 Prosciutto, often
16 Catch up with the class
17 "I'm countin' on it!"
18 With 24-Across, Fortune 500 company founded by two college dropouts
19 Began drawing
20 Tennis technique
22 Shah ___ Pahlavi
23 A lot of Tijuana
24 See 18-Across
25 Jams
28 Recourse?
29 With 37-Across, mid 20th-century avant-garde movement
33 Like a showstopper
34 Showstopper
36 Trevanian's peak
37 See 29-Across
38 Shingle abbr.
39 What cuirasses cover
40 See 51-Across
41 It may be pumped
42 Parliamentary doings, e.g.
46 Less sympathetic
48 ___ Pass (Candy Land shortcut)
51 Adm. Rickover of the 40-Across
52 1969 Frank Sinatra album featuring Rod McKuen songs
54 "John Q" actress Kimberly

55 Prowler avoided by prowlers
56 Some offshoots
57 Forsooth

DOWN

1 Parfait feature
2 Down ___ knee
3 Old Indianapolis-based automaker
4 It connects to the deltoid ligament
5 Project particular
6 English poet laureate of 1692–1715
7 Shingle abbr.
8 Had a cow?
9 They fight to the finish
10 Catch-22s
11 Curl units

12 Chronic fatigue syndrome, informally
13 Due
14 Mall rats, typically
21 Settings for some special deliveries: Abbr.
23 Toulouse-Lautrec hangout
25 Headline
26 Japanese computer giant
27 Psychiatric discipline pioneered by Margaret Naumburg
28 Tennessee
29 Subject of 2004's best seller "American Dynasty"
30 A cut above?

31 Well-suited for an office
32 Stirred drinks
33 Fishing corks
35 Like some paychecks
39 Help line?
41 Mulcts
42 "How to Read a Book" author Mortimer
43 Saffron sources
44 Like Chinese, as a language
45 It's not original work
47 Santa's drawer
48 Blowout
49 Butler, e.g.: Abbr.
50 Big club
53 National Ski Hall-of-Famer Tommy

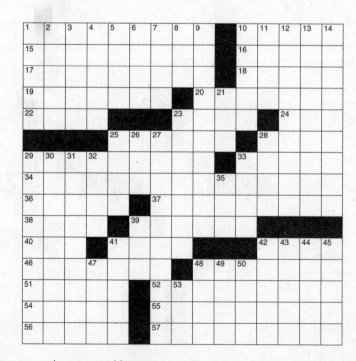

by Byron Walden

ACROSS

1 Training session
9 Rain forest denizens
15 Opportunity for a radio talk show caller
16 Rock's Dee Dee, Joey, Johnny or Marky
17 Got going after a crash
18 2006 World Cup runner-up
19 Sign before a crossing
21 2000 film "Billy __"
22 Author of "Oedipus at Colonus"
27 Many a quarter back?
32 On point
33 Took on
35 Reagan adviser Michael
36 Do well
37 Figures above a line
39 Covered (for)
40 Alexander and others
41 What gradeability is a measure of
43 Memory imprint
45 Resort town northwest of Naples
54 Having little talent for
55 Type of salad dressing
56 Before the deadline
57 When many Veterans Day ceremonies are scheduled
58 Like fourth-down yardage
59 Insects that walk on water

DOWN

1 Promise
2 Abbr. to the right of a star
3 Hart family sitcom
4 Have in one's head
5 Person with no hang-ups?
6 Billboard listing
7 Hollywood's Ed and Jennifer
8 Hawk
9 Monteverdi opera
10 Block splitter
11 Mother's helper in Madras
12 Corn __
13 Temple of the Sun worshiper
14 Bracket position
20 Long and short of it
22 Surprise visitor to Israel in 1977
23 Many Molly Ivins writings
24 Label in a Lauren Weisberger title
25 Protect, in a way, with "over"
26 Magical in
28 Highest point on the Ohio & Erie Canal
29 Smooth move
30 Weekend wear
31 Garden spots
34 Trying person
38 U.S.A.F. rank
39 Condiment in gourmet cooking
42 Copies, in a way
44 In the public eye
45 D.J.'s offering, informally
46 Dynamite
47 Memory work
48 Like most of Mongolia
49 Sitarist Shankar
50 __'Orléans, Québec
51 Musical based on a Fellini film
52 Growl
53 __ Club

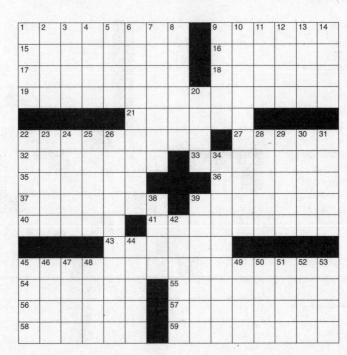

by Randolph Ross

80

ACROSS

1 Table saver
7 Gauged
15 Cosmetics dye: Var.
16 Primitive
17 Up
18 Refuse
19 Powers that be
20 Asylums
21 Twin killings, in baseball: Abbr.
22 Unidentified person
23 Louvre Pyramid designer
24 First name in courtroom drama
25 Mats
27 Like many leases
29 Language from which "kayak" comes
31 Last name of Dickens's Little Nell
32 Wallet loser's concern
36 Measure of pleasure
37 Far from laid-back
38 Barely eats
40 Praise to the heavens
45 Three-time speed skating gold medalist Karin
46 Cry of facetious innocence
48 They may accompany sitars
49 A.L. Central team, on scoreboards
50 Drive, e.g.
51 Complete
52 Gave what for
54 Lévi-Strauss of France
55 Player of Principal McGee in "Grease"
56 Secondary
57 Alternative to a box of chocolates
58 Joins

DOWN

1 Cause anguish in
2 Miss Ravenclaw, who co-founded Hogwarts School
3 Rectangle or square
4 One on a longship
5 Hostile territory is behind them
6 Catfish Row in "Porgy and Bess," e.g.
7 "What __ of the face is here!": Thomas Paine, "Common Sense"
8 Cast in a certain role
9 Absorb
10 Stationery store stock: Abbr.
11 One more than cinque
12 Shore border built up by waves and currents
13 Ratatouille ingredient
14 Something a loser may skip
24 Lake __, lowest point in Australia
26 Be just right for
28 Victorious soldier in May 1775
30 Plural suffix?
32 Cry after falling hard?
33 Did some horse-trading
34 Sommer of "The Prize"
35 Feeler
36 Shade
39 Recompense
41 Russia's Rostov, e.g.
42 Top of a closet?
43 Knighted Scottish singer Harry
44 Lactates, e.g.
47 Makes some lines disappear
50 Early copter
53 Sound system component?

by Sherry O. Blackard

ACROSS

1 You can always identify a Republican by one
9 Buck
15 Beneficiary, of sorts
16 Dodger who threw the pitch Bobby Thomson hit for the "shot heard 'round the world"
17 Essays
18 Zips
19 Chow order?
20 Many Middle Easterners
22 "Mârouf" baritone
23 His, to Henri
25 Makeovers
26 Tommy gun?
27 Enterprise counselor
29 Roulette or vingt-et-un
30 It may be needed after an entrance
31 Ones not getting their deserved acclaim
34 Ancient
37 Treated fairly
38 "___ a Man" (Calder Willingham novel and play)
39 ___ Salvador
40 Seine feeder
43 Neighbor of Pol.
44 Grounds for a medal
46 But, to Brutus
47 Bit of pollution
48 Summer Olympics participant
50 Main
52 With 36-Down, "Very strange . . ."
54 Maturity
56 Mean
57 Creepy feeling
58 Grain fungi
59 In harmony

DOWN

1 Ones doing a balancing job?
2 Oil worker
3 Worker with a wheel
4 The Beatles' "___ Mine"
5 Curry and Rice
6 According to
7 Remark introducer
8 Where no one has any business going?
9 Cousins of bassoons
10 Some arguments
11 Nonstick spray
12 Like the Coast Guard
13 August Wilhelm von ___, leader of German Romanticism
14 Indifference
21 Ones who can handle adversity
24 Hip-hop's Sister ___
26 Grave
28 Pakistan's chief river
30 Boulez's New York Philharmonic successor
32 Swedish flier
33 Laugh sound
34 City of 1.1 million named for the wife of King William IV
35 Ominous
36 See 52-Across
41 Suit, old-style
42 Early center of Christianity in Mesopotamia
44 Directional devices
45 Magazine proof
48 Nicky of "Boston Public"
49 Pull (in)
51 P.T.A. part: Abbr.
53 ___ Canals
55 Bristol-to-Leeds dir.

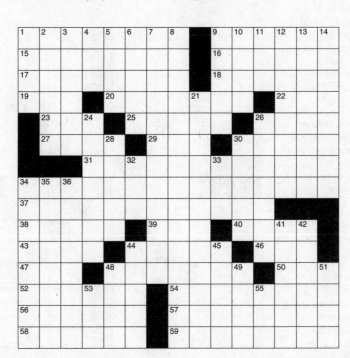

by Manny Nosowsky

ACROSS

1&8 Comic named one of Time's "100 most influential people" in 2006
15 Versatile weapon
16 Shrinking body
17 Do over
18 Entertainer whose last name is the past tense of a synonym of his first name
19 Chiang __-shek
20 Slice, e.g.
22 Unit in acoustics
23 Saskatchewan station name
25 Pretend
26 Central: Prefix
27 Sporty car features
29 Scatting syllable
30 One with concrete ideas?
31 False front
33 Victorian type
35 Quite bright
37 Their scores may accompany transcripts
38 X Games racers
42 French fashion
46 Prepare to shoot
47 Balance provider, briefly
49 They're between shoulders
50 Sitcom cross-dresser portrayer
51 Nannies' nightmares
53 He bought Vogue in 1909
54 New Deal org.
55 It's usually lost before reaching school age
57 Nova Scotia's Bras __ Lake
58 1909 Matisse painting

60 Hoot
62 Ajman, for one
63 Henry Wade's opponent in a famous court case
64 Less clear
65 "We made the right choice"

DOWN

1 "The first network for men" sloganeer, once
2 As you like it
3 "Kyrie __" (Mass petition)
4 Through
5 Berkeley's __ School of Business
6 Acclaim
7 Vital
8 Systems of rotating wheels?

9 "Caddyshack" studio
10 Arctic native
11 Short order
12 1962 pop hit with a foreign title
13 Decoration behind an altar
14 Nudist's lack
21 Travel route with no points in-between
24 Feature of some political parties?
26 Virile type
28 Einstein essay "The World As I __"
30 Stuff in a mint
32 Longtime U.S. ally
34 Inits. at J.F.K.
36 Prohibition-era offering
38 Stumps

39 2002 FIFA World Player of the Year
40 "Oprah & Friends" airer
41 Deferral
43 Impetuously, perhaps
44 Adventurer and Airstream
45 Boss's address?
48 View from Lake Kawaguchi
51 Thrash
52 Dinner course in Dresden
55 Sons of, in Hebrew
56 Port vessels
59 Refuge
61 Medit. land

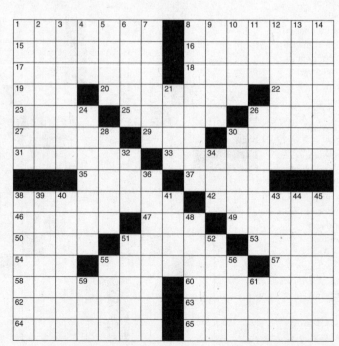

by David Quarfoot

ACROSS

1 Admirable people
10 Rope bridge sites
15 Formidable, as a task
16 Maker of the Jaguar game console
17 An unspecified number
18 Racing family surname
19 Ladies in men's rooms?
20 Air gun ammo
22 Problem fixable with a comb
23 Marionette parts
24 Thesis defender's prize, maybe
26 Assessment on out-of-state purchases
28 Disappear
29 Holds off
33 City where the Caesar salad was invented, 1924
35 It may have two sides
36 Option on an online order form
37 Highly recommends
39 You don't sit still in them
40 Prunes
41 One-horse town
43 Ingrid's "Anastasia" co-star
44 Theoretical massless particle
45 Cheers
50 Cage occupants
52 U.S. chief justice, 1953–69
53 Skillfully switch topics
54 People generally don't take it well
56 Surprising political move
57 Shoe insert
58 Seafood restaurant annoyances
59 Bagel variety

DOWN

1 Musical virtuosity
2 His statue (minus its head) can be found in Arlington's Freedom Park
3 Theater
4 Rub, rub, rub
5 It's nice to run these
6 Poor support
7 Big suit
8 Likely fossil location
9 Belittle
10 Dwellers in ancient Celtica
11 Magazine founder Eric
12 You'll find a trailer in it
13 Renuzit product
14 General address
21 Field-specific vocabulary
23 Film director Anderson
25 Gives someone a hand
27 Feature of the high church?
28 Musical genre featuring slap bass
29 Come back
30 Heading for
31 Upholstering tool
32 Goddess of the rainbow
34 "Heart of the Tin Man" author
38 Tropical fruit with white pulp and black seeds
39 Head up
42 Back-to-back action?
44 Narrow valleys
46 Figures in geometry
47 Not just put out
48 "When the ___ Breaks" (old blues song)
49 A big dummy
51 Inducement
52 1978–82 sitcom locale
53 Fill in
55 One who handles bookings

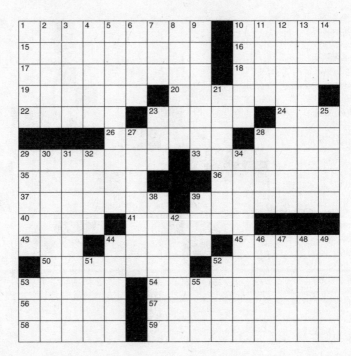

by Patrick Berry

84

ACROSS

1. Modern arts-and-crafts tool
10. See 56-Across
15. Present
16. Ecuador's Santa ___ Peninsula
17. Lingered past
18. Nonsense
19. It's extracted
20. Shakespearean title start
21. Small bay
22. Entangle
24. Graduate of Mount Holyoke
26. It may be rolled over
27. Having no gray area
29. 1941 musical comedy "That Night in ___"
30. Butcher's cut
31. Evasive tactic
35. Purple shade
38. Placed far in
39. Play things
41. Former European capital
42. Bit of mockery
43. Where the Peacock Throne was built
47. Mt. Tabor's country: Abbr.
48. Brief attachment to a report, maybe
51. Couple
52. Unanimously
54. Small amount
56. With 10-Across, stalemate
57. Fool
58. Like character actors
60. Dot follower
61. One studying camels
62. ___-face
63. Naive types, sometimes

DOWN

1. Pessimistic
2. "The Hustler" Oscar nominee
3. Comes out with
4. Saucerful?
5. ___ precedent
6. Air part
7. Rustic opus
8. Break
9. "The Spanish Tragedy" dramatist
10. Comedian/actress Wilson, an original cast member on "MADtv"
11. I, O or U, but not A or E: Abbr.
12. Coastal California colony members
13. Creator of the Mayfair Witches
14. Low-tech clicker
21. Current entry points
23. Guard
25. Guards
28. Disney's Princess ___
30. Ran out
32. Almost
33. Showy events
34. Action
35. Make campaign stops
36. Series opener
37. Tracts
40. Like Manhattan's Chrysler Building
44. Classic DuPont brand
45. Semi
46. "Leave business to ___, and wisdom to fools": Congreve
48. One easily pushed over
49. Like seconds: Abbr.
50. Lord Byron's "The Lament of ___"
53. Cracks
55. Speedy fish
58. Kid-___
59. Smidgen

by Rich Norris

ACROSS

1 Controversial court call?
9 See 36-Down
15 Bloody battleground for Lee
16 Affect sharply
17 Hit show with a colon in its name
18 Site of Atatürk's mausoleum
19 Series finale?: Abbr.
20 What a slasher usually gets
22 Top
23 Base for some decorations
25 Childish retort
26 Commanded
27 Means
29 Suburb of Melbourne, Australia
30 Many a surfer
31 First woman to appear on the front of a Wheaties box
33 Venus and others
35 Non-P.C. suffix
37 Target of a sweep
38 Musician known as "the Sound"
42 Treaded transport
46 Drops
47 Political columnist Thomas
49 Cry too readily, maybe
50 Further
51 Beat
53 1973 novel title character surnamed Peace
54 Drop
55 Setting of the FX series "Over There"
57 Area of responsibility

58 Jazz singer Reeves
60 "Yes, alas"
62 Draw
63 Offer that may be answered by "How much?"
64 Gave a hoot
65 "The situation looks bad"

DOWN

1 Drag performer?
2 Acting, say
3 Airport printout
4 Zip
5 Milldam
6 Breakout maker
7 Patterned fabric
8 Put out
9 Emmy-nominated "Hill Street Blues" actor
10 Hopper around a board

11 Cry of mock fright
12 "An American in Paris" song
13 Classic R&B song with the repeated lyric "See what you have done"
14 Trips might cause them
21 Midwestern tribe
24 Compact
26 Seats
28 Poker partner?
30 Not independently
32 Pilot's dir.
34 Attention-getters
36 With 9-Across, its images aren't hard to shake off
38 In time
39 Sprint competitor

40 Court embarrassment
41 Noted terrorist killed in June 2006
43 "Perhaps"
44 Country albums?
45 Bag holders
48 Lean
51 Put in a difficult position
52 Stock holders
55 About
56 Frog genus that's Spanish for "frog"
59 Nonexistent, in Nantes
61 Translated sum

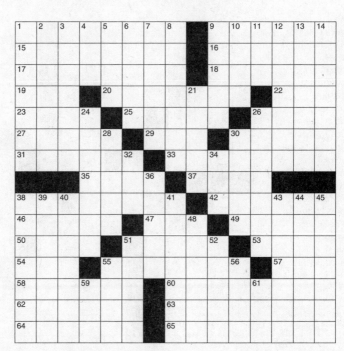

by David Quarfoot

86

ACROSS

1 Person who says one thing and means another
10 Crime lab items
15 & 16 Title time in a 1961 #1 hit by Gary U.S. Bonds
17 Language of 47-Down
18 "Homey!"
19 Contingencies
20 Public station
21 Not leave as is
22 Sitcom set in Houston
24 Percolate
25 Tears
26 Simeon the Great and his successors
28 Foul smoke
30 16-Across, in another way
31 Run
33 Terse identification
34 Rank informality?
35 Like the Supremes and the Go-Go's
38 Acoustic instruments
41 Band name heard in Morse code on its single "Secret Messages"
42 Tabooed
46 Grp. founded in part by the Y.M.C.A.
47 Time for a fresh start?
49 Like Eddie Murphy's Norbit
50 Parceled
52 Christian pop singer Tornquist
54 Brief salutation
55 Lighter
56 Devotee
58 Wee dram
59 Doesn't deviate from
60 Noted Joffrey Ballet dancer of the 1980s
62 Strikes abruptly
63 Flat, for example
64 Mississippi's ___ State University
65 Woman who flexes her muscles

DOWN

1 WD-40 applications
2 It's one funny thing after another
3 Classic chocolate treat
4 Foundation supporter
5 Nut full?
6 Olin and Horne
7 Bearded perennials
8 Say something to which people reply "Duh!"
9 Debussy's "La Mer," e.g.
10 Assumption subject
11 Question from the picked-upon
12 Place to spend drams
13 Spicy serving in a bowl
14 Plays, as a sub
23 Soprano's repertoire
27 Mr. Bill's outlet, once: Abbr.
29 Golden Slam winner of 1988
32 Rustic sounding man's name
34 Biggest part of a certain belt
36 Escape
37 McCallister of "The Story of Seabiscuit," 1949
38 Institutional investment
39 Fit
40 Lost the frivolity
43 Rear
44 Eighth-century pope in office for 23 years
45 Breathing trouble
47 Birthplace of Yakov Smirnoff
48 Hundred, in Honduras
51 The Bible's Mizraim, today
53 Register
57 Beard
61 Place to get five Jacksons, say

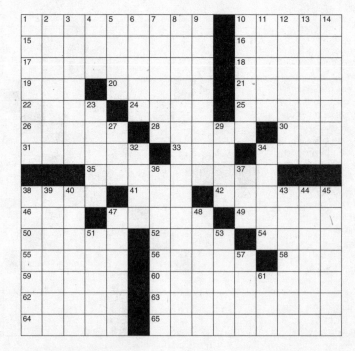

by Byron Walden

87

ACROSS

1 Actor with an L.A.P.D. auditorium named after him
9 Sell for
14 Words that often follow sweet offers?
16 One not mingling much
17 Flunkies
18 Vienna State Opera music director starting in 2002
19 It can have its charms
20 "Born from jets" sloganeer
22 One's native land
23 Fights
24 Key letters
25 Simple
26 Erstwhile grp. of 15
27 Bowl booster
28 Part of convention planning
30 Hurt
32 Relief providers
33 Subject of a financial report
37 Kind of port
38 Snide challenge
39 Guitarists, slangily
41 Shrink
42 Prayer opener
46 Starbucks option
47 Skill level option
49 Hamlet in 1969 headlines
50 Part of AIM
51 Look down
52 Source of sulfuric acid
53 World's second-highest capital

55 Feline gift
57 Open, in a way
58 Way of turning
59 They're perfect
60 Jazz greats, e.g.

DOWN

1 Crusades
2 It's less than perfect
3 Lulu
4 Sounds ominously
5 Its flag has a large red dragon
6 Mark up
7 Wood holder
8 Commits a logical fallacy
9 Mass
10 "Shoe" waitress
11 Not fully
12 Government reorganization
13 Good eggs
15 Plot target of the Decembrists
21 Like
24 Secretaries often hold them
25 Chuck, say
27 Relative of a fjord
29 2006 Oscar winner for his first film
30 Height
31 Expected before
33 One followed on horseback
34 Put on a pedestal
35 Interstate sight
36 Pres. appointee
37 Monkey with cheek pouches
40 Marxist leader?
42 Many a minstrel
43 Title pig of Ian Falconer kids' books
44 Like "The Godfather"
45 Double daggers, in printing
48 Volunteer baby sitter, sometimes
49 "Black Velvet" singer Alannah ___
51 Daddy-o
52 Tony who was the 2003 A.L. Manager of the Year
54 Kind of soldier
56 Cribbage jack

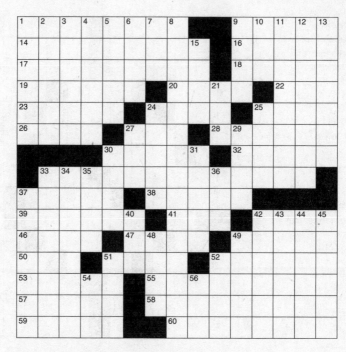

by Mike Nothnagel

88

ACROSS

1 Fandangles
8 It can aid one's climb to the top
15 With regard to worth
16 Smothering
17 DNA component
18 Fidgety
19 "The heck with it"
20 Come down briskly?
22 What might prevent you from staying out?
23 Semicircular room
24 Creaky
26 Swamp thing
27 Languish
28 Without repercussions
30 Massen of the 1940s film "Tokyo Rose"
31 ___ of assistance (search warrant)
32 Winter coat
36 Skips
38 Letter
39 Flatten
40 1992 Pulitzer poet James
41 Massenet's "Le ___"
42 How apples and oranges may come
44 Special treatment
45 Check
48 Series of six
49 ___ land
50 Precipitateness
52 It might be humanitarian
53 Inside look?
54 Thought
56 Like some tour buses
58 Fashionable part of N.Y.C.
59 ___ Island, N.C.
60 Brown foe
61 Displaying unmatched nimbleness

DOWN

1 Singer with the 1980 #1 hit "Upside Down"
2 Banked
3 Hyperbolize
4 "De Vulgari Eloquentia" author
5 First word of Oregon's Latin motto
6 Hound for bucks?
7 Makes sure something's done
8 Duty
9 Appreciative response to 38-Down
10 Designer Schiaparelli
11 Give a smooth and glossy finish, in a way
12 Woolly
13 Bank
14 Be apprehensive
21 Arizona's ___ Peak National Observatory
24 Compress
25 Like some plains
28 Faint
29 It might follow someone
33 Game in which crosses are used
34 Glares
35 Special kind of treatment
37 Bit of slapstick
38 Ones who accept charges
40 Waiter at a hotel
43 Schoolbook
45 Takes the edge off, maybe
46 Charged
47 River from the Savoy Alps
49 1974 Dustin Hoffman movie
51 Substitute for some names
53 Cherished
55 One-named rap star/actress
57 Some music

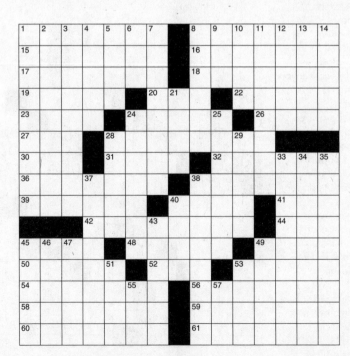

by Joe DiPietro

ACROSS

1 Mowgli's friend in "The Jungle Book"
6 Secondary education?
15 Half a robotic name
16 Besides
17 Pairing
18 "Just one cotton-pickin' minute!"
19 Changing places
21 Mature
22 ___ question (inquire)
23 Place to get a date?
24 Farm call
25 Hit list
27 Short shot, e.g.
28 Take the bait?
29 Goes quickly
30 Held up
31 Votes for
32 Time pieces
33 Bed occupant
36 Existed
37 Football Hall-of-Famer Blount
40 Satchmo, really
41 What you might give someone you don't like
43 Saw stuff?
44 Fix one's eyes
45 Grandson of Leah
46 Pump stuff
47 Sights before nights
49 Thoughtlessly
51 Indian tea source
52 On and on and on and on and . . .
53 TV sports personality Rodney
54 Quartz variety
55 Museum Folkwang site

DOWN

1 Flatter too much
2 Wisconsin city
3 Modern travel convenience
4 Consider
5 Bang-up
6 One-star hotel attraction
7 Sets of guiding beliefs
8 Certain winner
9 Coal sites
10 Pet food, maybe
11 ___ power
12 A fighting force
13 Strategist's creation
14 Like Polyphemus, in Greek myth
20 More wiry
24 Who's Who contents
26 "Now I remember!"
27 Secured by rope, e.g.
30 Fruitless
31 Slaving away
32 "Heavens to Betsy!"
33 Geezer
34 We
35 Figuring (out)
36 "How about it?"
37 Downsides
38 Issue
39 Photogs
41 Potsdam Conference attendee
42 Bronco actions
44 "The Lorax" author
47 Side track
48 Be wide open
50 Daisy ___

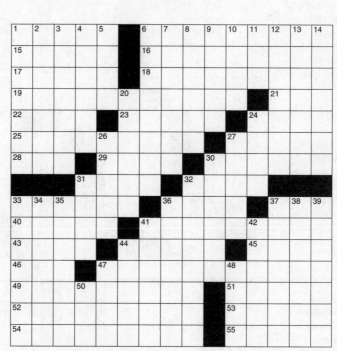

by Manny Nosowsky

ACROSS

1 Hardly poker-faced
6 Hamper contents
15 Nancy's friend, in the comics
16 It may be moderated
17 Hard to change
18 O.M.B. director under Carter
19 Word with heat or meat
20 Pays attention
21 16-team grp.
22 ___-wip
23 Back cover
24 Hirer of the stunt man in "The Stunt Man"
25 Dollar alternative
26 Skiing brothers of the 1984 Olympics
28 Excavation site
30 Course in African history
31 Go as far down as
32 Dialog box fill-ins
36 One may be hereditary
37 Give the benefit of the doubt
38 Upwardly mobile people
41 Tom Lehrer's anticensorship song
42 Yacht heading: Abbr.
43 Early '80s TV police comedy
44 Is touching
45 Separator of family names
46 Hot

49 Great-grandfather of David
50 Don't stop
51 Stop
52 From then on
53 In the main?
54 Many a conservative
55 Treasury

DOWN

1 Drought
2 Fizzled out
3 Tony winner for "Does a Tiger Wear a Necktie?"
4 Argued
5 It goes on and on
6 Help in constructing sites
7 They're made after a fight
8 A Manhattan restaurant is named for him
9 Angels' wishes
10 ___ parmigiana
11 They're obviously shocked
12 Progressing sequentially
13 Divertissement
14 Metric volume units
20 Hebrew tribe
22 Q-Tip, for example
26 Reason for a coup d'état
27 Many Pribilof Islanders
29 Ones making sports predictions

30 Connecticut resident
33 Frustrated cry
34 Screeners' targets
35 Make light of
38 Tool with a spiral
39 Swept off one's feet
40 Completely filled, say
41 Contact point?
44 Vanguard
47 Biblical verb
48 "Distant Correspondents" writer
49 Big loss
51 Campaign statement listing

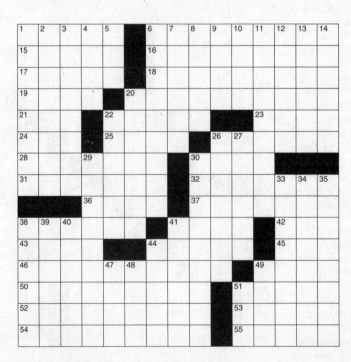

by Trip Payne

ACROSS

1 Brewer's need
5 Borderline
9 Salvaging aid
14 Strike
15 Art Spiegelman's Pulitzer-winning graphic novel
16 Show fear
17 Upper
19 Set free
20 Nice one
21 Sat. rehearsals, perhaps
22 Back up
23 Brand whose logo is a cone-headed character
26 Voltaire's "La ___ de César"
27 Electronic music pioneer
28 Culmination
31 Bring (out)
33 1990 #1 rap hit
36 Her name can be touch-typed with just the right hand
38 BBQ annoyance
39 Like kilts
41 Faux Japanese reply
42 Conductor's need
43 Prefix with -crine
44 Snarly sort
46 Biblical path to heaven
50 Pacific
53 RR sta. info
54 It's stranded
55 Hymn start
56 Bedtime cover
58 Fellow
59 React angrily
60 Pivot
61 Mythical reveler
62 Mice catchers
63 Spent

DOWN

1 Pedestrian
2 One whose flag features a dagger and two swords
3 Santa Claus, for one
4 Big race sponsor
5 Freshness
6 Events with tents
7 Offensive
8 Handbag monogram
9 Film attacker?
10 Postal unit
11 Like some troops
12 Homologous
13 English horn, e.g.
18 River whose mouth is near Nieuwpoort
22 Annual meeting attendees
24 Head-___
25 Dump (on)
28 They keep large flocks
29 Justice Fortas and others
30 Lighter, briefly?
31 Big Wheel rider
32 Jaffe who wrote "The Best of Everything"
34 Complex unit
35 Santa Claus feature
37 Poisonous ornamental
40 Not stay on deck
45 "Oh my!," for one
46 Erratic
47 Take second, e.g.
48 Result
49 Like baseball infields, before games
50 Is visibly miserable
51 Actress Raines
52 Etymology info
56 Sign of overfilling
57 Big Ten sch.

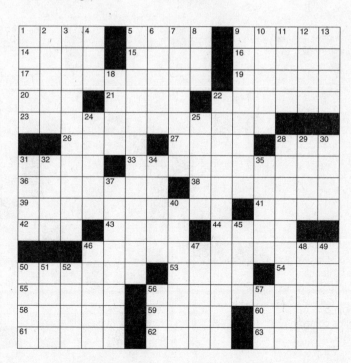

by Patrick Merrell

ACROSS

1 Cheerleader's syllable
4 "Aunt" with a 1979 best seller
8 Former Dodgers owner Charlie
14 Windowless
16 Where the Chiefs play minor-league baseball
17 Achluophobic
19 Wet
20 Works over
21 Lancaster's "From Here to Eternity" co-star
22 Formulator of the incompleteness theorems
23 Material for a dry cleaner
25 Country club figure
29 Peaks on a graph
30 Winner of all four majors
32 Look
33 Put away
35 Tree with roundish leaves
36 D. H. Lawrence's "The Rainbow," e.g.
37 Cuckoo announcement
38 Two-part
40 Showed
41 Calculus calculations
43 1960s–'70s vocalist known for his falsetto
45 Chieftains' groups
46 "___ Man" (1980s cult film)
47 Expo '74 site
50 New York river popular with kayakers

53 1988 film that precipitated the Buchwald v. Paramount lawsuit
55 Medium condition
56 Their work may involve banking
57 Touches (on)
58 Leftovers
59 Court sight

DOWN

1 Prajadhipok's kingdom
2 It's gathered by scouts
3 Unsuccessfully asks for a date
4 Where Tigrinya is an official language
5 Piece of pork?
6 Night light provider
7 Kennel sound
8 Medicine used to treat hypotension
9 Red meat sources
10 Like ghosts
11 Timeline divisions
12 It's worn on a road trip
13 Rival of Neiman's
15 Made better
18 Suit part
22 Biblical foursome
23 Futomaki or uramaki, e.g.
24 Long Island home of the Brookhaven National Laboratory
25 Clicker
26 Gibson garnish
27 À la king?
28 Gulf State resident

31 Pilots are found inside them
34 Demolition
39 Have a cow?
42 Bounce (off)
44 Not together
46 "Caddyshack" director
47 Where 46-Down got his start
48 Sweater?
49 Former Panamanian leader Torrijos
50 Goalie's feat
51 Planting unit
52 It goes on a break
54 Steering ___

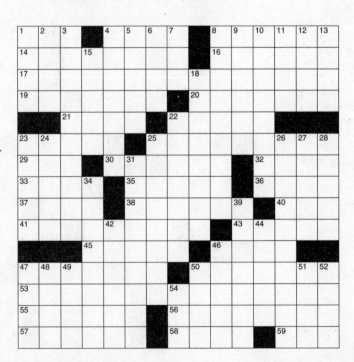

by Patrick Berry

ACROSS

1 Predicament
5 Tots' pops
10 See 12-Down
14 Metro Atlantic Athletic Conference team
15 Rice/Lloyd Webber work
16 It's part of P.R.
17 Backup troops
19 Dying words
20 Sweet German bread
21 Its use might leave you out of gas
23 Old computer networking protocol
26 One way to be repaid
28 Torment
29 Tiptop, in hip-hop
30 Steve ___, 1980 Olympic gold-medalist runner
31 "Fat chance!"
34 Musical instruction
35 Where "Aida" debuted
36 Captured, after "on"
37 In addition
38 Starch sources
39 Provide food for
40 Overseas carrier
41 Wags
42 Lincoln's description of pre-Civil War America . . . or a hint to the circled letters
46 Brown v. Board of Education city
47 Movable belonging
50 "___ charmant!"

51 Turn up on the beach
54 Religious inscription
55 Bypass
56 Enthralled
57 Shade of blue
58 Cries out
59 Junk

DOWN

1 Paul McCartney and others
2 Foot specialist?
3 Watching
4 Engine attachment
5 Stand up for
6 Opposite of après
7 Board member: Abbr.

8 Bill holder
9 Refuses
10 Lacoste-wearing, maybe
11 Affordable artwork, perhaps
12 One in a 10-Across
13 Baseball Hall-of-Famer Robin
18 Actress Verdugo
22 Fails to be
24 Literally, "little turnips"
25 New ___ (certain occultists)
26 "Well, well," to Wellington
27 Knot
30 Four-___ boat
31 Didn't like leaving

32 Little, e.g.
33 One of a matched set
35 Left
36 Words of defiance
38 Mission
39 Notes at the end?
40 Makes aware
41 Crusades
42 Where Christmas decorations go up in summer?
43 Ceratoid
44 Word with light or horse
45 Screening device
48 "Aeneid" figure
49 Endurance
52 Greetings from Galba
53 Staff note

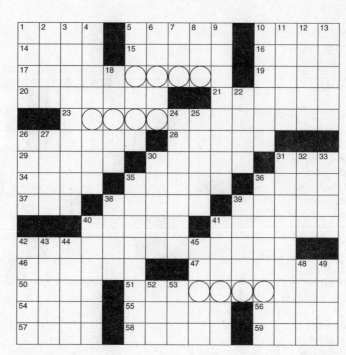

by Joe DiPietro

ACROSS

1 Big belt
8 Some ladies' men
15 Minnesota resource
16 Patent
17 Team members near the infield
18 Looks after
19 Longtime NBC inits.
20 Rave V.I.P.
22 Comedian who appeared on the cover of Time, 8/15/1960
23 Match
25 It may pick you up
26 ___ esprit
27 Capital on the Gulf of Guinea
29 Former grp. of 15
31 Adjure
32 Yahoos
34 Get blitzed
36 Electrical converter
38 Expression of bewilderment
41 Backup band in a 1960s R&B group
45 Keen
46 Minderbinder of "Catch-22"
48 Reserve
49 Nickname of B-western actor Robert Allen
50 Boots
52 Attraction at Chicago's Field Museum
53 Name of an Irish lass
55 One of five popes
57 Select
58 Made out
60 Court order
62 Annual White House event
63 Comparatively uncomplicated
64 Old "Your cup of inspiration" sloganeer
65 Grovel

DOWN

1 Site of a 1776 battle that gave New York City to the British
2 Major Atlantic Ocean feeder
3 Company picnic, maybe
4 Pop's kin
5 L'étoile du ___, Minnesota's motto
6 Religious denomination
7 Lumberjacks
8 "Keep your cool"
9 Judith ___, Tony winner for "Steaming"
10 42-Down ingredient
11 "The Wizard of ___" (short-lived Alex Trebek game show)
12 Old Buick
13 Busy, busy, busy
14 Bread with nuts and raisins
21 "Chill!"
24 Chicken-hearted
28 Sleep like ___
30 Center of power
31 Discarded
33 Like the Florida Straits, rarely
35 Self-proclaimed "singing journalist"
37 "Always Look on the Bright Side of Life" songwriter
38 Sentries
39 Extra
40 Necessary ingredients
42 Bar order
43 Punk, once
44 Authority on birds and bees?
47 How some books are sold
51 Roman general and dictator
54 Fuzz buster?
55 Popular magazine
56 Plane wing part
59 Indian state
61 Unburden

by Bob Peoples

ACROSS

1 Apes
5 Money in a Swiss bank
10 Athlete feted with a New York City ticker-tape parade in 1998
14 Home of the philosopher Parmenides
15 Be straight
16 Subj. of a makeup exam?
17 Cover sheet abbr.
18 Architect Jones
19 Store that offers Moo Malts
20 Single mujer: Abbr.
21 They may get engaged
22 Innovative chair designer Aarnio
23 Grammy-winning violinist Hilary
24 "Iceland" star, 1942
25 Place
26 Pennsylvanie, e.g.
28 Some hits: Abbr.
30 Seat of El Paso County
37 They help in making some calls
38 Norman Rockwell painted her eating a sandwich
39 General character
40 Way
41 Knock off
43 Tripartite treaty
47 Sun worshiper
50 Requiem title word
51 Not as exciting
52 Sometime today, say
53 Anjou pair
54 First name in 1950s politics
55 Up, in a way
56 Teri Garr's "Young Frankenstein" role
57 Best Actor nominee for "Affliction," 1998
58 Coven : witches :: clutch : ___
59 Slangy rejections
60 Bun component
61 Ready to be junked

DOWN

1 Chow line?
2 Super- relative
3 Ultimately triumph
4 Starting point of the Chisholm Trail
5 Follower of the captain's orders
6 Soprano Fleming
7 Like some zoo collections
8 Film vamp linked to Valentino
9 They have party restrictions
10 Roof sights
11 Jacqueline Susann best seller
12 New York skater
13 "Look ___!"
27 Where Orlando finds Rosalind, in Shakespeare
29 Encore elicitor
30 One that performs best when tired?
31 Iowa relative
32 Cartoon cry
33 Revealed, in verse
34 Sun. worshiper's focus
35 Educ. test
36 Old Black Sea borderer: Abbr.
41 Used for cover
42 Point of contention
44 Fire
45 Dijon daughter
46 Milk dispensers
48 Pointe-Noire's home
49 Calm's opposite

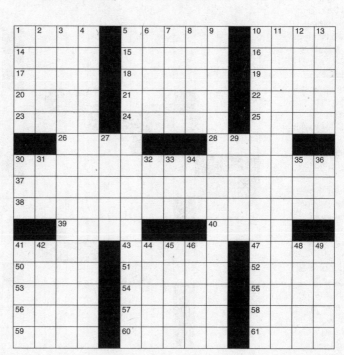

by David Levinson Wilk

ACROSS

1 Possible indicators of a change of heart?
12 Hang together, with "around"
15 "Dunno"
16 Pro
17 Tip-off
18 Easter bloom, in Évreux
19 TNT part
20 Things to stroke
21 Evidence of guilt, informally
23 Board
25 Computer security threat
27 Turns red, say
28 Japan's largest lake
30 Snap
31 "Moto Perpetuo" composer
35 "___ Autumn" (hit 1941 song)
36 Long-running TV show featuring match-makers
39 Hit the jackpot
40 He'd like you to put up with him
41 17-Across, perhaps
43 1990 Tony winner for "Gypsy"
44 Masterpieces
48 Passing notes?
50 Lure
51 With 47-Down, speaker's place
52 Golfer Aoki
55 Religious reformer Jan
56 Agcy. headquartered in Knoxville
57 First to see the sun, maybe
61 "I am worse than ___ I was": "King Lear"
62 Fondue ingredient
63 2000 title role for Richard Gere
64 Activity during which the blinds are never lowered

DOWN

1 Went (through)
2 Full of complexities
3 Something not often seen in France
4 One-named rapper with a self-titled sitcom
5 "Les Misérables" locale
6 Hitch
7 Snowthrower brand
8 Hamburger's one
9 Controversial 1980s plan: Abbr.
10 Some people take it to relax
11 Hardly snug
12 Mexican War battle site
13 Environmental woe
14 Lets up
22 Be short
24 "Dream Job" network
25 Going around and around
26 Onetime name atop N.Y.C.'s MetLife Building
28 Not a big chicken
29 Chip maker
32 Essen cry
33 Keeper for a rock collector
34 -ess overseas
36 Visit
37 What many saucepans hold
38 William ___ Center for the Arts, in Kansas
39 Kind of yarn
42 Mother or sister
45 Parroted
46 Lock holder?
47 See 51-Across
49 Clarification lead-in
50 Singer backed by the Aliis
52 "___ bird! . . ."
53 Mtg.
54 Sly
58 Shock's partner
59 Pack quantity, perhaps
60 Football Hall-of-Famer Hein

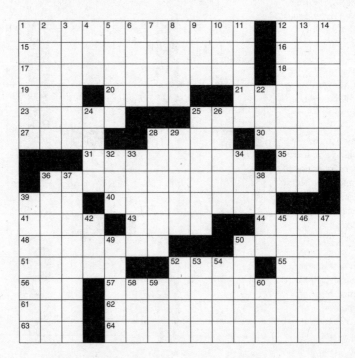

by Henry Hook

ACROSS

1 Dishes prepared alla Milanese
9 Some Western gear
15 "Heavens!"
16 Aloe soothes it
17 Call from Rocky
18 Lincoln is the only U.S. president to have one
19 Point pinpointer: Abbr.
20 Adequate, once
22 Renaissance fiddle
23 Interest
26 Attention-getting headline in a small ad
28 Neighbor of Rhône
29 One of three in eleven: Abbr.
30 Poor
31 Tart bar order
34 Eastern language
35 R&R sites
36 Santa ___, Calif.
38 Abbr. on a French envelope
41 Cry during crunch time
46 Runs into
48 Década divisions
49 Prefix with graphic
50 "Uh-uh"
52 Brains and beauty, e.g.
53 Skater Rodnina with three Olympic golds
54 Say you'll go, say
56 X
57 Compound used in aviation fuel
59 Roadblock
62 Words of clarification
63 Bridge opening
64 Roosevelt and Kennedy
65 Service station?

DOWN

1 Person of color?
2 Bit of wishful thinking
3 Under the table
4 Citation-filled ref.
5 Climber's prominence
6 One taking inventory?
7 Land with an exclave
8 Try to stab, e.g.
9 Big party: Abbr.
10 Modern greeting
11 Old empire members
12 Activity for little hitters
13 Calling up trouble?
14 1957 four-LP jazz set subtitled "A Musical Autobiography"
21 "Actually, you're right"
24 Refuges
25 Expressed uncontained joy
27 "Mefistofele" role
29 Assent for un hombre
32 Cartoonist Wilson
33 Bordeaux butters?
37 Teens might try to hide them
38 Handyman
39 Words with a nice ring to them?
40 Sent free of charge
42 Ace
43 Kind of soup
44 Out of action, in baseball lingo
45 "Uh-uh"
47 Actress Cusack, who married Jeremy Irons
51 21-season pitcher Darwin
52 Sleep clinic study
55 Grape or watermelon
58 A.P. exam org.
60 Reason to move forward annually?: Abbr.
61 Grp. concerned with m.p.g.

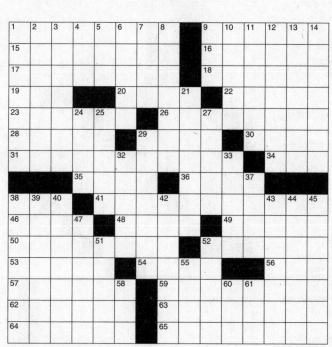

by David Quarfoot

98

ACROSS

1 "The Mod Squad" role
5 "Being John Malkovich" director
15 Clock starter?
16 Show in parts
17 Port whose harbor is in the crater of an extinct volcano
18 Rates
19 Missed the point of
21 Flying wedge members?
22 Larghetto
23 "Say __"
25 "Our Gang" dog
26 Long glove
30 Charity, often
31 Cuts out
32 Devon river
33 Those, to José
34 Those making firm decisions?
35 Aragón appetizer
36 Thonon-__-Bains, France
37 Stable arrivals
38 Host at church, say
39 Romantic
41 Like some points
42 "Crucifixion" artist
43 Suicidal
44 "Raising Dad" sitcom star
47 Naval escorts
49 Brew alternative
52 Low square
53 Garden transplants?
54 Highlander of old
55 BBC employee
56 Pieces of the past

DOWN

1 Put on
2 Unwilling
3 Style of pliers
4 Signifies
5 À la a stuffed shirt
6 Like some cleaning solutions
7 O.K., in a way: Abbr.
8 Little vixen
9 Abbr. in many dictionary definitions
10 Curél competitor
11 Situate
12 "Great shot!"
13 Puzzle pieces?
14 Sum, __, fui
20 Affectedly dainty, in Derby
23 Stands by
24 Hogans
26 Kind of trip
27 Folivorous
28 Go through
29 Fly
30 Torpedo's place
31 Seeming
34 It can be seedy
35 Ngorongoro Crater locale
37 Roller without sides
38 Rugby position
40 Revokes, as a legacy, at law
41 Not so slanted
43 Mark over an unstressed syllable
44 Pen, e.g.
45 __-mémoire (summarizing note)
46 Beleaguer, with "at"
47 Split
48 Large amounts
50 Not split
51 Site for Scheherazade

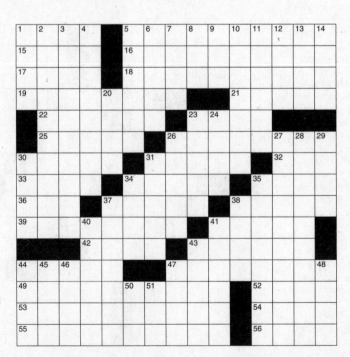

by Mel Rosen

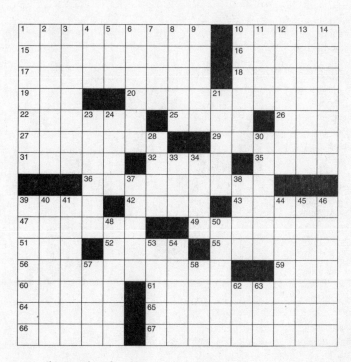

ACROSS

1 Manly attribute
10 Sailor's behind
15 It's frustrating not to get
16 In again
17 Like many an engine
18 Troubles
19 Road sign no.
20 Copier, of sorts
22 Correct à la a cobbler
25 Invoice abbr.
26 Mortgage org.
27 "The Three Burials of Melquiades ___" (2005 Tommy Lee Jones film)
29 Followed closely
31 Medicated
32 Stretch for the stars?
35 Dwarf planet in the outer reaches of the solar system
36 Candy jar classic
39 Copiers
42 Cryptozoological topic
43 Hippie sign-off
47 Hereditary
49 Basque, e.g.
51 Dog show org.
52 "Lobster Telephone," e.g.
55 Belfast's county
56 Like some sciences
59 Repeated bit in a song
60 Cremona artisan
61 Enthusiastic supporters
64 Wings, e.g.
65 Season openers?
66 Mars to mars, say
67 Sunscreen ingredient

DOWN

1 Fought
2 "Rather"
3 Hostilities
4 Duke's grp.
5 Density symbol
6 Were running mates?
7 One of two tumblers
8 Imminent, old-style
9 Doorstop, e.g.
10 Token place
11 Terribly tough task
12 Slightly
13 Top off
14 Dish with a side of guacamole
21 Blood of the gods, in myth
23 Bully's final words
24 Put great weight on
28 Sunscreen ingredient
30 Puzzle-solving level
33 Bank buildup: Abbr.
34 Year of Columbus's last voyage
37 Hamlet in 1969 news
38 Available
39 Where Enterprise is
40 Soldier armed with a spear
41 Subjugate
44 Small plane service
45 Having a stone heap as a landmark
46 As a body
48 Steer
50 North sea
53 George with a self-titled ABC sitcom
54 Many a Kurd
57 "Look ___!"
58 Score ___ (reach home)
62 Rescuer of Odysseus, in myth
63 One of two A.L. teams, informally

by David Bunker

ACROSS

1 Blockbuster
10 Inside job
15 "You'd better believe it!"
16 Hanging open
17 Base figure
18 Places for toupees
19 Victorian
20 Camp sight
22 Dirt
24 Thorny subject
25 Romance fiction award
26 Mocha setting
27 Neighbor of Draco
29 Mrs. Miller in "Ah, Wilderness!"
31 The Pleiades, e.g.
32 Noodlehead
35 Knock
36 Great time
37 Some E.R. cases
38 Dig
40 Thompson who played Fat Albert
42 Absorbent component of some cat litter
44 Thresholds
48 Rotten
49 #24 who played in 24 All-Star Games
50 Author Canin
51 His "J.B." won the 1959 Pulitzer Prize for Drama
53 Heart
54 Sticking point?
55 Odets hero Joe
59 Unhand

60 Smooth and white
61 Some nods
62 Warms up

DOWN

1 Displaying short-temperedness
2 County name in 17 states
3 Ratify
4 Well-groomed
5 It can turn over a lot
6 Head of lettuce?
7 Relieve
8 What there may be room for, barely
9 Fairy tale villain
10 Pops
11 Self-guided "tour"

12 Acquired with little or no effort
13 Having digital display?
14 Extra boots
21 Yuletide, e.g.
23 Some writers write this way
24 Remains to be seen?
28 Imperil
30 Makings of a hero, maybe
32 Knesset, literally
33 Noisy celebration
34 Goes after
36 They may shock you
39 Hamlet's cousin
40 Listening post?
41 Crank
43 Blowhard

45 Fan sound
46 Split
47 Derisive
52 "The Garden of ___" (Wilde poem)
56 Mr. Miller in "Ah, Wilderness!"
57 Workout target, for short
58 Stock figure

by Bob Klahn

ACROSS

1 Ones running things
16 It's black and tan
17 Rooster holder
18 Armies
19 Rooster holder, maybe
20 "Good for life" sloganeer
21 Passbook abbr.
22 Short units, perhaps
23 Not straight up
28 Coverage provider, briefly
30 Gone, and never to return
37 Where to see many rams?
38 Sulky racer
39 In need of a lift
40 Kind of inspection
41 Highly amusing
44 Sports supporter
46 Discontinuities
47 Brooklyn Dodgers pitcher Labine
49 Robert of Broadway's "My Fair Lady"
54 With nothing out of place
57 Flashlight alternative
58 Comment when something is over your head

DOWN

1 Dash part
2 Bygone cracker brand
3 Discord deity
4 Shut (up)
5 Some tributes
6 Took place
7 Professeur's charge
8 It covers the main points
9 Smith who won Wimbledon in 1972
10 TV component
11 It ended in 1806: Abbr.
12 1970–72 CBS sitcom
13 Like some pools
14 Is obviously happy
15 Lapses
21 Film director Vittorio
22 Passage preventer
23 Recipe direction starter
24 Come across as
25 Hobbling
26 Trail
27 In need of some color
28 Least bit of concern
29 President nicknamed Last of the Cocked Hats
31 Not much
32 Headache intensifier
33 Is left with
34 Belle ___ (Italian culture)
35 "Uh-huh"
36 Recitation accompanier
41 Charged
42 Nonparticipation declaration
43 Big note
44 Fox shelter
45 "South Pacific" role
46 Colette heroine
47 Pitcher's prize?
48 Afford
49 Athletic assoc.
50 "___ put it another way . . ."
51 ___-Neisse Line (border in Europe)
52 Time spent in a seat
53 Marine flier
55 It officially recognized Isr. in 1988
56 Literary monogram

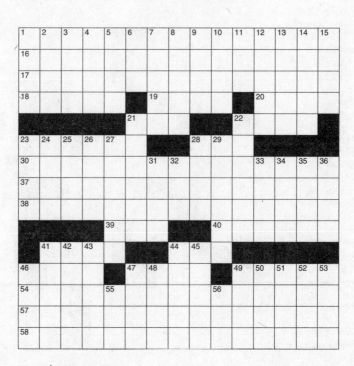

by Harvey Estes

ACROSS

1 Old afternoon TV staple, with "The"
6 Something light and soft?
14 Misrepresented
16 Prescription description part
17 Apprehensive
18 Joining-of-hands period
19 Number of the 2016 Olympics
20 Abbr. often before a name
22 Start of a critical call
23 Get worse
24 One of two extremes: Abbr.
25 Remains on the shoulder?
29 Retreat
33 Sore loser's cry
35 "Another Green World" composer
36 Island chains
37 It's held in an orbit
38 Inventor of a braking system for cars
39 The Rhineland Campaign was part of it: Abbr.
40 Tries to outfox
44 Curiously spelled 1960 Al Cohn tune
46 Somehow
47 One locked in a boat
48 Running things in a bar
49 Slime
51 "Now I get it"
52 Rake
56 Successful result in a DNA lab
58 Certain Ontarian
60 Three-time Emmy winner for "Nick News"
61 Drunken
62 Charges
63 Something struck from a book

DOWN

1 Big maker of small cars
2 Demographic group, briefly
3 Hoops Hall-of-Famer English
4 18-Across in France
5 Head shot?: Abbr.
6 Classic caution to a child
7 Start ___
8 Prefix with tourism
9 Where singles start out in love?
10 Lustrous
11 Mythical dweller across the Rainbow Bridge
12 Broad
13 Always, in verse
15 Try to profit from
21 Tiny waves
23 Calypso relative
24 Gooper's wife in "Cat on a Hot Tin Roof"
25 "The Old Swimmin' Hole" poet
26 Poem title start
27 Half-serious run?
28 Old Eur. money
30 Accepted
31 Hand and foot
32 "Munich" actor Ivgy
34 Spanish royalty
38 Have to return
40 Union organizers?
41 Always, in verse
42 They carry stigmas
43 Many men are registered with it: Abbr.
45 Having no charge
49 Molecular biology lab preparations
50 Some addresses
51 Unerringly, after "to"
52 Low in education
53 Frequent flier?
54 What comes to mind
55 Org. whose success is no accident?
56 Fabaceae family member
57 Breakers' equipment
59 Hardly a worthy competitor

by Michael Shteyman

ACROSS

1 Lake St. ___, between Michigan and Ontario
6 Ones turning on stoves?
14 Informal greeting
15 1966 Frank Sinatra hit
16 Exotic locale in old literature and song
17 Had nowhere to go but up
18 Boxer Tommy, loser to Joe Louis in a 1937 title bout
19 Successor to Goldberg on the Supreme Court
20 X-___ (big, in commercial names)
21 Popular weekend event
23 Arizona's ___ Canyon Dam
24 Where Dick Cheney grew up
25 Peak
26 Sidestepped
28 It may be found under an umbrella
29 Decorative covers
30 ___ acid (preservative)
31 Matched
32 Deeply tan
33 Very loosely knit
34 Emulate a base runner?
35 Lion prey
36 Sword swallowing, e.g.
40 W.W. II map: Abbr.
41 M-1 rifle inventor

42 Be in preparation
43 Totally unlike
45 Star of "The One," 2001
46 Free
47 Old-fashioned buildings in the English countryside
48 Excerpts
49 "Same Time, Next Year" happening

DOWN

1 Refuse
2 Major defense contractor
3 Omniscient
4 Name jewelry
5 Literally, "king"
6 Slipped out of

7 Magician's forte
8 Diamond datum
9 Chinese menu word
10 Last: Abbr.
11 Fifth of five
12 As above
13 Like some differences
15 Athletes Jim and Ian
19 Had nothing
22 Ghost of literature
23 Yellowstone sight
25 Lacks what it takes
26 1978 and 1986 World Cup winner
27 Masters
28 Reacted kittenishly
29 Bullied, in a way, with "on"

30 Hit with an errant pitch, maybe
32 Certain salts
34 Tower's end?
36 Carrier whose logo is an eight-pointed star
37 Like craft shows
38 Early Europeans
39 It's a surprise
41 Many a charity event
44 "Zoboomafoo" network
45 Bit

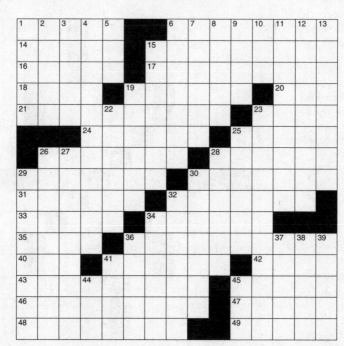

by Sherry O. Blackard

ACROSS

1&9 Informally, what aleph-null is, in mathematics
15 Old salts
16 "Willow Song" source
17 Rivals of the Buckeyes
18 Knights, by nature
19 "Modern Gallantry" essayist
20 Prefix with gram
22 Turn in a game
23 Yarborough of Nascar
24 Shy
25 On ___ (equipotent)
26 Antigen identifier
28 Sp. name preceder
29 Fourth número primo
30 Set
32 Like aleph in the central black squares of this puzzle's grid
34 Truncation indication: Abbr.
36 Certain jazz soloist
37 Face to face
42 Gerrymander, say
47 They're expected
48 By
50 Devil
51 On
52 Canal banks
54 Check inside?: Abbr.
55 Gush
56 Ballade ender
57 Lord's body: Abbr.
58 Cyberhandle
60 Performers
62 Fought
63 Revolt
64 & 65 What aleph begins, in linguistics

DOWN

1 Web site frequenters?
2 Neither here nor there
3 Not so stout
4 Like the Merkava battle tank
5 Basket material
6 Apples for the teacher, maybe
7 Positions
8 Trammel
9 Superbly pitched
10 ___ War in Colorado, 1879
11 Swimmer with three appendages
12 Hit a Texas leaguer
13 Buoy
14 Shade similar to cherry wine
21 Some British lines
27 Bad looks
29 Private instruction?
31 Parts of some grids: Abbr.
33 Cordial surroundings?
35 Group of 13
37 Hurried
38 A love of kitsch, e.g.
39 Certain Bartlett's listing
40 Montezuma, for one
41 Bliss
43 Bathysphere's place
44 Put off paying, perhaps
45 Grow together
46 Strongly built
49 Unlikely to preach
52 Moisten
53 Show sudden interest
59 Elvis Presley's "___ Lost You"
61 Girl chaser?

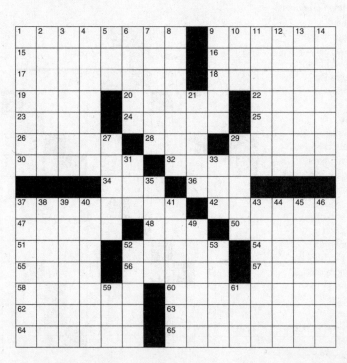

by Matthew Lees

ACROSS
1 78th Academy Awards host
11 Slugger known as the Big Cat
15 Honolulu Harbor landmark
16 "May It Be" singer, 2002
17 Modern loading site
18 Häagen-___
19 Retail chain started near Detroit in 1962
20 A person might drop one while dieting
22 Certain giftwrap design
24 "Bridal Chorus" bride
25 Bad: Prefix
26 It's like -like
27 ___ Gen.
29 Byzantine emperor called "the Wise"
31 Theo. Roosevelt Natl. Park locale
33 Admirer, and then some
37 "Any man who wants to be president is either an ___ or crazy": Dwight Eisenhower
39 Two-sided
42 Comanche relative
46 Fictional town in a 1945 Pulitzer-winning novel
47 Maze
49 Place to take stock?
50 N.H.L. star nicknamed St. Patrick
51 Pacer and Rambler
55 ___ Raiders (activist group)
57 It has a place in "herstory"
60 Étoile's field
61 Site of a 1992 Al Qaeda attack
62 Security alert
64 Zest
65 Conversation closer
66 Suffix with leather
67 Mae West, for one

DOWN
1 State capital on the Pearl River
2 Alternative to war
3 Rouyn-___, Quebec
4 Cheat, in a way
5 Percussion instrument
6 Sched. info
7 Promise
8 "Bird on ___"
9 Cut loose
10 Bit of salon waste
11 Pharmacy stock, for short
12 Helping
13 Destructive tropical American weevil
14 Starts gently
21 Dip choice
23 Cousin of a clog
28 First name in psychedelic rock
30 Fix firmly
32 New Jersey's ___ University
34 Something graded between E and F?
35 Bother, with "at"
36 German article
38 [Not more homework!]
39 Shakers and tongs, e.g.
40 Red Skelton musical comedy
41 It can make you square
43 Like some pumps
44 Rescuer of Andromeda, in myth
45 Wedges
48 A villain might come to one
52 Platform introduced in 1981
53 Relative of a rose apple
54 Nasal spray brand
56 Classic fantasy game, informally
58 "The Neverending Story" author Michael
59 Evil "Star Trek" group, with "the"
63 Eastern path

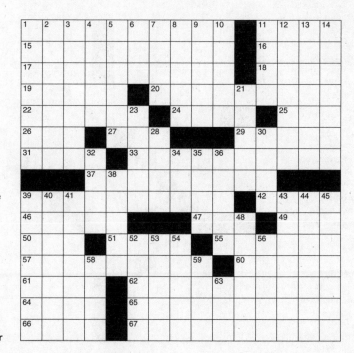

by David Quarfoot

106

ACROSS

1 Politically unstable area
8 2005's "Walk the Line" and others
15 Derived by logic
16 Fit for the stage
17 Goes home for the night, say
18 "Dig in, everyone!"
19 Actress with the memoir "Call Me Crazy"
21 Producer of the megaflop "E.T."
22 Film about a blind man for which the lead won Best Actor
24 After much delay
26 Like some calendars
27 Navigational aid
28 Repairs a leak, possibly
29 Snap ___
32 Classic pencil-and-paper game
33 Kiosk item
34 Mouthful
35 Signal
36 Lacking in resonance
37 Coin with a two-headed eagle on the reverse
38 Savvy film/TV character whose name, paradoxically, is Spanish for "idiot"
39 Bygone weapon
40 Some brass
44 Lose one's cool
45 Fiendish
48 Big farewell
50 1983 song that begins "Hate New York City"
51 Violinmaker Stradivari
52 Compared
53 Less natural
54 Brought to bear

DOWN

1 "Funny ___"
2 As yet undecided
3 Exchange words?
4 Brandy cocktails
5 Like a presidential suite, presumably
6 Help get settled
7 Color
8 With undisguised menace
9 Party supply
10 Council of Three Fires members
11 Flock's overseer
12 Rolled steel joist
13 Santa ___, Calif.
14 Arrive, as darkness
20 Exciting drive?
23 Auto racer Granatelli
24 Kind of adapter
25 Second person appearing in the Bible
28 Phrase in a police bulletin
29 Starting to mature
30 2004 title role for Anne Hathaway
31 Mountaineering goal
33 Car owner's annoyance
34 Swift traveler
36 Dessert topped with crumbled macaroons
37 ___ Colony (first English settlement in the New World)
38 Boss
39 Wordy
40 They're capped with caprock
41 "Aunts ___ Gentlemen" (P. G. Wodehouse's last complete novel)
42 Unelected officials
43 Former Lebanese president Lahoud
46 "Hard ___" (ship command)
47 "The Blue Dahlia" star
49 Cry of disgust

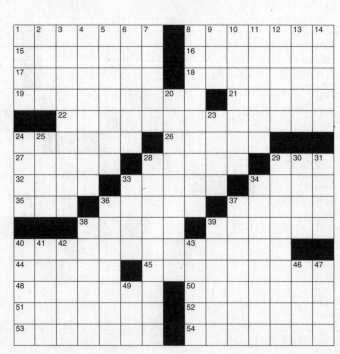

by Patrick Berry

ACROSS

1 George Orwell, e.g.
11 Hotel room amenity
15 Cabin locale
16 ___ di bravura (piece showing off a singer's vocal agility)
17 Oscar night activity, jocularly
18 Darn
19 Coil
20 American Indian organization
22 Honey, in prescriptions
23 Duct opening?
24 First name in country music
25 Take marks off
27 Red and white, e.g.
30 Universal Human Rights Mo.
31 Middle measure
32 Settled
34 Will do
36 Mob money units
38 Breeze (through)
39 King or queen
43 "Goodness gracious"
47 Modern site of ancient Thebes
48 Drum part
50 U.S. ___
51 Serotonin, e.g.
52 Breezed through
54 Kind of test
55 Hardly a good friend
56 Nash contemporary
58 Awning site
59 Skinny
61 Animals that are nearly invisible to infrared detectors

63 Scotland Yard discovery
64 Cooler by the shore?
65 Tearing things?
66 Vocal pessimists

DOWN

1 Restaurateurs' banes
2 "Antony and Cleopatra" role
3 "___ what?"
4 Foreboding
5 Univ. dept.
6 Pirate tale feature
7 Some shoe material
8 Harmonious wholes
9 Crescent
10 It follows that
11 Sorry
12 Language of the Talmud
13 Smoothness
14 They're small and may be golden
21 Some eastern Canadians
26 Denounce
28 Encourages
29 Blows a gasket
33 Party person, informally
35 Texas hold 'em, e.g.
37 Spring training site for the Cincinnati Reds
39 "The Silence of the Lambs" role
40 Within the realm of people's capability
41 Investment sales charge
42 Cage in Hollywood
44 Queen Elizabeth I had this
45 Holiday spot in el Mediterráneo
46 Slips by
49 Assayer's area of expertise
53 Andrea ___
57 Huge
58 Delight
60 Pained replies
62 Outlaw

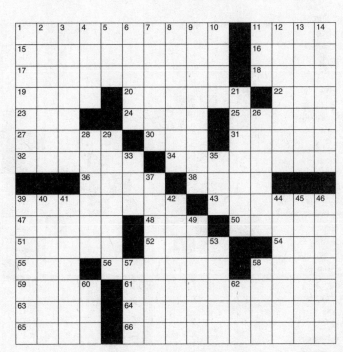

by Nancy Joline

ACROSS

1 Specialty of some bakers
9 Fictional N.Y.P.D. cop
14 Absolve
16 "Good alone is good without ___": Shak.
17 It's not meant for a 3-Down
18 Corral
19 Wine holder
20 Smart, in a way
22 Facial pair
24 Shift
25 2001 album that debuted at #1
26 Doughy
28 Sixth in a pledge's recitation
29 Break
31 Chase scenes were once common here, informally
33 Part of a fault line?
36 Answer to "Good enough?"
37 Awesome, in slang
39 Very wide, in a way
40 Amtrak abbr.
42 Inquisitor's quarry
43 A long one may have legs
45 Author of "The Gremlins" and namesakes
46 Writer LeShan
49 Brain, heart, liver, etc.
51 Not rot
52 One subjected to disarmament?
55 Kind of dye
56 Expensive string
57 Hiree after a move
59 Word before or after nothing
60 Wooded area surrounding a community
61 Dine, in Düsseldorf
62 Once

DOWN

1 "Oh well"
2 Choice
3 See 17-Across
4 "Nacho Libre" actress ___ de la Reguera
5 Jazzman Saunders
6 "___ you loud and clear"
7 Flip
8 Put in a ship's hold
9 Shot
10 "The ___ Love" (1987 hit)
11 Tylenol maker, for short
12 "Entrapment" director Jon
13 "Way of the sword" sport
15 Ornamental plume producers
21 It's big in Latin America
23 Convince
27 Zip
30 Hot
32 Enrich
33 Timeworn
34 Writer interred in the Panthéon
35 Longtime Indy 500 airer
38 Schnozzola
41 Completely clean
42 Some springs
44 Modern helmet add-on
46 Shake
47 Aspiring bands make them
48 1994 Noël Riley Fitch literary biography
49 Symbol of success
50 Astringent fruit
53 Olio magazine
54 Little ___
58 Typing letters?

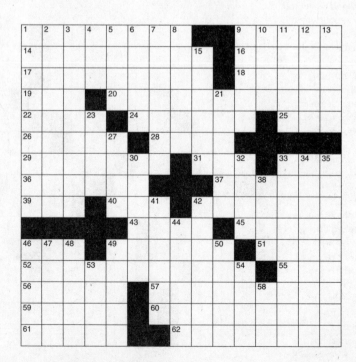

by David Quarfoot

ACROSS

1 It's just one thing after another
7 Sitcom character in apartment 5B
13 No longer minding one's business?
14 Animator
16 Vent, e.g.
17 Student of Titian
18 Group that shares its name with a 1930 Howard Hughes film
20 Series
21 Regard
22 Connections
23 Frightener
24 Bring (up)
26 Subject of an encoded message, maybe
27 Aircraft engine holder
30 General Mills cereal trademark
32 Adam or Eve vis-à-vis 6-Down
35 Deprive by force
36 Gun-toting types
38 Matter at court
39 Cacophonous
40 High points
43 P.O. items
44 Abbr. in a personals ad
45 Ducks
49 George Sand's "Elle et ___"
50 Torch carriers
52 Kind of set
54 ___ Novotny, 1950s–'60s Czech president
55 Frederick IX's land
56 Some wide-angle pics
57 Doesn't seem right
58 Qajar dynasty's domain

DOWN

1 Subject of the biography "Road to Peace"
2 Not straight up
3 Went through, as someone else's drawers
4 Person in the morning
5 32.81 feet
6 See 32-Across
7 Bedside container
8 Moon valleys
9 Some baseball stats: Abbr.
10 ___ de Glace, glacier on the north slope of Mont Blanc
11 Athlete's snack
12 Indefinitely repeatable
13 Mies van der ___
15 1960s girl group, with "the"
19 1958 Vincente Minnelli film
23 "Awake, arise ___ forever fallen!": Milton
25 Studio behind "American Beauty"
26 Smear
27 Like bicycles and organs
28 Negotiation preceders
29 Addle
31 Staying someplace temporarily, after "in"
33 Calculating types
34 Three times: Prefix
37 Potty
41 Snake, e.g.
42 Options
44 Picnic implement
46 Magicians' magazine since 1936
47 The woman in "An Unmarried Woman"
48 Figs. with two hyphens
50 A "South Park" kid
51 Mud dauber, e.g.
53 Year Louis III became Holy Roman emperor

by Eric Berlin

ACROSS

1 Hospitable host's invitation
10 Maid in "Die Fledermaus"
15 Notable return of 1969
16 Kick back
17 Modern flapper
18 Old "It's smart to be thrifty" sloganeer
19 Form 1099 amt.
20 Codswallop
22 "Snakes on a Plane" menace
23 Some bottled waters
27 Stuff sold in rolls
28 Kung ___ chicken
29 ___ cit. (footnote abbr.)
30 Part of an 800 collect call number
31 Japanese aborigine
32 Planners' paths
37 Intro to ancient history?
38 Numbers on the radio?
39 Supply center?
40 Blonde ___
41 M. equivalent
42 ___ volatile (pungent-smelling solution)
43 Black-and-white flash?
44 Pigged out
48 Writer LeShan
49 Comparable to a rose
51 ___ dye
52 City of Invention
54 George W. Bush, for one
58 Not made of brass
59 Like Argus
60 Louis Quatorze, for example
61 Pressed flowers, perhaps

DOWN

1 Pleasing to the palate
2 "Brusha, brusha, brusha" brand
3 Stuff of which some suits are made
4 ___-weekly (newspaper type)
5 Like some devils
6 Hawaiian juice brand that lent its name to a 1990s fad
7 Leavings
8 Line into N.Y.C.
9 Burlesque legend seen in "The Naked and the Dead"
10 Packing
11 Bona ___ (goddess also called Fauna)
12 Yosemite peak
13 Fails
14 Members of an old union
21 Entree from the oven
24 Self-titled 1991 female debut album
25 Playground yell
26 Postgame treatments for pitchers
30 French river that was the site of three W.W. I battles
31 Capella's constellation
32 Trade places
33 Something darn useful?
34 Ragtag force, say
35 Reading event?
36 Certain navel
43 Owner of The History Channel
44 Buffalo
45 Kind of surgery
46 Ultraviolet light filter
47 Home bartender's tool
50 Self-descriptive French name
53 See 57-Down
55 Power tested with Zener cards
56 French possessive
57 With 53-Down, ingredient in some soaps

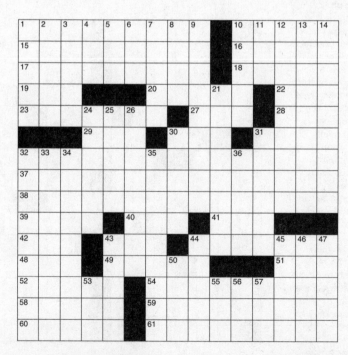

by Byron Walden

ACROSS

1 Suit protector?
16 2003 Pancho Villa portrayer
17 Some European political leaders
18 Book of the Book of Mormon
19 Powers that be
20 Spread stick
21 French shaker contents
22 Large number
24 Exerciser's target
26 Word repeated in "The Whiffenpoof Song"
27 Something that might roll over, briefly
28 J.F.K.'s U.N. ambassador
31 Statement subsequently belied
37 Locale of more than 50 volcanoes
38 Classic piano tune first recorded in 1921
39 The "gods" in "Chariots of the Gods?," in brief
40 Lover of Orion
41 Places where organs may be seen: Abbr.
42 Radio station expense
43 Charge of Moses
45 Letter getters: Abbr.
48 Goldfish in "Pinocchio"
51 Claret alternative, briefly
52 It's drawn for the dirty
53 Isn't pleasant to remember
58 Illegally
59 Time in Times Square

DOWN

1 Exhausts, say
2 "___ hand . . ."
3 Blake on "M*A*S*H," e.g.
4 Two, in Brazil
5 Bambi's aunt
6 Nonexistent
7 Conductors' places
8 Evening, in Emden
9 Natural butters
10 "Is that ___?"
11 Agcy. founded to help fight malaria
12 Lengthy meals?
13 Orsk is on it
14 Poet who wrote the novel "The Fathers"
15 Brand with a tiger mascot

22 Like some onions
23 Ones associated with wheels and deals
24 Where you may see a bust
25 Crybabies
26 Spell
27 Start of a 20 Questions question
28 1948 Chemistry Nobelist Tiselius
29 Swirl
30 Deflation indicator
31 Deceptive play
32 Hopped off
33 Team with a bridge in its logo
34 Its flag has a big white circle in the middle
35 Novelist Packer
36 Kentucky ___, annual Louisville race

42 Really fancy
43 Is in harmony
44 Pass
45 Kind of salad
46 Lustrous fur
47 Dig discovery: Var.
48 Lead
49 River through Yakutsk
50 St. Louis bridge designer
51 Newscaster Paula
52 Company
54 Long intro?
55 Symphony score abbr.
56 Beyond medical help, for short
57 Beer holder

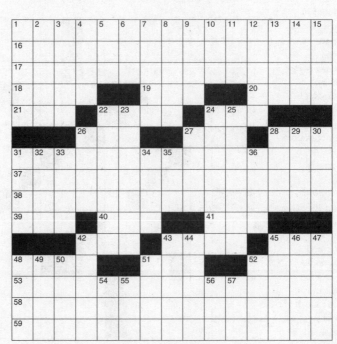

by Ed Early

112

ACROSS

1 Out of the woods
9 Peel provider
15 Pitched
16 "Immediately, boss!"
17 Bolts
18 Adenosine component
19 It may be found in an elevator
20 They're taken out in alleys
22 "___ hoppen?!"
23 Vaporize
25 Apocalyptic topic
27 Boost
29 Trendy
30 Musical syllable
31 As a friend, to François
33 Oaf, slangily
34 Capital of Manche, France
36 Some cap tossers
38 Nostalgic person's response
41 Saskatoon-to-Calgary dir.
43 Jam
45 Matter of debate in a sénat
46 Opposite of dolce
49 Delivery aid
51 "Go for it!"
53 Performer after whom a clone was named
54 Shape ender
55 MTV segment?
56 Crane's place
57 Had too much of, briefly
59 Go back further than
62 Turn (to)
63 Start of a rhyming taunt
64 Strict Sabbath observer of yore
65 Marketing mantra

DOWN

1 Fictional school whose motto is "Draco dormiens nunquam titillandus"
2 Bridge opening
3 Important person on the stand
4 Seigneur de Montaigne's output
5 Payment that won't change
6 Inexperienced
7 Old queen of Spain
8 Sporty Jaguar model
9 Full skirt with a tight waistband
10 1839 revolt site
11 Ruffian, to a Brit
12 Winter track
13 Directed a cry of contempt at
14 Not tense
21 Helping
24 Foo ___ (Chinese dish)
26 Radio talk host
28 Make uncomfortably hot
32 Yvette's evil
35 Bone head?
37 Old English poet
39 Totally lose it
40 Matching pair, informally
42 Opposite of peaceful
44 Family in a 1979 Oscar-winning film
46 First-ever speaker on C-Span, 3/19/79
47 Some fancy paperweights
48 ___ et quarante (card game)
50 ___ of civilization
52 Tolls
58 It might go for a buck
60 Never abroad
61 Take a toll on

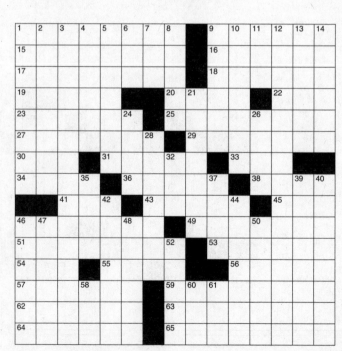

by David Quarfoot

ACROSS

1 "King Kong" co-star, 2005
10 Magazine subtitled "The Horse Owner's Resource"
15 Son or daughter, usually
16 Aachen appetizer
17 Fictional king with an enormous appetite
18 "Passion" actress, 1919
19 It had "three deuces and a four-speed and a 389," in song
20 Yachting event
22 Thousandth of a yen
23 Has a yen
25 Showy
26 One hanging around the house
27 Napoleon biographer Ludwig
28 Maker of a small purchase, sarcastically
30 Buttonwood
32 Bakery gizmos
33 Fire
34 Writer Jaffe
36 Like some antes
39 Arboriculturist
43 "The Fearless Vampire Killers" actress
46 First name in design
47 More than plenty
48 Claptrap
49 Turkish province or its capital
50 Some income: Abbr.
51 Unfair
53 Opened
54 "Dilemma" rapper
56 Superlatively stout
58 Newsman Roger
59 Fiancée, say
60 Popularity
61 Operation in 1998 news

DOWN

1 Shakes
2 All the things you are
3 Prolonged
4 It's tapped
5 Chutzpah
6 Propositional phrase?
7 Cry to an obedient dog, maybe
8 Heart
9 African livestock pens
10 Feudal worker
11 Lab. neighbor
12 Better model
13 Opposite the current
14 Some fishing boats
21 It's often put on backward
24 Bakery gizmos
26 Protected
28 Campy wear
29 A single, in Stuttgart
31 "Love ___" (1964 hit)
34 Contributions to them are not tax-deductible
35 It may have a lead part
36 "Memed My Hawk" director and star, 1984
37 Cell assignment: Abbr.
38 What a toddler might pull
39 What a scammer might pull
40 Brewed bit
41 Former Mexican president Zedillo
42 Drivers' duty
44 Its members may be seen traveling: Abbr.
45 Sluggish
49 ___ nothing
51 1944 Pulitzer correspondent
52 "Look ___!"
55 N.Y.C. school
57 N.Y.C. subway

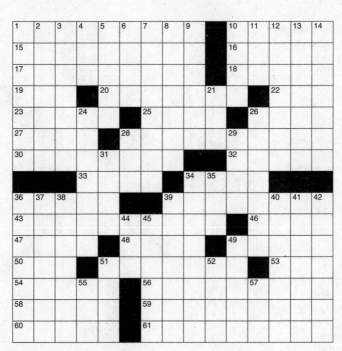

by David Bunker

114

ACROSS

1 Longhorns' rival, briefly
8 During
14 Leading evidence
16 Overnight success
17 "Way to go, bro!"
18 TV title role for Brandy
19 Film title role for Richard Gere
20 Agreement from the other half
22 Intimate
23 Brentford and Isleworth in the Thames, e.g.
25 Small finch
26 Anatomical term that's Latin for "hollow"
27 32-Down's place, briefly
29 Religious purview
30 Ursula's nemesis in "The Little Mermaid"
31 Hiding place, sometimes
33 Kahlúa's cousin
35 Wrestler once called the "Irresistible Force"
37 Comment when the shooting starts
40 Warren resident
44 Word with light or rock
45 Farming area: Abbr.
47 Sticker
48 Choler
49 Flexible weaving material
51 Daughter of Phoebe
52 Touchdown info
53 Working as a rep
55 River tower
56 Aged
58 "Impossible!"
60 1991 horror sequel
61 Rémoulade ingredient
62 Progressively smaller, in a way
63 Cursed

DOWN

1 Primes
2 Wifely
3 Move to and fro
4 Rag on
5 Something to bid on
6 14-year-old Grammy winner of 1997
7 Equilibria
8 City known in ancient times as Philadelphia
9 "Is it just ___ . . ."
10 Follower of McCarthy
11 Bad thing to sink into
12 "Me too"
13 "An American in Paris" song
15 Wrestler once called the "Immovable Object"
21 Follower of ducks, sheep or pigs
24 Start of a reprimand
26 Heady?
28 Anatomical hanger
30 Menotti boy
32 Dubya, once
34 Years ___
36 Russian fermented drink
37 Lake in Mist County, Minn.
38 Beau ideal
39 Connects (to)
41 Comment when you're almost done
42 Influence
43 Latter part of the Tertiary period
46 Web browser command
49 How many films are released
50 Like flip hairdos, say
53 Arthur lost to him at the 1972 U.S. Open
54 Prominent puppet show producer
57 Sioux Lookout setting: Abbr.
59 A nymph she's not

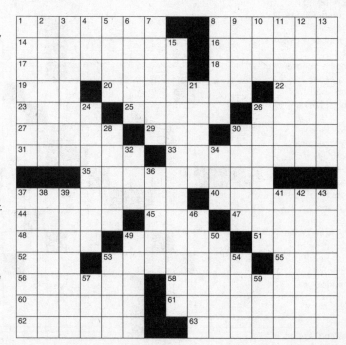

by David Quarfoot

ACROSS

1 Santa ___
7 Like an absent-minded professor, maybe
15 Souls
16 Winter race vehicle
17 Most decent
18 Bachelor, e.g.
19 Try to win
20 Breathing aid
22 Gillespie, to friends
23 Duck: Ger.
25 Crackers
26 Crack the whip at, perhaps
27 "Absolutely Fabulous" role
29 Yellow Pages info: Abbr.
30 Pulitzer-winning columnist Jim
31 Longtime musical group with a world capital in its name
34 "Well, looky who just came in!"
38 Floor it
39 Penicillin target
42 Cabinet acronym, once
43 Baddies
44 Bounced checks, hangnails, etc.
45 Do a new geographical survey of
47 Good names for old flight attendants?
48 ___ pro nobis
49 Reindeer herder
51 Suffix with prefect
52 Sign of spring

54 "Already?"
56 Subject to customs
57 Ones getting the show on the road
58 How déjà vu often occurs
59 Picked up

DOWN

1 Units of work
2 Party bowlful
3 Source of addiction
4 "___ Mine" (George Harrison book)
5 Home in Havana
6 Sean of "Encino Man"
7 Exactly
8 Over there

9 Not fine
10 A following
11 Charlie of the '60s Orioles
12 Not long from now
13 "Don't bother me, I'm in a rush!"
14 Eccentric sort
21 Mediocre
24 Meshes
26 Breakfast order
28 Invite to one's apartment, say
30 ___ harm (was innocuous)
32 Gob
33 Riddle-me-___
35 Chaste
36 Taking a grand tour

37 Ebbed
39 Toledos, e.g.
40 Hurt bad, emotionally
41 Lecture, in a way
45 Literally, "my master"
46 Tormentors
49 Good, long bath
50 Noted 19th-century French illustrator
53 Madeira, e.g.
55 II or III

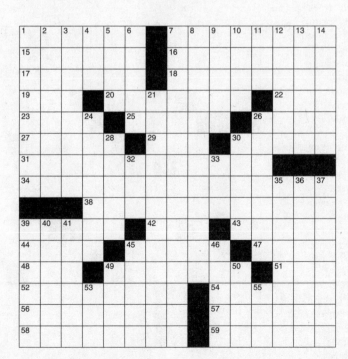

by Manny Nosowsky

116

ACROSS

1 Words accompanying a flash
11 Dickens's pen?
15 Drifting time?
16 "Three Sisters" sister
17 "Huh?!"
18 Troubles
19 Mil. title
20 High roller?
21 Female donkey
23 Freshness
24 Composer Boccherini
25 Words to a boxer
28 Hand over
29 Use unlimited minutes, say
32 "___ Ordinary Man" ("My Fair Lady" song)
33 Without vigor
36 Relish
38 Custodian's charge
39 Literally, "god," in Sanskrit
40 Anti-apartheid org.
41 Wasn't true
42 Comparatively unadorned
43 Comes down
45 Big name in footwear
47 Antilles tribe
49 Worn smooth
50 Kind of case in gram.
53 Conclusion
54 Man on the street
57 Converse
58 Nobel Prizes, e.g.
59 Fictional sailor
60 Geometric figures

DOWN

1 One may help support a nest egg
2 Screen
3 Not excluded from
4 Boarding place: Abbr.
5 Emergency discards
6 Impulses
7 Comes (from)
8 Capuchin monkey relative
9 Former name in tyranny
10 Court figures
11 Successful
12 It may be pulled
13 Eye
14 Wear
22 Nonsensical refrain
23 Loi maker
24 Like a Rockettes show
25 Standard deviation symbol
26 Explanation starter
27 Children's game for two
28 Preserved, in a way
30 "___ Supreme" (classic Coltrane jazz album)
31 Easily
33 Inventory ___ (euphemism for shoplifting)
34 Finger ___
35 Arab League member
37 "Drink to me only with thine eyes" dedicatee
42 Some stars
44 Up
45 Calendrier column
46 Squeeze
47 Follower of John
48 Drift
49 Carillon component
50 California's ___ Valley
51 Forward
52 Old heavyweight champ Willard
55 TV control: Abbr.
56 Japan's ___-Tokyo Museum

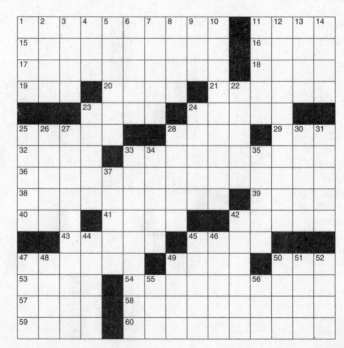

by Rich Norris

ACROSS

1 Emotional mess
11 Like Manhattan's G.E. Building
15 Cause of a split decision?
16 2003 and '05 A.L. M.V.P.
17 Process of elimination?
18 Racecar driver Ricky a k a Iron Man
19 Let go
20 Big shakeup?
21 Diaper bag supply
22 Clears
24 First name in comedy and conga lines
25 One way to be divided
26 Real shocker
28 Propels
30 Big game org.
31 Novelist Arundhati ___
33 Assignments done in class
35 Standard operating procedure?
39 Wounds
40 Evidence tester
42 Clunker at sea
43 Nutty Nickelodeon character
44 Court star who won bronze at the Sydney Olympics
46 Do not disturb
50 ___-American
52 Remembered family member?
54 Streamlet
55 Back, in a way
56 Drift
58 "Gnarly!"
59 Modern journal
60 Token taker
62 Siberian river
63 Column reply opener
64 Place of temptation
65 Glitterati

DOWN

1 American Film Institute's "greatest male star of all time"
2 Loss of muscle coordination
3 Particles
4 Mauna ___
5 Newton-meter divisions
6 "Ring" leader
7 Some knitted pieces, in Britain
8 Gets together
9 Otto Preminger directed him in "Exodus"
10 Pilothouse abbr.
11 "18 Yellow Roses" singer, 1963
12 Dermatological problem
13 It may not mean what you think
14 Matchless attire?
21 Pensive
23 Infection injection
27 Emperor Jones portrayer
29 Touched
32 Kind of log
34 Composer of the opera "Euryanthe"
35 Where you might get a word in edgewise
36 Having gaps in the top, as a castle wall
37 Cell phone selection
38 Spot for a date
41 Fierce fighter
45 Slide preparations
47 Oratorical outburst
48 Plaintiff, e.g.
49 Experienced advice-givers
51 Canada's highest peak
53 Surrealist Breton
57 Outdoor bite preventer
60 Dictionary abbr.
61 Piece of a hood?

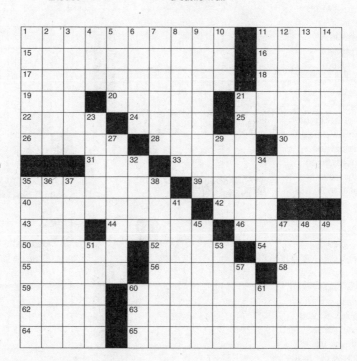

by Lynn Lempel

ACROSS

1 They might be protected by an 8-Across
8 See 1-Across
15 Sites for small schools
16 Like rubble, often
17 Kind of grape
18 Where Marat was murdered
19 Associate
20 Haunted house worker's job
21 One may get pins and needles
22 Flowering plant with two seed leaves
24 "As I Lay Dying" father
25 Up
27 Editor Talese
28 "___ where it hurts!"
29 German chancellor after Kohl
31 Tabloid fodder
32 Villain
34 Villain
38 Ones in hip joints?
43 Curtain shades
44 Indicator of canonización
45 Trunk coverer
46 "Take heed ___ any man deceive you": Mark 13:5
47 Good
49 Mars: Prefix
50 It may be a bear to throw down
52 1984 movie with the tag line "It's 4 a.m., do you know where your car is?"
54 Google company
55 Varnish material
56 People described by Josephus
57 Classic R&B tune that inspired the "stroll" dance craze
58 Ice, e.g.
59 Appropriately named band with the 1984 hit "Drive"

DOWN

1 Some laryngitis sufferers
2 Marine, maybe
3 Member of the sedge family
4 Less together
5 Home of the Zagros Mountains
6 Like antlers
7 St. Louis Arch designer
8 Big name in guitars
9 "It's all ___"
10 First name in espionage
11 Biblical kingdom of the Hebrews
12 Slammed
13 1970–71 winner in Johnny Lightning
14 "Baseball Tonight" segment featuring the day's best defensive plays
23 Simón Bolívar's birthplace
26 Spanish uncle?
28 Projects
30 Hangout
31 Flying Cloud of autodom
33 Term paper?
34 Secured while rock climbing
35 Needlelike
36 "The King's Stilts" author, 1939
37 Changes
39 All over the place
40 Fleet of warplanes
41 Sugar daddy, e.g.
42 Jam band fans, stereotypically
44 Like the best advice
47 Arrowroot, e.g.
48 "Ugh!"
51 Something written in stone
53 ___ Noël

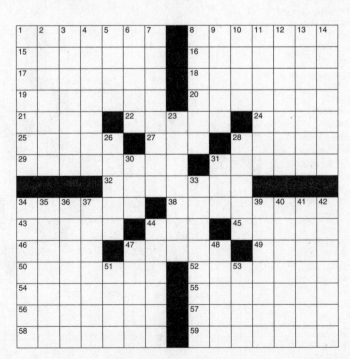

by Brendan Emmett Quigley

ACROSS

1 Six-story, say
8 Like some curves
15 Team the Mets defeated in the 1969 World Series
16 A couple may be in it
17 Not all there?
18 Kind of camp
19 Fulcrum locale
20 "C'est la vie"
21 Nickname for Mike Krzyzewski of Duke basketball fame
23 Captain's ___ (naval disciplinary hearing)
27 Intake optima: Abbr.
28 Jazz genre
33 Johnny Nash hit written by Bob Marley
35 State on the Gulf of California
36 Fictional adventurer with a map and a backpack
38 Sometime
39 Possible result of an accident
40 Commemorative meal
41 Ox driver
42 Classic singer with the 2005 album "Rock Swings"
43 Talked up?
45 Case
50 Product of hindsight, sometimes
55 Ointment base
56 Offense
57 By and by
58 Prime example
59 Informational/ marketing tool
60 Down

DOWN

1 Objects of some hand-wringing?
2 Requiem Mass hymn word
3 Grave
4 Deteriorates
5 ___ artery
6 Fit to be untied?
7 What an alien might take: Abbr.
8 Miller alternative
9 Mideast V.I.P.
10 Significance
11 Cut ___
12 When doubled, a Pacific capital
13 Modern pentathlon event
14 Lock changers?
20 Patsy
22 Together, in music
23 Old PC platform
24 Square things
25 Brought forth
26 Sports news
28 Yellow's opposite
29 ___ Gay
30 A metalloid
31 Hoover rival
32 Weatherproof wear
34 ___-Tass news agency
35 Sticky-fingered guy?
37 Look into?
41 Rock variety
43 Detail
44 Messing with lines
45 Lot
46 Attention
47 Seat near the front of a plane
48 The in crowd?
49 Wellsian race
51 Five-time U.S. Open champ
52 Classico competitor
53 Designer von Furstenberg
54 Piece of cake for a marathoner
56 Wire provider: Abbr.

by Beth Hinshaw

ACROSS

1 Interviewer in some mock interviews
9 Point in the wrong direction
15 Grad school administration
16 Eponym for an annual literary award since 1919
17 Attention-getter
18 Goal-oriented activity
19 Balmy
20 Actress who made her big-screen debut in "Julia," 1977
22 Inits. in a 1948 upset
23 It's often taken in night sch.
24 Like germs
25 Bubble
26 Souvenir shop staples
28 Rather, musically
29 Border
30 "Shake Loose My Skin" poet Sanchez
32 Losers
34 Able to draw
36 Captain's charge
38 Something to part with
40 ". . . lived in ___"
41 Envoy and others
43 Point in the right direction?
45 Look
46 Asian city heavily bombed during W.W. II
47 Alex Box Stadium sch.
48 Knock hard?
49 Ending words of inclusiveness
51 Millinery
52 Pungent cheese
54 Some cats
56 Enclosing rim in which a jewel is set
57 Longtime play-by-play announcer Chris
58 Works with one's hands
59 It may be planned before a move

DOWN

1 Clothing item with strings
2 Gets excited
3 Admiral Nelson victory
4 Expression of unhappiness
5 Natural trap
6 Cans
7 "Are you up for it?"
8 Scene of many demonstrations
9 Amble
10 Chain letters?
11 Tick
12 Earthquake Park setting
13 Quitter's cry
14 Allspice and clove, e.g.
21 Name on a historic B-29
25 QB Kosar
27 Easily attachable
28 Cousin of an agouti
29 Cancel
31 Resort site
33 Subway map array: Abbr.
35 How some trust
36 Cram
37 Boomer born in the 1960s
39 Pittsburgh giant
42 Car model beginning in 1970
44 Scrap
46 Tough posers
49 Like some cigars
50 Garland co-star of 1939
51 Nesters
53 ___ provençale
55 Pill, e.g.

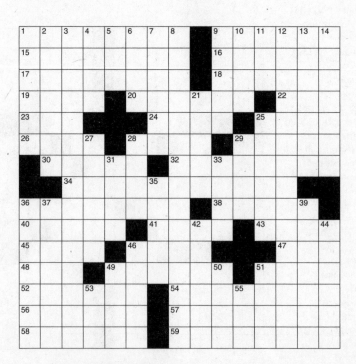

by Victor Fleming

ACROSS

1 Some Italian baby food
8 Company that owns the brands Kiwi and Hillshire Farm
15 Product of yeast fermentation
16 Old Olds
17 Enjoy perks
19 Star of "The Gene Krupa Story," 1959
20 Let off steam
21 1998 Sarah McLachlan hit
22 Stand standout
25 ___ Ray of the Indigo Girls
26 Frees
27 Pastoral warrior of Kenya
29 Musician with the 1974 album "Here Come the Warm Jets"
34 Things that are picked up and kicked
35 Shower activity
36 Olivine variety
37 Sales rep's file label
38 Scamperers in the woods
39 Baseball Hall-of-Famer Tim
40 ___ de cebolla (onion rings, in Spain)
41 It's often next to a phone
42 Where women's biathlon was introduced as a medal event
49 Hardly Mr. Personality
51 Like some pirates
52 "___ to recall . . ."
53 Where Mae West did jail time
56 Still below the horizon
57 Accord
58 Place out of order
59 Decides not to quit

DOWN

1 Makes wavy, in a way
2 Took the loss
3 Former "60 Minutes" debater Alexander
4 Attenuate
5 How mom often has the kids
6 Eastern drama
7 Paul Revere's midnight duty
8 Script makeup
9 Some volunteer baby sitters
10 Itinerary abbr.
11 "Bravo" preceder
12 Put in abeyance
13 One who's not being precise
14 Some bloggers
18 Bygone railroad
23 Castle in a dance hall
24 Sophisticated
28 Some
29 A shoe presses against it
30 Quaker product
31 Department store section
32 "Yeah, right!"
33 Big name in skin care
34 Job
36 Gives out appropriately
38 Fish basket
40 Without
43 Two-time U.S. Open winner
44 Prospect
45 Longtime R&B family name
46 Relies (on)
47 Slow
48 North Sea port
50 Greek letters
54 What that is in South America
55 Bank buildup: Abbr.

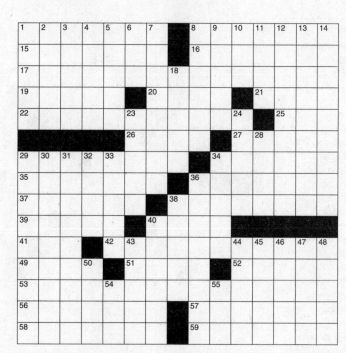

by Dave Mackey

ACROSS

1 See people
8 Like Baylor University
15 Shows that one is in?
16 Either of two track stars
17 1970 B.B. King hit
19 Prepare for planting, perhaps
20 Legionella and listeria
21 Pro ___
22 English agriculturist and inventor
24 Wouldn't stop
25 Company acquired by Mattel in 1997
26 "___ directed"
28 Code on some N.Y.C.-bound luggage
29 High kingdom
30 It may be fit for a queen
32 To a greater extent
33 Claims
35 Faux family name in rock and roll
38 Peak east of Captain Cook
42 Co-star of Marcello in "La Dolce Vita"
43 "Mathis ___ Maler" (opera)
44 Put up with
45 Sunroof option
46 Actress Lords
48 Like a retired prof.
49 Billet-doux recipient
50 Catnip relative
52 Hi-tech organizer
53 "Believe you me"

56 Destroyed little by little
57 Galley of yore
58 Result of doing the twist?
59 1979 #1 song with the chorus line "Turn the other way"

DOWN

1 Novelty race vehicle
2 Staff-produced
3 Prepared for bad news, say
4 Worked (up)
5 Dept. of Labor arm
6 Less sinful
7 Went around and around
8 100 centesimos

9 Strange
10 Kisser
11 "Star Trek" series preceding "Voyager," for short
12 Duplicate specimen, in biology
13 Native New Yorkers
14 Voice lesson topic
18 Ways back
23 Rail
25 Like soybean leaves
27 Leg
29 Highest points
31 End of a race?
32 Spartans' sch.
34 Spirit transporters

35 Sound of a woodpecker pecking
36 Spiritedly
37 Handle
39 Aquatic sucker
40 Words under "E pluribus unum"
41 Pitching stats?
43 Utilized
46 "___ relax"
47 Chief god of early Hinduism
50 Upscale hotel chain
51 "The Wizard ___"
54 Autobahn hazard
55 Something to pick

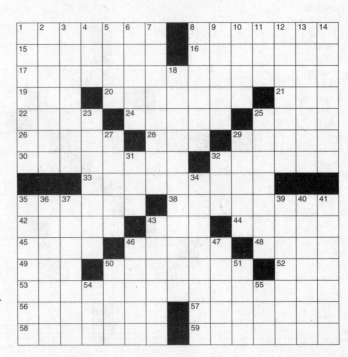

by Sherry O. Blackard

ACROSS

- **1** Hit Japanese TV import
- **9** Part of a B major scale
- **15** Celebrated smiler
- **16** Slave
- **17** Place to put buttons
- **18** High-priority task
- **19** Calm
- **20** They're acquired in some unions
- **22** Manager of a two-party system?
- **23** Tassels, e.g.
- **25** Bribe
- **26** ___ case
- **27** Screen
- **28** Bring down
- **30** Follower of Mao?
- **31** It goes around at a construction site
- **33** "Interesting . . ."
- **34** Red Cross mission
- **35** Gusto
- **41** Scratch
- **44** "Herman" cartoonist Jim
- **45** Division du Mexique
- **46** Town SE of Sacramento
- **47** ___ Miguel
- **48** Fleet that was very fleet
- **49** Ukrainian hub
- **50** You can bet on it
- **54** Rap
- **55** Many a posting
- **56** Where to taste tostones
- **59** Begin operating, datewise
- **60** One-room schoolhouse features
- **61** Failed to be
- **62** Close watcher

DOWN

- **1** "Seriously!"
- **2** Stick alternatives
- **3** Like some bridges
- **4** Blanket artisan
- **5** Grass alternative
- **6** Big royalty generator
- **7** "Cómo es ___?" ("How come?," in Córdoba)
- **8** Comic collected in "The Chickens Are Restless," with "The"
- **9** "You looking ___?"
- **10** Short course
- **11** Express disapproval
- **12** Cannonball Adderley played it
- **13** Cold symptom
- **14** Boom
- **21** Some snoops
- **23** School composition
- **24** Glass component
- **28** Valentine for Valéry
- **29** A spade, e.g.
- **31** One reporting to a capt.
- **32** Foods with fillings
- **33** Part of a snicker
- **35** Even as we speak
- **36** Tethered
- **37** Match, for one
- **38** Grant
- **39** Comment when no one is up
- **40** Plant container
- **41** Not fixed
- **42** Blip
- **43** Coin part
- **46** "Maybe"
- **51** Reduced sentence, maybe
- **52** High-school class, informally
- **53** Paltry payment
- **54** Turn on the waterworks
- **57** Gasteyer of "Mean Girls"
- **58** FedEx pickup: Abbr.

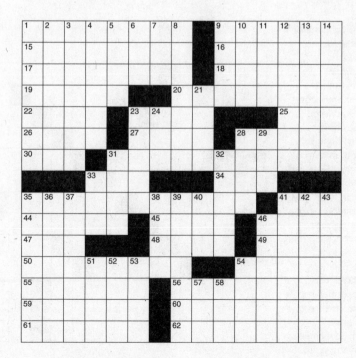

by Mike Nothnagel

124

ACROSS

1 Closing bars
5 Leaves for dinner
15 "The Green Hornet" trumpeter
16 Mixed drink?
17 Whereabouts
18 Roosevelt Island locale
19 Boxer on the cover of "Sgt. Pepper's Lonely Hearts Club Band"
21 Battle of Endor fighter
22 Submit
23 Brand of chips
24 Thin fastener
25 Anita Loos's autobiographical "A ___ Like I"
26 Lots
28 Musical notation pioneer
29 Blows
30 Hamper
31 Legs
34 Light housecoats
35 It's said to be everything
36 Third highest trump in card games
37 Saxophone great, familiarly
38 Common reply to a parent's demand
42 Plain sight
43 Inner ears
44 Ranger, e.g.
45 Alexander Pope's "Solitude," e.g.
46 Unlocked?
47 Hybrid women's clothing
48 Jackpot

51 Actress Petty of "A League of Their Own"
52 Park Avenue retailer?
53 Cross
54 Not the biggest thoroughfare in town
55 Flap

DOWN

1 Name shared by a Grace and a Muse
2 Putting on
3 Fast
4 Attitude
5 Sweet ___ of Avon (epithet for Shakespeare)
6 One in column A?

7 Washington posts
8 Main lane
9 Provincetown entree
10 Tilt
11 In
12 One making excuses
13 Black box
14 Decide by chance
20 Conservative
24 Dessert whose name means "peasant woman"
25 English composer of the opera "The Perfect Fool"
27 Kind of bean
28 Regular container?
30 Amateurish
31 Columbus discovery of 1493

32 Wiped
33 Alabama slammer ingredient
34 Toaster setting?
36 Author of the memoir "One Soldier's Story"
38 Thing that shrinks when inflated?
39 Cheap cigar, slangily
40 Monopoly's railroads, e.g.
41 "If music be the food of love, play on" speaker
43 Addition symbol
46 Sacks
47 G.E. Building muralist
49 Spring
50 Grand finale?

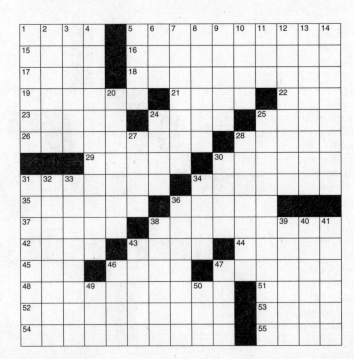

by Bob Klahn

ACROSS

1 "Hoc __ in votis"
5 Six-Day War hero
10 Eponym of a classic Minnesota-brewed beer
14 Specify, in a way
15 Pungent fish garnish
16 Novel of the South Seas
17 Implement with a serrated front edge
20 Forestalled potential impediments
21 Stink
22 Fresh
23 Biblical possessive
24 Start of a new season: Abbr.
26 R. J. Reynolds brand
29 Sound associated with a 40-Across
31 Shark's activity
37 "Dies __"
38 __ Krispies
39 "Dial __ Murder"
40 Doctor's tool
43 __ Center (Chicago's second-tallest building)
44 End of abnormalities?
45 Little __
46 It's read for a price: Abbr.
48 Bad thing to live in
51 Whip
53 Lightheaded people?
59 A century in American politics
60 Big dot-com headquartered in San Jose
61 Like some paper

62 Track star elected to Congress in 1996
63 HDTV component
64 Quick scorers on the court
65 Store advisory

DOWN

1 Hwy. dept. employee
2 Opera __ (classical music record label)
3 Passage leading to Panama?
4 Halfhearted
5 Crackers
6 River of Leeds
7 Bar line
8 Common biography subtitle
9 Munitions compound

10 Bad thing to abandon
11 Quite some time
12 Bum
13 Composition of some rolls
18 Japanese mushroom
19 Sp. misses
24 Bar in a bar and grill
25 Dollar rival
27 Hardly at all
28 Start of an invocation
30 Tourist stop conveniences
32 Big name in blocks
33 Swells
34 River to the Rhine
35 Time to draw?
36 Goes off
41 Flabby, e.g.

42 These, in Cádiz
46 Underdog's thrill
47 Newbie, of sorts
49 "Waterworld" girl
50 Goldfinger's first name
52 End of __
54 Diggs of "Rent"
55 Champ who lost his title to Braddock
56 Geo. Washington and M.L.K. Jr. were awarded them
57 German iPod holder
58 Form data: Abbr.

by Harvey Estes

126

ACROSS

1 Mathematical grouping
6 Is dishonest with
12 Climbers' goals
14 Illinois home of Rotary International
16 Friend you may never have met
17 Write seperately, say
18 Cinch
19 Altogether
20 Russian writer Andreyev famous for his horrific tales
21 Creepy crawler?
22 Some pizzas
23 Mason, at times
24 It's a sign
25 Chaplet relatives
26 "Le Mur" writer
28 Goya, for one
33 Connectors
35 Some vertical lines
37 Peaceful place
41 Row
42 Bull __
43 Appellation for winter
44 Shade provider
45 Somewhat green
46 Note
47 Rejoinder to a doubter
48 Dark
49 It can be carved out
50 Things found by hounds
51 Orchestra section

DOWN

1 Auriga's brightest star
2 Full attention
3 Stimuli-perceiving brain parts
4 One who strikes out
5 Least joyful
6 Taps, in the British military
7 Unmoved
8 Wit
9 Knighted essayist
10 Quasimodo, notably
11 But
13 Winter Olympics equipment
14 Surface
15 Locales for trellises
25 Sentencing judge's prerogative
27 Points from which light emanates
29 Light hybrid vehicle of the 1910s
30 Trophies in a tournament, informally
31 Patient at a doctor's office
32 Lapped again
34 Freshwater fish of the perch family
36 Men of Manáos
37 Minute
38 Fix, as an old swimming pool
39 Baseball Hall-of-Famer Joe
40 Undesirable part of a record
41 Kind of barrier
44 Tax, in Tottenham

by Robert H. Wolfe

ACROSS

1 Threatening to sue, maybe
12 Portrayer of Clouseau's superior, in film
15 Versatile modern device
16 She played Eloise in "Mogambo"
17 Stalled
18 Tapping target
19 Knock-down-drag-out
20 "Where ___ was thickest fight": Milton
21 Adder's-tongue or Venus's-hair
22 "Je vous en ___" ("You're welcome": Fr.)
23 "Take ___," 1985 #1 hit
24 Words before may or might, in verse
25 Final finisher, in Falmouth
26 Not buying it
28 Bavarian keepsake
29 Yet
30 Multiplication table, e.g.
32 Under the table
33 Prominent Quebec City daily, with "Le"
34 Pocket holders
35 Not have to check bags, say
37 It turns out looies: Abbr.
40 Ran
41 Crash sites?
42 Kind of score, for one doing postgrad studies
43 Classic PC's
44 Mayor who co-wrote "Murder at City Hall"

45 Pink-pulped produce
46 Air Tahiti ___ (carrier to Papeete)
47 Soon to be heard
49 Coast Guard figure: Abbr.
50 Go downhill
51 One target of Rachel Carson's "Silent Spring"
52 Mysterious swimmers

DOWN

1 Seafood entree
2 Supplies
3 Charlotte ___
4 Ally's roommate on "Ally McBeal"
5 City on Presque Isle Bay
6 Piper topper
7 Add-on
8 Procter & Gamble brand
9 Junks
10 One may be technical: Abbr.
11 It'll easily pass you
12 Like some resorts
13 Budget figure
14 Blow up
21 Seafood entrees
23 "Beyond the Horizon" writer
24 Charged
26 Comment after bombing
27 They may take a toll
28 Allen and Rossi
30 Stagnant
31 Fearmonger

32 Line on an application
33 Like many aprons
34 Recipe amounts
36 "No Escape" star, 1994
37 Dweller on the Yodo River
38 TV host with two Emmys
39 Convention roll call
42 Profit
44 Gonitis target
45 Tar, e.g.
47 Some E.R. cases
48 Part of a board: Abbr.

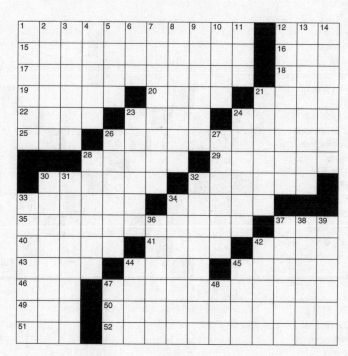

by Levi Denham

128

ACROSS
1 Faux finish
8 Ancient fertility goddess
15 A position of prominence
16 Fundamental group
17 Pedigree, e.g.
18 Father's Day gift, perhaps
19 Prefix with center
20 Bowwows
22 Wait at the motor vehicle bureau, say
23 Ball material
25 Closer to perfection
26 Its motto is "Lux et veritas"
27 Capri, e.g.
29 Identify
30 Alter
31 Scarlatti's "Capriccio," e.g.
33 Composes
35 Kind of support
37 When doubled, a shore dinner order
38 1988 Burt Reynolds flop
42 Persian attraction
46 Time after retiring?
47 General Mills brand
49 Tundra or rain forest
50 1960s soul record label
51 Back parts of keels
53 Suffix with game
54 Flight board abbr.
55 Headdress wearer
57 Call
58 Home of the Moai statues
60 Certain Playgirl centerfold
62 Trapped
63 French politician ___ de Silhouette, from whom the word "silhouette" comes
64 Italian city, setting of a Walpole novel
65 Like some couples

DOWN
1 Martyred bishop of Paris
2 Wishful reply
3 Shackle
4 With 61-Down, 14th president's inits.
5 Informal denial
6 March
7 Struck
8 Where to work out, maybe
9 Less social
10 "___ bon"
11 Post-Manhattan Project org.
12 Issue
13 French poetic form
14 Cable program with team coverage?
21 Political suffix
24 Recurring economic proposal
26 Answer to "No, that's not!"
28 1980s TV quartet
30 Doctor's order
32 Maryland and Virginia are in it: Abbr.
34 Campaign grp.
36 Seikan Tunnel terminus
38 "Will & Grace" maid
39 Competitor
40 Like some bond prices
41 Debarking point
43 Intersection interdiction
44 Last song recorded by the Beatles
45 Puzzle
48 Annual competition since 1995
51 Surgical implant
52 A little, colloquially
55 Nabokov novel
56 Corey of "The Lost Boys"
59 Grp. concerned with defense
61 See 4-Down

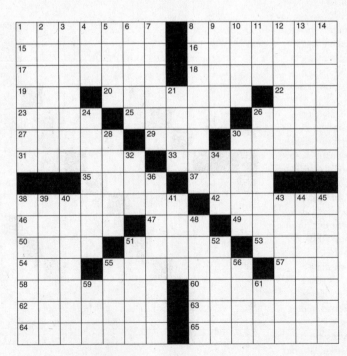

by David Quarfoot

ACROSS

1 Seminal computer game of 1989
8 Special delivery?
14 Shop steward, briefly
16 When some hands join
17 "Sold!"
18 Touching
19 1982 Richard Pryor flick
20 Kick in
22 It's east of Mayfair
23 Farm stand units
24 Spider's legs, e.g.
26 Article of apparel akin to a tarboosh
27 Dump
28 Entangles
30 Wonderland directive
32 Relaxed
33 Take the top off
34 Superstition that a rookie's second season will fail
37 Under the table
38 Key of the "Eroica"
39 Kind of blade
40 Break or time follower
41 Go bad
44 Slangy intensifier
45 Tallinn's St. __ Church, once said to be the tallest building in Europe
47 Turn over
48 Saragossa is on it
50 Squeeze
51 Major milk maker
53 Met who won the 1985 Cy Young Award
55 Doesn't let differences cause conflict
57 Stumblebum
58 Show stopper?
59 Catering aid
60 Took over

DOWN

1 Some executive offices
2 Because
3 Good thing to be put out of
4 Lab wear
5 Chinese leader?
6 Small heart, say
7 It helps in passing
8 Lecture follow-up
9 Language related to Bannock
10 Band featured on the reality show "Rock Star"
11 Rarely
12 100%
13 Went out for a while?
15 Clinical trial phenomenon
21 Problem while drying out
24 Utah city
25 Party hiree
28 Rescuee's cry
29 It can help you carry a tune
31 Take __ (suffer loss)
32 Highlighted rte. on a map
33 Hungarian filmmaker Tarr
34 It may be found in a slip
35 Just out, maybe
36 Some mail services: Abbr.
37 Breakfast order
40 An oenophile might detect a hint of this
41 Winner of the first World Series (as the "Americans")
42 "Swan Lake" princess
43 Stiffened
46 Slow
47 It may appear on a record
49 Something picked up in a gym
51 Universal Postal Union headquarters
52 Strong team
54 It's a big stretch
56 Large cells

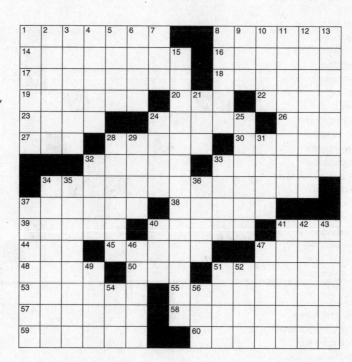

by Mike Nothnagel

130

ACROSS

1 Did some court work
11 Cow: Sp.
15 Set of routine duties
16 Argonaut who slew Castor
17 Locks up?
18 Things usually held while facing backward
19 Architectural projection
20 Ones with well-defined careers?
22 Farm sound
25 Players' tryouts
27 Fish also called a Jerusalem haddock
29 Play mates?
30 Alma-___, city where Trotsky was exiled
31 Walgreens rival
33 Separates
37 Not necessarily against
38 Hang out
39 Rock formation, to geologists
41 Contemporary correspondent
42 Saint-___ (France's West Point)
43 A following?
45 Formal introduction?
46 Couple in the news in 1945
50 Health reporter Blakey
51 Fly (by)
52 President between Farrell and Lonardi
54 1968 album with the song "John Looked Down"

55 Interested
60 One with special insight
61 Fails
62 "Look ___ . . ."
63 Carrots and mashed potatoes, e.g.

DOWN

1 What passes may lead to, quickly
2 Charge on a record
3 Crowd in old Rome?
4 Nevada county or its seat
5 Tannery workers
6 Monkey, so to speak
7 Stuck
8 "Royalty of the garden"

9 Twice 58-Down
10 Minute Maid Park's former sponsor
11 Dwarf plant of the eastern U.S.
12 Mr. Deeds player
13 Sign that something's missing
14 Clubs: Abbr.
21 Lago di Como locale
22 "Woman With a Pearl" painter
23 Foucault's "This Is Not ___"
24 Dispenser of gossip?
26 Image on Australia's coat of arms
28 Abstract sculptor whose work is seen at Lincoln Center
32 Consoles popular in the '80s

34 Like fashionable apparel
35 Word in several Dunkin' Donuts doughnut names
36 Its flag has two green stars
40 Low ___
41 Iran-contra figure
44 Filched
46 Swimming
47 Lithium, on the periodic table
48 Waste at the polls
49 Lifetime winner of the most Grammys (31)
53 Intelligence
56 Island staple
57 Quote from Homer
58 Amount past due?
59 Accepts

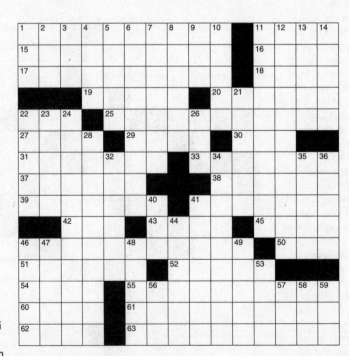

by Myles Callum

ACROSS

1 "Have some"
6 Slate, e.g., informally
10 One to grow on?
14 Whom a leader follows
15 Recently departed
16 Unfrequented
17 Expected
18 Weightlifter?
19 Not just surmise
20 Insult from a fashionista
23 KNO₃
24 Prayer wish
25 Lair
28 Runner in "The Sun Also Rises"
29 "Stuart Little" inits.
30 Less refined
32 Part of some joints
35 Dr Pepper Snapple Group brand
37 They couldn't be further apart
39 Like the sea
40 Rancher's charge
42 Bugged, with "on"
44 Spigot site, maybe
45 Move easily
47 16th-century Spanish mystic
49 Conference planners' needs
52 Pioneer in the math of sudoku
53 Bartender's query
57 Makeshift pencil holders
58 1814 Byron poem
59 Gas bill factor
60 "Lean __"
61 Not name

62 Pushes
63 "The Phil Harris-Alice __ Show" of 1940s–'50s radio
64 Hip
65 Namesakes of Perry's creator

DOWN

1 Bit of hardware
2 Hebrew for "beginning"
3 Retort to an improbable threat
4 Drawn
5 Newsmaker in space, 1962
6 Bygone Cadillacs
7 Send off
8 First string
9 Is in on the joke

10 Romper room
11 Starry-eyed sentiment
12 10-year-old Oscar winner of 1973
13 Land overseas
21 Clinch
22 Bring (out)
25 Some lobsters
26 "Ri-i-ight"
27 Pound sounds
31 Emphasize, in a way
33 Partners' word
34 Tot watcher
36 "It's dark in here!"
38 Frame job
41 Farm young
43 Nitpick?
46 Knock down

48 Hunt's sitcom co-star
49 Wowed by, after "in"
50 Home of the Ashanti
51 Copycat's comment
54 "Redemption" novelist, 1995
55 Eye
56 Sad ending?

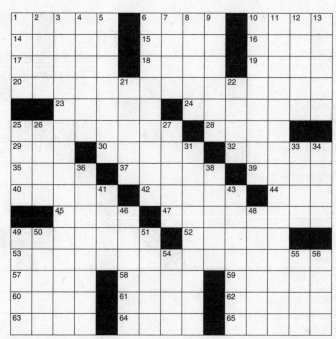

by Seth A. Abel

132

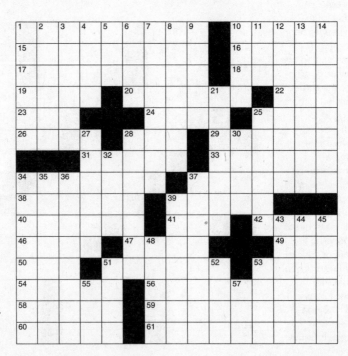

by Rich Norris

ACROSS

1 Better Business Bureau concerns
6 Hefty competition
10 What someone who is out might be in
14 Put through the mill?
15 Legal cover-up?
16 Robert Burns title starter
17 1986 rock autobiography
18 Member of a small family
20 "Six Degrees of Separation" family name
22 Suitor's presentation
23 Where to spend birr
24 John of Parliament
25 It's projected
30 Browsers' place
32 Sturdy building material
33 Pique experience?
34 Make a stink?
35 Density symbol, in physics
37 It may follow an etym.
39 Ottoman officer
40 Utter
42 Special ability
44 Burrowing animal
46 Mysterious letter writer, maybe
49 Lyricist Dubin and others
50 Come this close
53 Take, as a life
56 Humored
57 Curved wall used as a stage background
59 Actress Georgia ___ of "The Mary Tyler Moore Show"
60 "Flower Petal Gown" sculptor
61 Not easily angered
62 Surgical tube
63 Ones that may get ticked?
64 Gathering suffix
65 "Me, too"

DOWN

1 Sudden increase
2 Get the job done
3 Putting two and two together, say
4 Bring up
5 Pirate
6 "Beethoven" star, 1992
7 Time of many a fairy tale
8 Good enough to 2-Down
9 "The Partridge Family" actress
10 Collusion
11 Votes overseas
12 M.'s counterpart
13 Contributes
19 Swamp thing
21 Bad words
24 "Me, too"
26 See 51-Down
27 Not mincing words?
28 European capital
29 Virginie, e.g.
30 Dos into seis
31 "If a ___ is happy, it cannot fit too close": O. Henry
36 Mama bear, in Madrid
38 Keep
41 It can be semiattached
43 "The Murder Room" novelist
45 Token
47 Kids' TV character voiced by Kevin Clash
48 One of "Them"
51 With 26-Down, it may be used in a pool
52 Longtime Chicago Symphony conductor
53 Sent a duplicate, briefly
54 Invention of Hermes, supposedly
55 ___ gratuit (something done without apparent motive)
56 Give up, slangily
58 Make calls

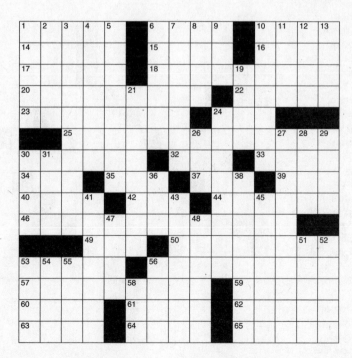

by Eric Berlin

134

ACROSS
1 Popular Bravo series, 2003–07
9 Quaint hairstyle
15 Outraged
16 Insight
17 "Servant of the Bones" writer
18 "This I gotta hear"
19 It's flaky
20 Like a certain complex
21 Per __
24 March sound
25 Weeklong holiday
26 "The Wizard of Oz" co-star
27 Of the bicuspid valve
29 Annual contributions may be made to them
30 One of 51 in Atlantic City, once
34 First name in horror
35 Dries up
36 Maupassant's "__ Vie"
37 Where a specialist has expertise
39 Develop
40 Develop
41 Develop
42 Way off
44 Like Brahms's Symphony No. 3
45 Workers' incentives
46 Things included in a count
48 Bristol locale: Abbr.
49 Join forces?
50 It may raise the roof
54 Hebrew title of respect for God
55 Rosary bead representation
56 Zapper
57 Serves

DOWN
1 In the capacity of
2 Broadcaster since Jan. 1995
3 Article of Cologne
4 They may be sworn
5 Hole-in-one, e.g.
6 Pine Valley soap siren
7 Place to work out
8 A storm heading: Abbr.
9 Caused to swell up
10 Snake or eel, e.g.
11 Assign an alias
12 Delicate breakfast item
13 Bravura
14 Break
20 Performed better than, in a way
21 Kind of powder
22 R.B.I. recordholder
23 Annual, e.g.
24 Dialectal pronoun
27 Bidding doers
28 Oils and such
30 Baking holder
31 Masters
32 __ side (askew)
33 Axolotl look-alikes
35 Bug-eyed cartoon character
38 Irish game resembling field hockey
39 Charging
41 They come from Mars
42 "9 to 5" co-star
43 Fusion
45 Title girl in a Left Banke hit
46 Kind of nectar
47 Levi's uncle
48 VCR alternative
50 Monetary unit?
51 The Rams of the Atlantic 10: Abbr.
52 Yes, in São Paulo
53 Martial arts word meaning "trample" in Korean

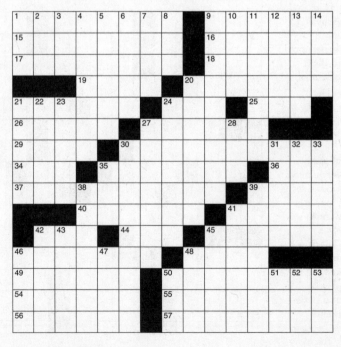

by David Liben-Nowell

135

ACROSS

1 Athletic supporter?
10 Electric meter inventor __ Thomson
15 Viniculturist's sampling tube
16 Join securely
17 It remains effective until filled or canceled
18 Places to set geraniums
19 Hardly a Yankee fan
20 Flatten, in metalworking
21 Near
22 Brand in the freezer section
24 Prima donna
26 "The Neon Bible" novelist
28 Union foe
29 Shrimp
30 Those with 48-Acrosses
32 It may have reservations
34 Vital
36 Most numbers have two or more
39 Enliven
41 Gym amenities
43 Year in Severus's reign
46 Letterhead?: Abbr.
48 See 30-Across
49 Pros at increasing profits
52 Railroad necessities
53 Series finales
54 Guffaw
56 Setting for St. Paul: Abbr.
57 Country lass
58 Rush hour, in adspeak
60 1,000 millimes
61 Ride
62 Catcher
63 Horoscope data

DOWN

1 Affirmed in court
2 "Put a lid on it!"
3 Not as a group
4 TV dog
5 'Vette option
6 Bit
7 Those who wait
8 Play again
9 About 20% of the earth's land: Abbr.
10 Footnote abbr.
11 Disco-era duds
12 Rather than, with "of"
13 "Stalag 17" star, 1953
14 Still waiting to go out
21 They're changed frequently
23 Option for some long trips
25 "Terrif!"
27 One of die Planeten
31 Antique photos
33 Stink maker
35 Flashy basket
37 Seductive
38 Drummer
40 Male character in French pantomime
42 Some stanzas
43 Ochlophobist's dread
44 Finished
45 "The Third Man" setting
47 Three-person team
50 Three-time World Cup skiing champion
51 Hero, at times
55 Play directors
58 Infielders' stat.
59 Honey eater of New Zealand

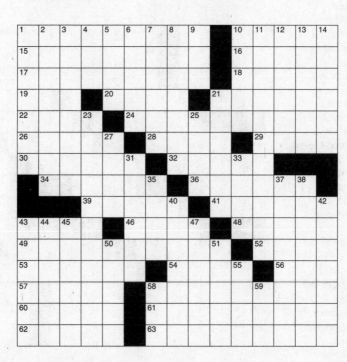

by Bob Peoples

136

ACROSS

1 Not blocked
5 Knocked completely off one's feet
15 What a card reader may do?
16 For love or money
17 Dejection interjection
18 It's used to make carbon black
19 Pool opening
21 Like some hands
22 It's nice when prize winnings come with lots of these
23 Meddle managers?
24 Town near Perugia
27 Blazed
28 Wars of the Roses battle site
31 Coupe complement
34 Permanently undecided
35 Gallery item
36 1969 target
37 Head up North?
38 Noted 2003 Eton graduate
42 Pan, e.g.
43 Peak
44 Application after a break
47 Reason to put on a collar
49 Sash accompanier, maybe
50 War game
54 Line of sight?
56 Inter ___
57 Events for potential bidders
58 Artery
59 Using big words?
60 Lively

DOWN

1 Moore verse opener
2 Counseling, e.g.
3 Bring up
4 Expanding
5 Punch with punch
6 Aviator ___ Balbo
7 "Princess Caraboo" star, 1994
8 Currency unit in Harry Potter tales
9 Strathclyde port
10 Some earth movers
11 Francis of old TV
12 Probe
13 Florida's ___ National Forest
14 Exploits
20 Make a home
23 Thither
24 Contemporary of Emerson
25 Bellow in a library
26 Send down
27 Barber's supply
29 Cut off the back
30 Crib
31 Reason to press a suit, perhaps
32 Sported
33 Black
36 Nougat-filled treats
38 Dash
39 Progress preventer
40 Superlatively smooth
41 Pressure
42 Activity on a range
44 Milker's aid
45 Browning title character
46 "Ciao!"
47 Persian
48 Rouse
50 Fear, to François
51 Cockeyed
52 Iago, e.g.
53 Disney dog
55 Letter lineup

by Craig Kasper

ACROSS

1 National service
9 Buggy
15 How some entrees are served
16 Cut aid
17 "Don't sweat it"
18 Palace figures
19 Mass apparel
20 Part of a column
22 Animal that Poseidon turned Theophane into, in myth
23 Year in Nero's reign
24 Land
25 Unrest
26 Lamp sites
28 All over
29 Biblical verb
30 Bash
32 Neutral shades
34 Fork-tailed bird
35 Ending of some plant names
36 Classic convertible name
39 Murphy's portrayer
42 Dredge (up)
43 They're all for it
45 A month abroad
47 Somalian-born supermodel
48 Swinger
50 "Cupid is a knavish __": "A Midsummer Night's Dream"
51 Part of a footnote abbr.
52 Jewish village
53 Zaire's Mobutu __ Seko
54 One to watch in a pinch?
56 Matter of course

58 Attach securely
59 Drinkers, at times
60 Magnetic induction units
61 Cruising

DOWN

1 Presidential first name
2 Unfolds
3 Wimp
4 Speaker of note
5 Cape Tres Puntas locale: Abbr.
6 ". . . but no __"
7 Environmentalist's concern
8 Grooves on a coin's edge
9 Snack named for a Massachusetts town
10 Like Hawaiian shirts
11 Boise's county
12 Relative of a bug
13 Back to back
14 Takes off wrongly
21 Period of darkening
24 "Rich Man, Poor Man" actor, 1976
25 Recluse
27 Term of affection
31 Surprise court actions
33 Warwickshire forest
35 Accusatory question
36 Fair

37 "It's Too Late Now" autobiographer
38 Camel performers
39 Totals
40 Former name of Sulawesi
41 Sign of a slip
44 Mus. slow-up
46 Texas city named by Russian immigrants
49 __ once
52 Old gathering place
53 1960s–'70s Japanese leader
55 NATO member since 1999: Abbr.
57 D-Day vessel: Abbr.

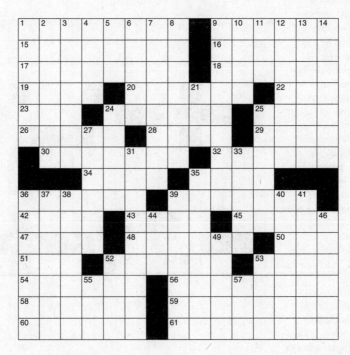

by Rich Norris

ACROSS

1 Home of America's first automatic traffic light, ca. 1920
16 Declaration of independence
17 Store something away, in a way
18 Raised rumblers
19 "One Mic" rapper
20 Western N.C.A.A. powerhouse
21 Workout unit
22 Southpaw Shawn
24 N.S. clock setting
27 ___ Drake, longtime illustrator of "Blondie"
30 Actor Corey ___
34 Mrs. Reed's creator
39 "That's my final offer"
40 It's surprising when played
41 Record problem
42 Shift very carefully
43 Fronted
44 Personal assts. keep track of them
48 A question of self-examination
51 Follower of Christ?
52 Cartoon hit
55 Sun Devils' sch.
58 Superpowers often have them
62 1959 pop hit that asked "Why?"
63 Infatuation situation

DOWN

1 Element of change
2 Series follower: Abbr.
3 "Bad!" sounds
4 Explorer of the Canadian Arctic
5 P. D. James's "Death ___ Expert Witness"
6 "Garfield" waitress
7 Tight ends?
8 What androphobes fear
9 Metrical stress
10 Vacation locale, with "the"
11 Mozart's portrayer in "Amadeus"
12 Vacation spot
13 Classic cars that were the first to have Ram Air engines
14 Giotto's work
15 Reply put in by Putin?
22 Some like them hot
23 Be rude in line
24 Be temporarily
25 Radio ___
26 Original "Star Trek" actor
27 Bad thing to have showing
28 Threatener of Miss Gulch
29 Buckets
31 Slippery as ___
32 Stick-to-___
33 Dealt
35 Commits to another hitch
36 The lady in "The Lady From Shanghai"
37 Former first lady's first name
38 Breathing abnormality
45 Firing places
46 Zhou ___
47 Think fit
48 Politico Hutchinson and others
49 Slugger Williams
50 Virginia willow
52 Universal Postal Union headquarters
53 Japon's place
54 Range: Abbr.
55 "That's not ___!" (parent's admonishment)
56 Golf's Ballesteros
57 Handles
59 Suffix with cannon
60 ___ Fabi of auto racing
61 It contains about 6% alcohol by volume

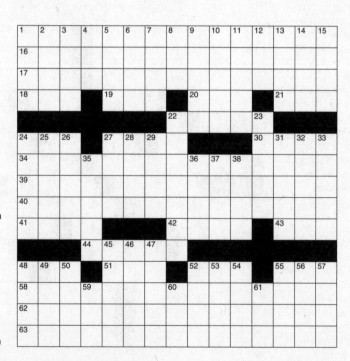

by David Levinson Wilk

ACROSS

1 Polo alternative
5 Food item whose name means "slice"
9 The "C" of C. S. Lewis
14 Composition of some ladders
15 Gray ode subject
16 Soda pop purchase
17 Abbr. that may precede a colon
18 Fast talker
20 Like some architectural designs
22 Checks
23 Leading the queue
24 Honolulu's ___ Tower
26 Pulls the plug on
28 Liberal
32 Executive attachment
33 Quaint taletellers
34 ___ mater
35 Divvy up
37 Old faces in workplaces, perhaps
39 Where to go in Gloucester
40 Schubert's "___ sentimentale"
42 In a safe place
43 Lamp locale
45 Pick-me-up
46 Time's partner
47 End of Missouri's motto
48 "The View" co-host
50 Lonely
54 Mom or dad
56 ___ jure (legal phrase)

57 Sipowicz player on "NYPD Blue"
58 "What ___?"
59 Commend, as for outstanding service
60 Rosalind's cousin in "As You Like It"
61 Terrarium youngsters
62 Are, in Arles

DOWN

1 Gasconade
2 Learning may be done by it
3 Like a troublemaker
4 Not so tough
5 Spreads
6 It has its notions
7 Fantasia's cousin
8 Dove's helper, in an Aesop tale
9 Person likely to have a big closet
10 Unlike a plane
11 Point
12 Flashed signs
13 Need to be set straight
19 Legendary Irish princess
21 Really big show
25 "Mad Love" star, 1935
26 Red ___
27 Red ___
29 Laetrile source
30 Flower girl, sometimes
31 Stunner
33 Ruby's defender

36 Armor coverer
38 Sooner than soon
41 Dispatch
44 Falafel sauce
45 Plagues
48 Empty
49 Notably secure carrier
51 Put out
52 Town in the Euganean Hills
53 Pulls off
54 One overseen by a sgt.
55 Name associated with anonymity

by Dana Motley

140

ACROSS

1 Much-seen figure on a security cam
10 "Look out below!," e.g.
15 Going
16 Mann who sang "Save Me," 1999
17 Ninnies
18 Quintain rhyme scheme
19 Make a face
20 Pound sound
21 Old-fashioned news announcer
22 Got down
24 "No kidding!"
26 A or B in blood typing, e.g.
29 Kin of hagfish
30 Kick, in a way
31 Usual
33 Nice amount of moola
36 Eur. kingdom
37 Hardly the screaming type
38 Let go
39 Off one's feed
40 Fuel type, informally
41 They have plans, for short
42 Longtime Delaware senator William
43 Place name in '90s TV
45 Kid's taunt
49 Feature of an exit strategy?
50 "The African Queen" co-star, informally
51 Farm male
53 Bang up
56 __ Corning, fiberglass maker
57 Integrated with
59 Amtrak station west of Grand Forks
60 Drawing room?
61 First name in sewing
62 [See above]

DOWN

1 Goes up and down
2 Sometime soon
3 Zero
4 Beggar's bearing
5 Baseball hero called "Gibraltar in cleats"
6 Wear and tear
7 Not home
8 Transmit
9 Calling a Jaguar XK a jalopy, say
10 Certain battery
11 Fall guys?
12 Kind of address
13 Not stand for oppression
14 Demonstratively sad
23 Stretching quality
25 Flinched, maybe
26 Prefix with syllabic
27 Wassailer's song
28 Pretty good
32 Preschoolers?
33 Attorneys' productions
34 Some people cry when these are said
35 __-humanité
38 Major export of Albania and South Africa
40 "No legacy is so rich as __": Shak.
42 Three-toed critters
44 Was beaten by
45 Certain W.M.D.
46 "That hurts!"
47 Broker
48 Nymph in Muslim paradise
52 Paw
54 Energize
55 You can hang your hat on it
58 "Saving Private Ryan" craft: Abbr.

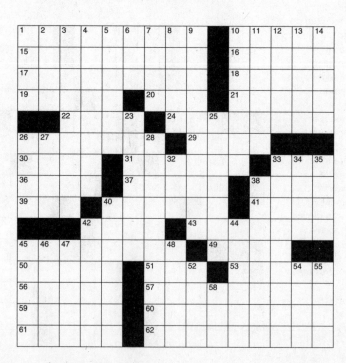

by Manny Nosowsky

ACROSS

1 1971 Bond girl portrayer
11 It's often given a red coat
15 Something that may be twisted apart
16 Deal
17 Fancied
18 Language of the 1983 film title "Koyaanisqatsi"
19 Contracted into folds
20 They may be blowing in the wind
22 Plus-or-minus fig.
23 1998 name in the news
26 Get set to shoot
27 It may put you in a difficult position
29 Modest
31 Thackeray's "The Book of __"
33 "It's all __"
34 Dungeons & Dragons co., once
35 Kind of story
38 G.E. co-founder
41 It may fill up your tank
42 Keep from desiccating
46 Jet-setters
49 Ballyshannon's river
50 Corn problem
51 Conical dryers
53 It's hard to get a grip on
54 Over
56 Shirt that leaves the midriff exposed
58 Applied oneself (to)
59 Request to a cabby
62 Capacity
63 Oscar nominee for "A Man and a Woman"
64 Soprano Ameling
65 Untold

DOWN

1 They're usually short . . . or shorts
2 Affixes, in a way
3 "Move on"
4 Senator who succeeded John Stennis
5 "Gladiator" director
6 Some cartridges' contents
7 Famed streaker of 1941
8 Let pass
9 Chart maker
10 Hardly classicists
11 Making a comeback?
12 Punching bag, so to speak
13 Kind of court
14 Expert, slangily
21 One who may marry repeatedly
24 Supercontinent of 200+ million years ago
25 1998 Ice Cube film, with "The"
28 Exerciser's pride
30 Plasma alternative, for short
32 Lift passages
36 Tied, in a way
37 Thou
38 Globe, e.g.
39 Send a jet over?
40 Dim sum selection
43 Correspondence request
44 Added numbers
45 Mobile homes
47 Something to play
48 Forty-niner's fantasy
52 Aid in removal of mines
55 Arch
57 "Buck Rogers" novelist Nowlan
60 Big name in Burmese history
61 Actor in Pink Panther films

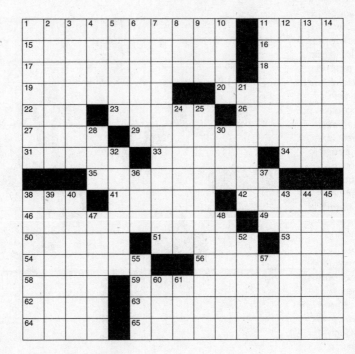

by Byron Walden

142

ACROSS

1 Holder of a lot of hidden dirt
8 Cajun condiment
15 Basement feature, sometimes
16 Not quite direct
17 Took some of
18 Bass offering
19 Shellback
20 Swear
22 By and by
23 Big name in home furnishings
25 Accommodate, in a way
26 "The 5,000 Fingers of ___" (1953 film musical)
27 Emulates a wolf
29 Roller coaster feature
31 Quintillionth: Prefix
32 Implant deeply
34 One and only
36 Efficiency option
38 Available from, as a product
41 Winter weather wear with adjustable straps
45 Eliminates as unnecessary
46 Old Testament figure
48 Insinuating
49 Year in St. Gregory I's papacy
50 Old World grazers
52 Formerly, once
53 Duffer's obstacle
55 Isn't up
57 Bird of the genus Corvus
58 Approach in a hurry
60 Sure shot
62 Wearing
63 Get behind
64 Sports physicians' concerns
65 Coty fragrance

DOWN

1 Like some egos
2 Indicate
3 Molson product
4 Something to thank God for: Abbr.
5 Historic Hebrides monastery site
6 Mississippi senator's family
7 Gushed
8 News leader
9 Makeup course?: Abbr.
10 "Up the Down Staircase" novelist Kaufman
11 Like some salts
12 Keep at steadily
13 Development of the 1950s
14 Like some mules
21 It's not too bright
24 Baking by-products
28 Essential element
30 18-Across offerers
31 Renaissance edition of a classic
33 Every family has one
35 Cries of alarm
37 Optimist in "Candide"
38 Masters
39 Good-for-nothin'
40 Record player
42 Ones who pay attention to bills
43 "Sounds about right to me"
44 Linking
47 They have naps
51 Knackered, as a Brit would say
54 Long-lasting, in commercial names
55 Cold-cock
56 "Vic and ___" of oldtime radio
59 Samoan staple
61 Point of "view"

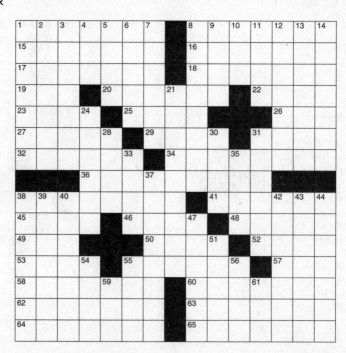

by Bob Peoples

ACROSS

1 Xerophyte
7 Demands
14 Surfing, say
15 Outside-the-box
16 Nation with a red-crested crane on its flag
17 Strewn
18 Good things
19 So to speak
20 Oktoberfest duds
22 Talented
23 Song that ends "Bless my homeland forever"
24 Certain charity event
25 Supporter
26 ___ special
27 Like a junker's engine
30 Dumpster lifters
31 Free-for-alls
32 Blood line
33 Resin from ancient trees
34 Dead giveaways
39 Show of absolute power
40 Corresponding
41 Regrettable occurrence
43 Hand-decorated
44 Auto part you shouldn't tamper with
45 Preshow ritual
46 "___ is knowing that your worst shot is still pretty good": golfer Johnny Miller
47 Cover
48 Matricide of Greek myth
49 Record producers

DOWN

1 Dance team
2 Like hockey sticks
3 18th-century French artist Gillot
4 Decorative threads
5 Masks are worn here
6 Oldest known form of currency
7 Surfaces
8 Became widespread
9 William of TV's "The Greatest American Hero"
10 Some Amtrak employees
11 Vessel that pumps the water it's floating in
12 Sheets used in four-color printing
13 Cashes in
15 Upmarket
21 Lubricative
24 Bridge hand assessment
26 Morning routines
27 Note on the fridge, maybe
28 Relative of a bigeye
29 Certain club reservations
30 1965 #1 hit with an exclamation point in its title
31 Family member
32 Church committee
34 What a creed is composed of
35 Pronto
36 Mystery author ___ Jackson Braun
37 Despite what you say
38 Swamp grasses
40 Secure anew
42 Ding

by Patrick Berry

144

ACROSS
1 Edelweiss source
5 First name at Woodstock
9 "That really happened!"
14 Give rise to
15 National competitor
16 Harped
17 Bridge words
18 Gubernatorial right
19 À la King
20 Ship damaged in the attack on Pearl Harbor
22 Fact finder, say
24 Islamic Republic Day observer
25 Follower of a wondrous feat
27 "Mystic River" co-star, 2003
28 Boxing historian Fleischer
29 Upright relatives
32 Bill of Rights subj.
33 Political symbol
35 Political symbol
37 33- or 35-Across?
39 Military shell thrower
41 Popular furry 1980s toy
44 1990 Hollywood autobiography subtitled "My Story"
45 Took up
47 1988 purchaser of Motown
48 Gospel singer Winans
50 Zip
51 Collars may cover them
53 Naive
55 Special Forces wear
56 55-Across's lacks
57 Reliever's triumph
60 Tough test
61 Olympics array
62 Quaint outburst
63 Parcel
64 Hot time in Argentina
65 Film, in Variety-speak
66 Father of Harmonia

DOWN
1 Sans sense
2 Bounteous
3 A doctor may open one
4 Driver's choice
5 Site of a famed fossil find
6 It may be added to impress
7 "Good Will Hunting" setting, briefly
8 King Mark's bride
9 Noodle product?
10 Weenie
11 He played a monocled colonel in a sitcom
12 Legal heir, at times
13 One way to issue a warning
21 Kitchen sink sight
23 Grovel
25 Causing squinting, perhaps
26 Settler in a drugstore
30 Regulars
31 Unnamed source
34 Way to stand
36 Nail
38 Dog of literature
39 À la King
40 Engulfed
42 Transparency
43 Scraps in the backwoods
46 Loafer attachment
49 One known for stick-to-it-iveness?
52 Dining room drawer
54 Brand with a tiger slogan
55 Inn inventory
58 Biographical bit
59 Delivery aid

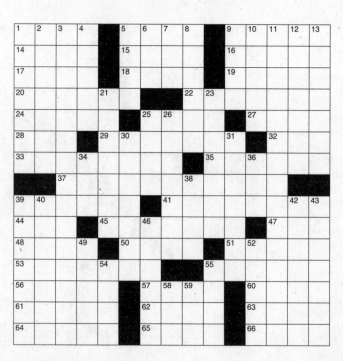

by Harvey Estes

ACROSS

1 Fill
5 Puppets
15 Blockage
16 Question from the back seat
17 Excitedly
18 Napery
19 Decrease the production (of)
21 Beginning of time?
22 Fancy
23 Fire extinguishers
25 Foes of the Seminoles
27 3.7×10^{10} to the 10th power disintegrations per second, to a physicist
28 Certain Arab
29 Ideal match, it's said, for a Cabernet Sauvignon
33 Kind of seat
34 Break time, often
35 Buddy, in slang
36 Wasn't generous with
39 Group belonging to the same rank
41 Top spot?
42 Give
43 1997 Stallone film
46 Thomas Mann novella "___ Kröger"
47 "I'm gone"
48 Flip over
51 Temporary lodging
54 1950s–'60s TV horse
55 Having little support
56 Sailing along

57 Good bettors follow it
58 Shockingly bright

DOWN

1 Cozenage
2 Eukaryotic organism
3 Went faster than by foot, say
4 Exhorted
5 Mums
6 Wipe
7 Bills
8 Symbol of Minerva
9 It's often fixed
10 Super Bowl champs of 2000
11 Not laid on thick
12 She played Irene in "Me, Myself & Irene"
13 Backward
14 Proceeds
20 Romance author Foster
23 Longtime Leonard foe
24 Its nickname is "Family City, U.S.A."
25 A lot
26 Crazily
27 Woodskin, e.g.
29 Made over
30 Feature of good design
31 Start of a show
32 Biting
34 It has a forked tail
37 Foulness
38 Robert Burns, the ___ Bard

39 Galilee town in John 2:1
40 Follower and then some
42 Obtain
43 Family heads
44 Loathing
45 Noted Italian marble
46 "Careless Hands" crooner, 1949
48 Show of amusement
49 Wafers-and-creme treat
50 Baseball's first $1 million/year player
52 Topper
53 "Olé ___" (1976 rock album)

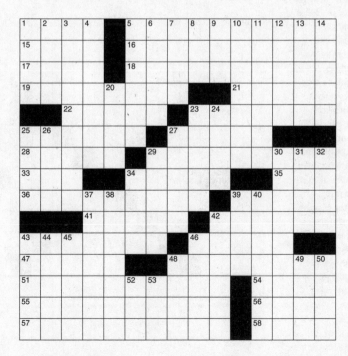

by Joe DiPietro

146

ACROSS

1 Like some doughnuts
16 It'll do your heart good
17 They have to listen
18 Letters of royalty
19 Doesn't get everything one wants
20 Mushroom part
21 Those in La Mancha
23 Breeds
24 Runner's goal
25 Chief Justice in the Dred Scott case
27 Some are odd: Abbr.
28 Stuff in a closet
29 Blood pressure readings
31 Pulled tight
32 They may be draining
33 Counter's start
34 They're fed at curbside
37 War game
41 Unearthly
42 Italian pronoun
43 One who made Ulysses fit to be tied
44 Pitcher Maglie and others
45 Emulates a 43-Across
47 Prefix with language
48 Radar, e.g.: Abbr.
49 Cloak
51 Harris of Hollywood
52 Choice words
55 One with a poll position?
56 Classic Frank Loesser song from a 1950 musical

DOWN

1 Distinguishing marks
2 Court no-no, usually
3 "Father Murphy" extras
4 Simple sack
5 Eastern ties
6 Video game allotment
7 Thinner components
8 Where óperas are performed
9 Crows
10 Yields
11 ". . . __ it me?"
12 Rare driving result
13 They inspired Andy Warhol
14 Coop flier
15 Hysteria area
22 Parlor fixtures
24 1960s falsetto singer
26 Colloquial possessive
28 Actress Headey and others
30 Abbr. for dumbbells
31 Thrice. Lat.
33 Tchotchke holders
34 It may run in the rain
35 Ran out
36 Farmer's fieldwork
37 Open
38 Taker of a religious vow
39 Pay someone back
40 Watching
42 Stamped out, in a way
45 Longtime Chicago maestro
46 C.D. source
49 Latin quarters
50 Composition of some beds
53 Lacking value
54 Boy whose name is repeated in a nursery rhyme

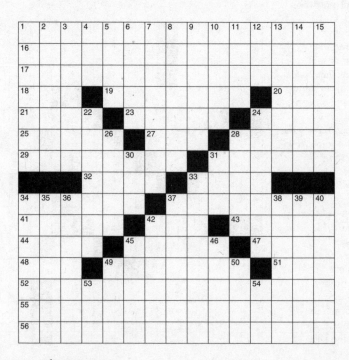

by Harvey Estes

ACROSS

1 Old-time poacher deterrents
9 Doesn't do enough
15 "That was the last straw!"
16 Ready to be engaged
17 Heat shield location
18 Disturbed the peace
19 Overdrawn
20 Wife to José
21 It's sold in sticks
22 Jets player whose jersey #12 was retired
24 Rest
25 "Drat!"
27 Sailor's punishment
28 Funny ___ (2003 Derby winner)
29 Addressed flippantly
31 Hang-ups
33 Some people can wiggle them
35 Another name for Cupid
36 Singer with the 1994 #1 hit "Stay"
40 Where people get loaded on trains
44 Building block
45 The Sudanese Republic, today
47 He said "The only alternative to coexistence is co-destruction"
48 Sportscaster Allen
49 Duds
51 Takes a powder
52 Female patron saint of Ireland
54 Dismissive remark
56 Alchemic knowledge
57 One of Rome's seven hills
58 Examine
59 What Vito Corleone's company imported
60 Hard to please
61 Stand in the great hall?

DOWN

1 Big wheel's entourage
2 L. M. Montgomery book "Anne of ___"
3 Empty ___
4 A bad situation, slangily
5 People
6 Trim
7 ___ gland (melatonin secreter)
8 Longtime beau of Oprah
9 Big digit?
10 Turnover
11 Restaurant chain, for short
12 Process by which one cell becomes two
13 Officiate
14 Knocks out
23 Perplexed
26 Part of a dollar bill
28 Spots connections between
30 Caravan carrier
32 Gray-spotted horse
34 Clothing line?
36 Lower back pain
37 Mistaken
38 Element used to make semiconductors
39 Two-layered candy
41 Certain two-wheeler
42 Neighbor of Georgia
43 ___ Long, Louisiana senator, 1948–87
46 Gulp
49 Makeup item
50 100%
53 Yielded
55 Yield

by Patrick Berry

148

ACROSS

1 Bar stools, e.g.
8 Like show horses
15 For fun
16 Early art supplier
17 Basketball Hall-of-Famer Dick, who played for the 1950s Knicks
18 Former British royal house
19 Prominent schnauzer feature
20 Chap
21 Quarter of M
22 Wet bar?
23 Cartoon character whose first name is Quincy
26 The pit
27 Refreshers
31 Hungry person's hyperbole
34 Order of business?
35 Communication ender
36 Cheers
37 Do
38 Tightens, as a belt
39 Ones yelling 36-Across
40 "Dude," in Kingston
41 Marigolds, e.g.
45 Mars Bars, e.g.
49 Tim'rous one, to Burns
50 Where to spend kroons
51 Setting for Longfellow's "The Wreck of the Hesperus"
52 Ill-used
53 Celeb-to-be
54 Light, with "to"

DOWN

1 Apple, to a botanist
2 Suffix with consist
3 It may make your face red
4 Two-door closed cars with back seats
5 Ash, e.g.
6 Morris who directed "Fog of War"
7 Bias
8 One quarter, maybe
9 Skipper's run
10 Supermarket chain
11 P.S. on an invitation
12 Serenader's sentiment
13 Zeno's home
14 Sew up
22 Ushers
23 It has little meaning
24 Get ___ reception
25 Pig out
26 Miraculous
27 Dozing
28 Eagerness
29 False front?
30 Some Rockefeller Center murals
32 Write quickly
33 Haunt
39 Calamitous
40 ___ Sharett, Israel's first foreign minister, 1949–56
41 Kid's recitation
42 How Scotch may be served
43 Wine area
44 One with ulterior motives
45 Promontory
46 Con
47 Bank
48 "The Sweetest Taboo" singer, 1985

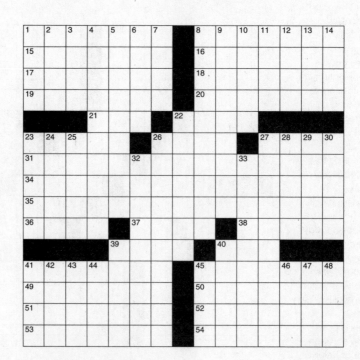

by Manny Nosowsky

ACROSS

1 Kind of engr.
5 Quiverful, e.g.
10 Cudgel
14 String of numbers?
15 Col. Klink's secretary
16 Brutus's blood vessel
17 It's full of cuts
19 Lift innovator
20 Green shade
21 Editor's request
23 One may carry off carrion
25 Pseudologue
26 Europeans, to colonial Indians
29 Bagatelles
33 Lew Wallace's "Ben-Hur: ___ of the Christ"
34 Position
35 Dr.'s order
36 It may be in a split
39 Physics 12-Down
40 Blois is on it
41 1953 Louis L'Amour novel
42 Follower
44 Conversation opener
45 It'll give you the edge
46 Economizes, with "down"
48 Boilerplate word
51 Like some kings
55 Rods and such
56 Sequin alternative
58 Trough site
59 Gone, in a way
60 Degas detail
61 African antelope
62 Some gowns
63 Wedding couple?

DOWN

1 N.Y.C. tourist attraction
2 Peak stat.
3 Giorgio's greeting
4 It may have an alarm rating
5 Window shopper's purchase?
6 Marsh fisher
7 Forest ranger
8 "Happy Days Are Here Again" composer
9 Indicator of success in life, to a palmist
10 "Songs My Mother Taught Me" composer
11 It's no longer working
12 See 39-Across
13 Kind of pay or path
18 Big makeup maker
22 Porch item
24 Arrays
26 On disk, say
27 Combat producer
28 Is very burdensome
30 Run for the money
31 Reciprocity
32 One who says a lot?
34 Make a wake
37 Like a basset
38 "The Blessed Damozel" poet
43 Learning center
44 Department store section
47 Company avoider
48 Vincent van Gogh's brother
49 Sense, in a way
50 Alternative to Chinese or Indian
52 Common contraction
53 Inner opening?
54 Evan S. Connell's "___ lo Volt!"
57 Drafter of the Meiji constitution

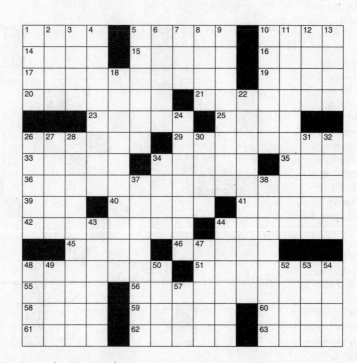

by Dana Motley

150

ACROSS
1 Playfully roguish
5 One up
11 Mountain pass
14 Owner of the Y?
15 Saint said to have been martyred by Huns
16 Ex of Mickey
17 Ready to get drunk, perhaps
18 Sports film that was a 2003 Best Picture nominee
20 Like a smoker
21 Pollute, say
22 Winner of nine golf majors
23 Tough
25 Fox's relative
27 Remote choice
28 Like retirees
30 Nottingham nursery needs
32 Article written by Kant
33 Running things in a bar
35 In things
36 Oddball
38 Ward of the screen
41 Like many hearths
42 Court people, for short
45 Is faithful (to)
47 Life saver
49 Twin
50 Code word
52 Shake, to some
53 It's divided into 24 books
55 Mend
57 Berth place
58 Novel featuring the madam Dora Flood
60 A famous Amos

61 Took the cake, say
62 Richard's "On Your Toes" collaborator
63 Sister on "The Waltons"
64 Marshaled
65 Unfortunate things to have to count
66 Homes in the woods

DOWN
1 Rolled up
2 Old bar material
3 One working on the spot?
4 Person who won't commit
5 Like a fox
6 Country statistic

7 Bygone leaders
8 Abolitionist Harriet
9 Certain Ivy Leaguer
10 Dermal development
11 "Ia Orana Maria" painter
12 Kept one's nose in the air?
13 Glib quality
19 Drive
24 Lose the freshness of youth
26 Be out briefly?
29 Corporate inits. since 1924
31 Talking up?
34 Retiree server: Abbr.
36 "Riverdance" composer Bill

37 Something to believe in
38 Extreme
39 Admire to a fault
40 Like Prometheus
42 Really regret
43 Heart protector
44 Short panties
46 Don Juans
48 Stewed
51 Lagomorphic leapers
54 29-Down competitor
56 Corn ___
59 Outback critter

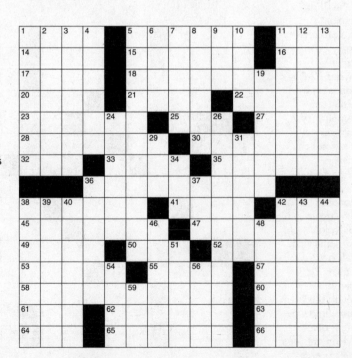

by Edgar R. Fontaine

The New York Times

CROSSWORDS

SMART PUZZLES PRESENTED WITH STYLE

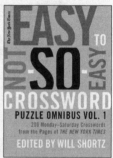

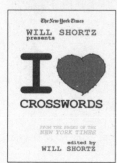
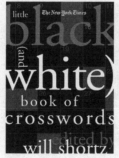

Available at your local bookstore or online at nytimes.com/nytstore.

St. Martin's Griffin

1

S	C	A	L	A	R				I	V	I	N	S
E	A	S	I	N	E	S	S		C	A	N	O	E
E	P	I	C	T	A	L	E	S		U	P	T	H	E
M	O	V	I	E	F	O	N	E		O	H	O	H
S	T	E	A	D	F	A	S	T		C	R	E	P	E
		O	N	E	S	T	R	I	P	E	R
	W	H	E	R	E	S	T	H	E	F	I	R	E
	S	H	A	M	E	S		H	E	M	I	N	S
S	C	A	R	E	S	T	H	E	H	E	C	K
P	E	R	P	E	T	R	A	T	E
I	N	F	E	R		E	M	A	I	L	L	I	S	T
K	E	R	R		E	M	B	R	O	I	D	E	R
E	X	A	L	T		T	E	L	E	S	C	O	P	Y
T	I	T	E	R		D	E	S	C	E	N	T	S
V	I	S	E	S		S	H	Y	E	S	T

2

S	K	I	N	N	Y	B	I	T	C	H		E	P	I
I	L	T	R	O	V	A	T	O	R	E		L	O	L
T	E	A	C	H	E	R	S	P	E	T		C	U	L
K	I	L		A	T	T	Y		W	E	B	A	R	T
A	N	O	I	N	T	S		S	C	R	A	P	E	R
	D	D	E		F	L	U	O	R	I	D	E
L	O	S	E	S		B	O	A	T	S		T	O	A
A	X	I	S		T	E	X	T	S		H	A	U	T
K	Y	L		S	I	R	E	E		F	O	N	T	S
E	M	I	R	A	T	E	S		L	O	O
T	O	C	E	L	I	A		H	A	R	D	C	A	P
A	R	A	B	I	C		E	A	S	E		R	E	A
H	O	G		N	A	S	T	Y	H	A	B	I	T	S
O	N	E		A	C	U	T	E	A	C	C	E	N	T
E	S	L		S	A	V	E	S	T	H	E	D	A	Y

3

S	O	L	A	R			T	I	R	E	D	O	F
K	N	I	F	E		O	P	E	R	A	T	I	V	E
A	T	S	E	A		M	A	L	E	M	O	D	E	L
T	H	A	W		S	E	R	E		S	N	O	R	T
E	E	K		S	Y	N	A	P	S	E	S
	L	U	B	E	D		D	A	W	S		T	S	A
G	O	D	E	L		Z	I	T	I		S	H	I	N
M	O	R	A	L	H	I	G	H	G	R	O	U	N	D
A	S	O	K		O	N	M	Y		E	A	M	E	S
N	E	W		S	A	C	S		B	A	R	B	Q
	Z	E	R	O	H	O	U	R		S	U	B
A	W	G	E	E		X	I	N	G		A	D	A	R
T	H	A	T	S	L	I	F	E		S	C	O	N	E
R	E	L	A	T	E	D	T	O		O	H	W	O	W
A	W	E	S	O	M	E		P	E	N	N	S

4

K	I	C	K	S	T	A	R	T		S	P	L	A	T
C	L	E	O	P	A	T	R	A		P	E	A	B	O
A	L	L	C	O	M	E	R	S		E	R	N	I	E
R	E	S	H	I	P	S		D	E	F	I	E	S
	L	E	T	S	L	I	D	E
S	C	O	R	E	R		M	T	P	O	C	O	N	O
H	E	R	O	D		R	E	G	I	S	T	R	A	R
E	D	E	L		S	A	L	O	N		T	A	D	S
R	E	A	L	I	T	Y	T	V		A	E	R	I	E
M	D	D	E	G	R	E	E		A	S	N	E	A	R
	R	O	A	D	R	A	G	E
S	H	E	B	O	P		C	A	P	E	C	O	D
P	I	L	A	F		F	I	R	S	T	T	A	K	E
E	F	I	L	E		R	A	I	S	I	N	P	I	E
W	I	E	L	D		I	N	D	I	C	A	T	E	D

5

M	A	G	N	E	T	I	S	M		C	H	I	C
A	L	L	A	T	O	N	C	E		P	H	O	N	O
D	O	I	T	A	G	A	I	N		H	A	M	A	N
E	N	D			S	N	E	A	K	I	N	E	S	S
	G	E	T	A		E	N	G	E	L		L	E	I
	I	R	R		C	E	Y		N	A	R	D
	T	H	E	M	I	S	E	R		G	E	N	I	E
P	I	E	R	O	G	I		I	N	O	R	D	E	R
O	M	A	R	R		D	R	E	Y	F	U	S	S
S	E	R	A		B	E	E		C	A	D
I	S	T		M	I	S	S	M		R	A	H	S
T	H	E	P	R	O	P	H	E	T		O	W	L
R	A	N	E	E		I	O	N	I	A	N	S	E	A
O	R	E	A	D		N	O	S	E	C	O	N	E	S
N	E	D	S		S	T	A	R	T	W	I	T	H

6

A	Z	T	E	C	S	■	■	S	A	M	P	A	N	S
R	E	H	E	A	T	■	H	A	V	E	A	C	O	W
A	R	E	O	L	E	■	E	X	I	T	V	I	S	A
B	O	B	■	L	E	E	R	■	D	R	E	D	A	Y
I	Z	O	D	■	P	A	C	T	■	O	D	I	L	E
S	E	X	E	S	■	T	U	R	I	N	■	C	T	R
T	R	E	B	L	E	■	L	I	M	O	S	■	■	■
■	O	R	I	E	N	T	E	X	P	R	E	S	S	■
■	■	S	I	T	U	P	■	S	T	R	A	T	A	■
F	G	S	■	G	O	G	O	L	■	H	I	F	I	S
L	O	A	T	H	■	S	I	A	M	■	F	E	L	L
O	N	F	I	R	E	■	R	Y	E	S	■	A	L	A
R	E	A	D	I	N	T	O	■	D	E	A	R	E	R
A	I	R	E	D	O	U	T	■	E	N	B	E	R	G
S	N	I	D	E	S	T	■	A	T	E	A	S	E	■

7

S	A	D	R	C	I	T	Y	■	B	E	I	G	E	S
T	R	U	E	L	O	V	E	■	E	L	N	I	N	O
A	T	A	L	A	N	T	A	■	E	M	A	J	O	R
T	I	L	■	M	I	R	R	O	R	■	R	O	T	E
E	C	R	U	■	C	A	N	A	■	Q	U	E	E	N
S	L	O	P	E	■	Y	E	R	O	U	T	■	■	■
M	E	L	O	T	T	■	D	E	S	E	■	S	K	Y
A	V	E	N	U	E	C	■	D	O	N	T	L	I	E
N	I	S	■	D	A	R	E	■	S	C	R	I	M	S
■	■	■	C	E	L	I	C	A	■	H	A	D	J	I
S	O	N	Y	S	■	E	S	T	D	■	P	E	O	N
T	E	A	R	■	I	S	E	E	I	T	■	I	N	D
A	S	H	A	R	P	■	G	A	S	R	A	N	G	E
I	T	U	N	E	S	■	A	S	C	O	T	T	I	E
D	E	M	O	D	E	■	R	E	I	N	H	O	L	D

8

C	O	O	K	I	E	J	A	R	■	N	O	R	M	S
O	P	P	O	R	T	U	N	E	■	U	B	O	A	T
R	E	C	O	V	E	R	E	D	■	R	I	O	J	A
E	R	I	K	■	S	Y	M	S	■	S	E	T	O	N
S	A	T	Y	R	■	B	I	T	T	E	■	C	R	I
■	■	■	E	C	O	C	A	R	■	F	A	D	S	■
J	U	N	K	F	A	X	■	R	E	T	I	N	O	L
E	N	U	R	E	S	■	P	A	J	A	M	A	■	■
A	D	M	I	R	A	L	■	M	A	N	I	L	O	W
N	E	B	S	■	B	U	S	O	N	I	■	■	■	■
G	R	E	■	B	A	R	Q	S	■	A	B	B	A	S
E	R	R	O	L	■	C	U	E	S	■	L	I	Z	A
N	A	O	M	I	■	H	I	L	L	S	I	D	E	S
E	T	N	A	S	■	E	N	L	A	R	G	E	R	S
T	E	E	N	S	■	S	T	E	V	I	E	R	A	Y

9

A	S	S	U	A	G	E	■	G	R	A	P	P	L	E
P	O	U	R	C	O	L	D	W	A	T	E	R	O	N
I	M	A	G	I	N	A	R	Y	F	R	I	E	N	D
E	B	B	E	D	■	P	E	N	T	A	■	N	E	Z
C	E	L	S	■	A	S	S	N	S	■	P	A	S	O
E	R	E	■	E	L	I	S	E	■	R	A	T	O	N
■	■	■	C	R	O	N	Y	■	S	E	S	A	M	E
W	I	S	H	I	N	G	■	G	E	N	T	L	E	S
A	C	T	O	N	E	■	D	I	R	T	Y	■	■	■
T	E	R	M	S	■	H	O	F	F	A	■	J	E	D
C	H	I	P	■	R	U	N	T	S	■	M	E	M	O
H	O	C	■	R	E	N	E	W	■	C	I	R	C	E
O	U	T	R	I	G	G	E	R	C	A	N	O	E	S
U	S	E	D	C	A	R	S	A	L	E	S	M	E	N
T	E	R	S	E	L	Y	■	P	I	N	K	E	S	T

10

A	D	E	■	R	O	L	O	■	C	O	R	N	E	R
D	J	S	■	E	L	O	N	■	A	R	E	O	L	A
Z	I	P	P	I	E	S	T	■	J	E	S	T	E	R
■	B	R	I	N	G	T	O	J	U	S	T	I	C	E
P	O	E	T	S	■	O	P	E	N	■	A	M	T	S
R	U	S	T	■	A	N	O	N	■	N	T	E	S	T
O	T	S	■	R	E	F	E	R	E	E	■	■	■	■
M	I	O	■	R	E	S	T	S	O	N	■	S	T	U
■	■	■	P	A	S	C	H	A	L	■	T	I	S	■
A	B	R	A	M	■	O	E	I	L	■	M	A	R	E
D	E	A	D	■	R	O	W	S	■	F	I	R	E	D
V	E	N	T	R	I	L	O	Q	U	I	S	T	S	■
I	T	C	H	E	S	■	R	U	N	F	O	R	I	T
S	L	O	A	N	E	■	L	O	O	T	■	E	A	R
E	E	R	I	E	R	■	D	I	S	H	■	K	S	U

11

```
M R I S . . E G O B O O S T S
A I N T . . P A T E N T L A W
D P L U S . O Z O N E H O L E
L E E . T A X E S . N E W M E
I N A N E L Y . . F I R E U P
B I G A P E . B L O G . R D S
S N U F F . H A I G H T . . .
. G E T O N T H E S T I C K .
. A R O M A S . S E A N S . .
P R O . D E L I . S T O P I T
R E N E W S . . P L A N S T O
E L E M I . D E I O N . I T O
C A P E V E R D E . D A Z E D
I T I N E R A N T . . J E R I
S E N D S A W A Y . . A S S N
```

12

```
S A R C A S M . E M P O W E R
A Q U A R I A . T E A T I M E
N U L L I T Y . I N T E R I M
J A E . D U B U Q U E . E N E
O M O O . P E R U . R A M E N
S A U N A S . B E D S T A N D
E N T E R . S A T E . O N T .
. . . G I G A N T I S M . . .
. S T A . E L I E . K A F I R
S C H M A L T Z . C A N A D A
P R I E D . W E A R . T R E N
I O N . R O A D B E D . S A P
C O M F O R T . I W O J I M A
E G A L I T E . D E R I D E S
S E N A T O R . E L E M E N T
```

13

```
P A S S E D U P . S T U P I D
A R T U R O T O S C A N I N I
C L E R I C A L C O L L A R S
M E R G E . H A I R L I N E S
A N N E . C A R O N . M O P E
N E O . F O G I N . N I K O N
. . N A M E S . C U T E S T .
M A D I G A N . S A D E Y E S
C L O N E S . D O M E D . . .
E G G O N . L O C U S . M U D
N E W T . H U L K S . T I L E
T R A C T A B L E . P U N T S
I N T H E N E A R F U T U R E
R O C K A N D R O L L S T A R
E N H A L O . S O U P I E S T
```

14

```
G E T S M A D . C E R E A L S
A C E T O N E . U T E N S I L
B U R E T T E . C H A T T E R
F A R T H E R . H Y D R A S .
E D I T E D . D I L . A I L S
S O N I A . O R F E . P R O W
T R E N T . P O R N O . E W E
. . . G E N E V I E V E . . .
U M P . N O N E T . E X A C T
K I R S . C L I O . R I S H I
E N O L . H E N . P A S S E L
. E X O C E T . T A C T U A L
T R I P L E T . S A T I A T E
V A M O O S E . A V E N G E R
S L A N D E R . R O D G E R S
```

15

```
S A D B U T T R U E . L O D I
G R E E N B E A N S . A V O N
T E N N I S A C E S . R E T E
M O V E . P R O V E . K N O X
A L E T A . D O I N G . M A C
J A R . T B O N E . U N I T E
. . . M E O W S . C N O T E S
S O D A C A N . L O C A T E S
T H E A R T . J O N A H . . .
A R E S O . L A W N S . N O R
M E R . W H O M E . E V A D E
P A S T . A V E R T . I P O D
A L K A . L E S L E Y G O R E
C L I P . A L V I N A I L E Y
T Y N E . S L I P N S L I D E
```

16

```
F A T B A C K   N E T F L I X
A R E A M A P   A N A L O G Y
S O L D E R S   R E M O V A L
O N E L E G   S I S   R E V E
      A R O M A S   H A R E M
A T T N   P A C   D E L
R O A D W A R R I O R   J A M
C O N S E N T I N G A D U L T
H T S   S T A L A C T I T E S
      X E S   E W A   R E S T
Q A T A R   I G E T I T
U L A N   P R E   C A R T E L
A V I A T O R   S H M O O Z E
K I L D A R E   S E S A M E S
E N S U I N G   E R O D E R S
```

17

```
I M A C   S K A T E O V E R
N O N O   M A I D E N N A M E
A N O N   A L P H A T E S T S
P O T T E R   S O R R I E S T
O P H E L I A   C O O L
T H E S S A L Y   S P L A T
H O R S E   G O R E Y   T A B
E N Y A   C A K E S   M A K E
R I O   B L E E P   V A L E T
C U R I E   L E M O N L A W
A F A R   L E T I T B E
B E D C O V E R   R E T I R E
I C E I C E B A B Y   O M E N
T H E N A T U R A L   B E A U
S O R E L O S E R   A S K S
```

18

```
P U B Q U I Z   U N S N A R L
A N O U N C E   G O T F R E E
P I L A T E S   G N O C C H I
A C E S O U T   B E A T S I T
D O R A   P E R O T   E I R E
O D O R S   D E O   C A N E R
C E S S N A   S T J A M E S
      A L R O S E N
  H A I R G E L   W I N D O W
G O R M E   D E B   D U E N A
A P I A   R A D I I   M R E S
M I S D E A L   P D Q B A C H
E N T E N T E   E S T E L L E
S T A I N E R   D A Y S T A R
T O S T A R T   S Y S T E M S
```

19

```
  C L A I M T O F A M E
  T H E W O M A N I L O V E
J E A L O U S M I S T R E S S
A N N A L S   P O K E I N T O
M A N N S   B E N E   A B A B
I C E D   E A R S   C R E T E
E E L   S L U R   C U T T E R
  D I M M E M O R Y
N F L E R S   S I Z E   H E P
B L O T S   A I R Y   B O N O
C O C O   O R S O   B E T T E
T R A N S E C T   G A S L I T
V I T A L S T A T I S T I C S
  N O T A T A N Y P R I C E
  R E G E N T S P A R K
```

20

```
S P L A S H G U A R D   S R S
T O U J O U R S G A I   E E C
U N P A T R I O T I C   A S U
A G O   S T E P   L E G S I T
R E N     R E M B R A N D T
T E E D U P   N E A   G A U L
    A N A   S S R   S K E E
L I M N I N G   H O S T E S S
I L E T   C I A   N E E
E L L E   A V I   S E R B I A
A T T A C K E R S     E N G
B R O N Z E   B A E R   A G E
E E R   E D G A R B E R G E N
D A M   C A E S A R S A L A D
S T E   H Y M E N O P T E R A
```

21

```
U S B A N K ■ S O A P S U D S
N O R T O N ■ A P P L E P I E
C H A M P A G N E B O T T L E
L E S ■ E C A R D ■ W A I L S
E L S E ■ K E E P S ■ E L O I
S P R A T ■ A M A T E ■ T N N
A M A T O L ■ O G R E S ■ ■ ■
M E T O N Y M ■ E U R O P O P
■ ■ N O M A D ■ M I L A N O
N I M ■ F A R E D ■ E A R E D
E D A M ■ N Y L O N ■ R O T C
B A Y A T ■ J U T E S ■ D O A
U H O H S P A G H E T T I O S
L O R R A I N E ■ D E C E N T
A S S E R T E D ■ A M U S E S
```

22

```
G A Y I C O N ■ S E A W E E D
O P E N E R A ■ I N R A N G E
K E A T O N S ■ X S A N D O S
A S H ■ S O D A P O P ■ N I K
R U M P ■ T A T A R ■ P O S T
T I A R A ■ Q V C ■ S E T T O
S T N I C K ■ S K I N D E E P
■ ■ ■ M E A D ■ S T A X ■ ■
L O S A L T O S ■ S K I H A T
A N I T A ■ E I S ■ E N O C H
T A L E ■ L A M I A ■ G E R E
E D E ■ B A D P E R M ■ D O C
R A N L A T E ■ R I O L O B O
A R T I S T E ■ R A C E W A R
L E A T H E R ■ A S S A N T E
```

23

```
R O S E B U S H E S ■ U S A F
E R A S E R H E A D ■ S Q M I
P O L A R B E A R S ■ A U E R
O S T ■ L A S T S ■ N I E L S
■ ■ ■ T I N A S ■ M A D E I T
A R O U N D ■ ■ S A M ■ Z O O
D A R T ■ E E Y O R E ■ E R R
A K A ■ O S M O S I S ■ B A D
M E N ■ L I E S O N ■ V O T E
A L G ■ M G R ■ C O A X E R
N E E S O N ■ A B O U T ■ ■ ■
D A Z E S ■ I N O U T ■ O J O
E V E R ■ O C E A N L I N E R
V E S T ■ T E S T T A K I N G
E S T A ■ B E T S Y W E T S Y
```

24

```
J A B B E R ■ C A R E S F O R
E Q U I N E ■ O N C A M E R A
L U R K E D ■ M T A R A R A T
L A S E R S ■ M I S P R I N T
O P T S O U T O F ■ S T A G Y
S L O T ■ N O D U H ■ ■ ■ ■
H A P A X ■ P E R I O D I D E
O N E N I L ■ ■ C H A N E Y
T E N D A Y W A R ■ S T A T E
■ ■ ■ ■ S I N E W ■ E N O L
N A P P A ■ S U P E R M I N I
O L E A S T E R ■ B O Y M A N
D I E T S O D A ■ E X M A T E
A T T H E G U N ■ R I O T E R
T O E S T O P S ■ N O M E S S
```

25

```
A C Q U I R E ■ S M A L L E R
T O U R N E Y ■ W E B S I T E
T M O B I L E ■ A T L A N T A
H E N ■ S O F T P R E T Z E L
E S S A ■ S U M M E R ■ ■ ■
S L E D S ■ L E E ■ M O W S
C A T H A Y ■ N E E D A N A P
E T H E N E S ■ T H E R E T O
N E U R O S I S ■ S W I P E R
E R T E ■ X E S ■ S N E R T
■ ■ W E T R A G ■ O R B S
S O U T H P H I L L Y ■ C O W
T H R E E P M ■ S E E H E R E
R O S A L I A ■ A N T E N N A
S H A R P E N ■ S N I F T E R
```

26

P	S	H	A	W	S		T	E	A	R	G	A	S
A	T	A	X	I	A		B	O	S	W	O	R	T	H
C	A	R	E	E	R		U	P	T	O	D	A	T	E
E	T	D	S		A	D	Z	E		R	E	N	E	E
C	E	T		W	H	I	Z	K	I	D		D	S	T
A	L	I	T	O		G	L	A	M		S	E	T	S
R	A	M	S	E	S	I	I		O	S	E			
S	W	E	A	T	I	N	G	B	U	L	L	E	T	S
	R	O	T		H	A	T	E	M	A	I	L
C	A	W	S		A	R	T	Y		D	A	R	E	I
A	R	A		B	R	E	Y	E	R	S		T	S	P
V	E	R	B	S		P	E	D	I		L	O	C	I
E	T	C	E	T	E	R	A		G	L	U	E	O	N
T	O	R	E	A	D	O	R		G	O	K	A	R	T
T	O	Y	S	R	U	S		S	T	E	R	E	O

27

A	D	A	M	S	A	L	E		D	E	V	I	L
L	I	M	E	T	R	E	E		U	R	S	I	N	E
D	N	A	T	U	R	A	L		S	U	P	E	R	G
A	T	T		D	E	N	S		S	M	O	R	E	S
		I	A	N		Q	T	S		
F	M	A	J	O	R		Q	U	E	E	N	M	U	M
R	O	L	O	S		Q	U	I	E	T	G	A	M	E
E	S	T	H		Q	U	E	L	L		A	S	I	A
R	E	H	N	Q	U	I	S	T		V	I	T	A	L
E	L	O	Q	U	E	N	T		K	I	O	S	K	S
	I	T	T		S	I	P	
P	I	Z	A	Z	Z		G	A	S	P		A	T	V
O	R	I	A	N	A		I	R	S	A	U	D	I	T
P	A	T	R	O	L		S	A	M	S	P	A	D	E
S	N	I	P	S		T	H	E	S	I	R	E	N

28

S	H	O	R	T	S	T	R	A	W		S	T	O	W
M	E	D	I	U	M	R	A	R	E		A	R	I	A
I	R	O	N	M	A	I	D	E	N		W	I	L	T
L	A	U	D	S		V	I	F	T		N	A	P	F
E	L	L	S		T	A	X	L	A	W		L	A	R
Y	D	S		D	O	L	E		T	I	G	R	I	S
	H	E	R	E	S	Y		S	P	U	N	K
S	T	R	A	P	I	N		A	S	H	A	N	T	I
T	I	A	R	A		T	O	R	T	E	S	
A	T	S	T	U	D		P	D	A	S		S	P	R
Y	I	P		L	A	T	E	S	T		O	T	O	E
S	C	U	M		B	E	N	T		O	C	A	L	A
M	A	T	E		B	R	A	I	N	C	H	I	L	D
A	C	I	D		E	R	I	C	T	H	E	R	E	D
D	A	N	E		D	A	R	K	H	O	R	S	E	S

29

H	A	S	A	L	O	T	G	O	I	N	G	F	O	R
I	M	P	R	O	V	E	O	N	N	A	T	U	R	E
P	O	R	K	B	A	R	R	E	L	B	I	L	L	S
R	F	Y		S	T	R	I	D	E	S		F	A	T
O	B	E	S		E	I	L	A	T		G	I	N	S
N	A	S	A	L		F	L	Y		F	A	L	D	O
E	S	T	H	E	S	I	A		M	A	R	L	O	N
	A	V	E	C		M	E	N	D	
P	U	R	R	E	D		C	O	N	T	E	S	S	A
O	N	E	A	L		L	A	V		A	N	I	O	N
L	S	T	S		T	O	T	E	M		A	G	H	A
E	N	O		C	E	R	A	M	I	C		N	U	L
N	A	T	I	O	N	A	L	E	C	O	N	O	M	Y
T	R	A	D	I	T	I	O	N	A	L	I	R	A	S
A	L	L	A	L	O	N	G	T	H	E	L	I	N	E

30

P	I	T	B	O	S	S		I	M	P	A	L	A	S
O	N	E	A	W	A	Y		F	A	R	P	O	S	T
S	T	A	T	I	N	S		O	N	E	O	N	T	A
T	H	R	E	E	D		C	L	E	M		G	E	T
P	E	D	S		P	A	D		I	S	E	R	E
U	S	O		G	R	I	P		K	E	A	R	N	S
N	E	W	F	R	O	N	T	I	E	R	S	
K	A	N	S	A	S	C	I	T	Y	C	H	I	E	F
	T	H	E	H	O	N	O	R	A	B	L	E
S	A	M	O	A	N		N	O	N	U		R	E	D
T	W	O	P	M		S	E	W		T	O	G	A
J	A	G		K	I	N	D		P	A	R	K	A	Y
U	K	U	L	E	L	E		T	O	L	U	E	N	E
D	E	L	I	R	I	A		A	C	T	N	I	C	E
E	N	S	U	R	E	D		T	O	O	K	T	E	N

31

32

33

34

35

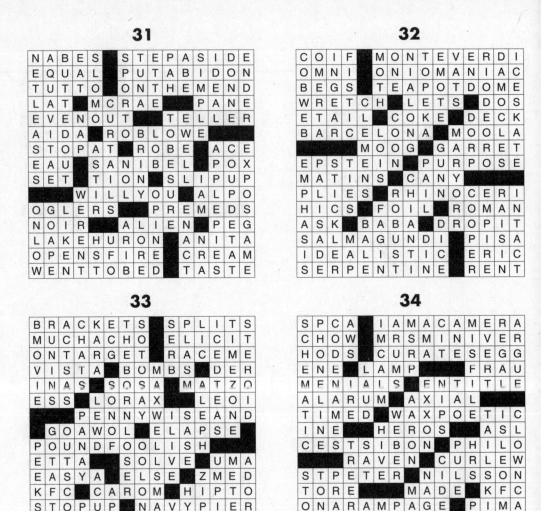

36

```
O P P O S E D █ A N D R E A
O R I G A M I █ A S H R A M S
H O N E Y B S █ S P L I T P S
L U B E █ A M A S S █ P A T E
A D A █ R A G E █ A S T I R
L O L L S █ Y E N T L █ A L T
A F L O A T █ S T R E E T Y S
█ E L I S █ S O R T █
H E R B A L T S █ I T A L I C
O L E █ R E R A N █ S T E A L
L E F A Y █ A L O E █ A C E
D A R N █ P U T I N █ A T O M
S N A K E I S █ S O U T H C S
T O I L E T S █ E L G R E C O
O R N E R Y █ S A H A R A N
```

37

```
H A I R R A I S E R S █ S D S
A C T I O N M O V I E █ M A U
S H E L L C A S I N G █ A R B
T E S L A █ G A L A █ E L K S
█ N E E D S █ P A L S Y
A R C A D E █ L A T H E S
P O R T █ L E I C A S █ O C T
R O O M T E M P E R A T U R E
I T S █ O R I O L E █ O R E M
C A S S I S █ D E I S T S
O R I E L █ G E N O A █
T O N E █ C O L E █ S P A T E
J U D █ H O M E T H E A T E R
A N E █ E L E C T R I C I A N
M D X █ P A R T Y S N A C K S
```

38

```
A C C T █ J E A N █ S A M B A
M O R A T O R I A █ E V I A N
O Z O N E H O L E █ T I A R A
R E A G A N S █ S E S A M E S
E N T E R K E Y █ A C T I N
█ L Y N █ A P P R O V A L
S E C O █ O S H A █ E R I K A
A R A █ E X I T R O W █ C E O
S I N E X █ C Z A R █ R E D S
S E A Q U A K E █ D O E █
█ C A U L K █ E M I R A T E S
R A N A T A B █ O N A G A I N
A N I T A █ Y O L A T E N G O
R A T O N █ R E A R E N D E R
A L E R T █ D O R Y █ T Y R E
```

39

```
J A C U Z Z I █ W H A S S U P
E V A S I O N █ A A M I L N E
T O P S P O T █ V I B R A N T
S C I █ S M I L E R S █ Y E A
F A T E █ S M I T S █ M E R L
A D A M S █ A N O █ C A R V E
N O N S T I C K █ P A R S E D
█ P O L Y █ G E M S █
S Q U A W K █ F A C E B O O K
O U N C E █ D I V █ L A N C E
D I K E █ D O J O S █ R E T E
A X E █ D O R I T O S █ M A P
C O M P I L E █ T O W L I N E
A T P E A C E █ E T A I L E R
N E T I Z E N █ S H Y N E S S
```

40

```
S H T E T L S █ T E C H I E
H E R S H E Y █ C H A G A L L
A S A T E A M █ L O U I S I I
R A C E D █ P L A N █ B K S
K I T E E A T I N G T R E E █
S D S █ A L O N G █ O N E I L
█ D I M E █ S W A N K Y
W A L T Z E S █ J A N S S E N
A L I S O N █ P U T A █
S L O A N █ B A S I N █ N A N
█ U N R E Q U I T E D L O V E
C D S █ A G R A █ G A M E R
R E D H A T S █ B R O C A D E
A T E A W A Y █ I O W E Y O U
W O N D E R █ T E N D O N S
```

41

```
S C A T H E   W H O V I L L E
S O T H E N   A U R E V O I R
M R T O A D   I S I T S A F E
I L E   P O R T H O S   F T C
N E S S   N O F U N   M E E T
N O T I T   G O P   S A R D S
O N E L I N E R   B A Y
W E D I D I T   J U J I T S U
    C E L   S O D A S H O P
S H O O S   P E A   K E E P S
C O N N   G R A N T   E A R S
A L L   L E I B N I Z   L A T
L E A N O N M E   R O M A N O
D U T Y F R E E   E N A M O R
S P E C T E R S   D E P O S E
```

42

```
G U E S S E R     D R O S S
U N S H A D E D   F A I S A L
N I C O T I N E   A S S T D A
M A R R I E D W I T H K I D S
A T O       I O W E   N E H
N E W S P A P E R A D   A N E
      W I S E R   L A T T E R
  S T A R T S   E L W O O D
I C A N S O   S P E A R
T H X   Q U A L I T Y T I M E
S A P   U N D O       N A M
L E A D A D O U B L E L I F E
O F Y O R E   C L O S E D I N
V E E R E D   H A M S A L A D
E R R E D     S E E R E S S
```

43

```
R I G M A R O L E   J E R K
O L E I C A C I D   P I X I E
B E E S K N E E S   A M O N G
E R S   R E A D E   S I N K S
    C O E N   L E T H E
  S T A Y S A T   L E E R A T
S T A N D   U R A L   N A P E
L O K I   S T Y N E   D T E N
A N E T   A S T A   F R E E D
T E T R A D   O B E L I S K
    H Y P E R   O R Y X
N T E S T   I S L E S   F A A
E R R O L   C H I C O M A R X
S E A M Y   C E S T L A V I E
T Y P E   I A M S O D E A D
```

44

```
F A T A S A H O G   A S S N S
I D O N T C A R E   D E A R E
N U N N E R I E S   I L I A C
K E I S T E R   I T L L D O
      S A D D E N   N I N
P I T T   G O I N G A H E A D
O N H I R E   E Y E T E E T H
S T I L E   S S A   N A D I A
T H R E E T O N   R O L L O N
M E D D L E S O M E   S E N D
O A F   N A N A N A
S I L E N T   L A P T O P S
A S O N E   P L A U S I B L E
I L O S T   B A W L E D O U T
C E R E S   S O I T S E E M S
```

45

```
A B B R   I R S   R E S E T S
C R E A M P I E   A G A T H A
T R Y G O O G L I N G T H I S
  O A T   H A L O   N O S
R U N S I N T H E F A M I L Y
E N D   F A A   A F L A C
D I S S   R R S   P I C O N
Y O U H A D M E A T H E L L O
E N S O R   L B O   R E E L
  P A T H S   D U G   A I T
D A I L Y O C C U R R E N C E
E N C   R A U L   A S S
B E I J I N G O L Y M P I C S
A R O U S E   M A D M O N E Y
R A N G E R   O H S   O G O D
```

46

```
A M O R E ■ S S S S ■ S C A M
L E N O X ■ C P O S ■ T O N I
S W E A T S H I R T ■ E L O N
■ L O R R A I N E ■ L A U D E
■ K A T Z E N J A M M E R ■ ■
R E M ■ V I O L ■ A K I N ■ ■
O Z A W A ■ I S O M E R I S M
T R I A G E D ■ L A T O S C A
C A N V A S S E D ■ I N T O W
■ L E N S ■ N Y E T ■ S T S ■
G R A F Z E P P E L I N ■ ■ ■
S U N R A ■ A L L O C A T E ■
U N D O ■ I T A L I A N I C E
I T E N ■ N I N E ■ C A N O N
T O R T ■ B O E R ■ A S Y L A
```

47

```
B E L C H ■ A L D O ■ S P I T
I N A N U P R O A R ■ A R N O
K E N N E L C L U B ■ R I S E
E M T ■ A H A B ■ ■ A M I ■ ■
S Y Z Y G Y ■ ■ E T H A N E ■
■ ■ A I M S ■ S P A ■ R C A ■
T A I L G A T E P A R T I E S
I L L T A K E Y O U T H E R E
R E L A T I V E C L A U S E S
E X T ■ O N E ■ K E R N ■ ■ ■
S A R O N G ■ ■ T S K T S K ■
■ N E A ■ ■ C H A T ■ A P U ■
R D A S ■ C R E P E P A P E R
A R T E ■ S A L E S A G E N T
M A S S ■ I M P S ■ M E R T Z
```

48

```
T R U T H I N E S S ■ A B B A
H A S A S H O T A T ■ C U R S
A M E L I O R A T E ■ C L I P
D A S K A P I T A L ■ E L B E
■ ■ ■ ■ I N L A N D E R ■ ■ ■
■ P I K E R S ■ A C T O R S ■
■ F E D E R A T E ■ A U G I E
C A R E E R S ■ G A R A G E D
A C T O N ■ A D A M I T E S ■
R E A L E R ■ E L I D E D ■ ■
A V I O N I C S ■ ■ ■ ■ ■ ■ ■
L A N G ■ S H O W C A S I N G
A L I I ■ K I T E R U N N E R
R U N E ■ I N O N E S E N S E
M E G S ■ T A S T E T E S T S
```

49

```
B U R S T S ■ ■ H A L F W A Y
O N E P I N ■ D A V E R A G E
T R U E T O ■ U N A W A R E S
T I N E ■ W Y N N ■ D I L L ■
O P E D ■ S E G A R ■ L O I N
M E D I C I N E H A T ■ C M A
■ ■ T A N T O ■ M U S K I E ■
C A J U N ■ A N T ■ T E S T S
E L O P E D ■ M A I E R ■ ■ ■
S L Y ■ S U Z A N N E V E G A
T A R S ■ H E S S E ■ E A R P
■ L I M B ■ S T Y X ■ T R I P
M O D E R A T E ■ A K I N T O
O N E L I N E R ■ C O M E T S
W E S T E N D ■ T I E D Y E ■
```

50

```
C D T ■ ■ A D D R ■ E L K S
L O W E ■ A R E W E ■ R E A P
A N O N ■ P R E E N ■ G A Z A
S O M E P E O P L E ■ D O W ■
P R I M A R Y E L E C T I O N
■ N Y C ■ O N O ■ A O N ■ ■
C A U L K ■ S S N ■ R I G E L
H I T I T ■ ■ ■ C L A R A
I R E N E ■ C U B ■ R E R A N
■ D E N ■ A P U ■ A T T ■
F I R S T I M P R E S S I O N
U N I ■ ■ M I S S T H E C U T
T U L L ■ P L A T A ■ A L T E
O S L O ■ E L L I S ■ T E D S
N E S T ■ L E A N ■ S O T
```

51

```
T I K I T O R C H █ C A T E R
I R E N E C A R A █ A R U L E
D O N T S H O U T █ F I R M S
E N O L █ R U D I █ T E N E T
█ █ H E L E N █ A S T R A
S C A L E S █ H O N █ O S U
C O M E R █ N E A R S █ M G R
R U I N █ J E N N Y █ H U L A
E R S █ P A W E D █ B O S U N
E T H █ I R S █ S A C H E T
N O B L E █ C R A I G █
T R U E R █ R O T E █ A C E D
E D G A R █ A M E R I C A N A
S E G N O █ W E A R S T H I N
T R Y S T █ L O M A L I N D A
```

52

```
Z I P L O C B A G █ H A R P S
O N I O N R O L L █ A G O R A
M R R O M A N C E █ Y O Y O S
B E A M E N G I N E S █ A T H
I A N █ O D D S █ P L E A
E C H O I C █ S O C K A W A Y
S H A F F E R █ W A R R E N S
█ N I L E █ E P O S █
A L C O V E S █ R E N E G E S
T A S T E S O K █ S A C R U M
E R L E █ T R E F █ A G A
I D E █ W A T E R H E A T E R
N E W D O █ S P E A R M I N T
T R I C K █ T U R N S T A I L
O S S I E █ O P E D E S S A Y
```

53

```
E L L I S █ O G R E █ M E N U
M O O C H █ T O O N █ I V E S
M O V E R █ R O T C █ T A T A
A M E R I C A F I R S T █
█ U M A █ N Y U █ S A D
J O H N P H I L I P S O U S A
E D A █ N O A █ T A H I T I
W O R S T █ U S A █ N O T U S
I N L A I D █ E R S █ U T E
S T A R S A N D S T R I P E S
H O N █ C R O █ A E C █
█ T H E M A R C H K I N G
U Z I S █ N A S A █ A I R E R
S A L K █ O D A Y █ N E M E A
A P E S █ T S P S █ G R A D S
```

54

```
E S T A S █ A L S O █ S T E M
C O R F U █ M O O N S T O N E
O L A F S █ I D L E H A N D S
N O V I S A D █ D A I R I E S
█ E D E R █ D I L A T O R Y
G A L A X Y Q U E S T █
L I E V █ A U E R █ S A S H A
A D R I A N I █ S K U L K E D
M A S T S █ Z H O U █ G Y R A
█ T O M A N D J E R R Y
S A B E R S A W █ Z E R O █
C L E R I C S █ A U R I C L E
U P A N D A T E M █ B A K E R
S E M I E R E C T █ O N E A M
I S E E █ S R O S █ A S T R A
```

55

```
A T M C A R D █ B A K L A V A
R E G A L I A █ E N C O D E R
C A M P I N G █ D N A T E S T
A P L O T █ G M A I L █ P T L
D O I N █ S E I Z E █ A T I E
I T O █ M E R T Z █ E M A G S
A S N E A T █ E L E V A T E S
█ A R O W █ E V E N █
L B J R A N C H █ I R A Q I S
A D U L T █ F O R T Y █ U M P
P A G E █ C I R C A █ R I P A
L L B █ B L E A R █ H E X E R
A T A B O I L █ U N I C O D E
C O N T E N D █ M I N U T E S
E N D U R E S █ B E D R E S T
```

56

```
C R A N K C A L L E R ■ H S T
W O M E N I N L O V E ■ E T E
T O S S E D S A L A D ■ A R D
S M O T E ■ ■ M I S A D D E D
■ ■ S H E B A T ■ S A S S Y
S T P ■ O L D S A W ■ N T S B
T R I P L E S ■ S A N T A F E
A I L E E N ■ ■ T I E R R A
L O O K S A D ■ F U N S T E R
E S T O ■ S A N E S T ■ S E S
M O L E S ■ R U B I E S ■ ■
A N I S E T E A ■ ■ N O A H S
T A G ■ ■ D I N N E R D A T E S
E T H ■ A V O C A D O P E A R
S A T ■ N O T E P A S S E R S
```

57

```
E S C A L A T E S ■ A M A T I
L E A V E H O M E ■ W A N E S
Y A K E T Y S A X ■ A N N A L
S T Y M I E ■ I L I K E I K E
■ ■ A N S ■ L I N E T E S T
O M A R ■ ■ E V A N ■
R A C I A L ■ D E L I M I T S
I N H A L E S ■ S I N A T R A
G O E S D E A F ■ E G G S O N
■ ■ E L M O ■ ■ N A T E
O U T E R E A R ■ A N E ■
F R O N T E N D ■ T O T E M S
M A N O R ■ T E S T P I L O T
A N I C E ■ H A P H A Z A R D
N O C H E ■ A D H E R E N T S
```

58

```
W E T T S H I R T ■ L E W I S
A Y E A Y E S I R ■ O M A H A
S E R E N G E T I ■ M O R E L
H E M ■ C O R ■ R I A ■ R A T
E X I M ■ T E L E G ■ T O R T
R A N O U T ■ I M O ■ H O Y A
S M I R C H ■ P E T E R M A X
■ ■ I L E T ■ S T L O ■
B O N S A M I S ■ H E W I T T
R H E O ■ I M P ■ E M I N O R
A C C T ■ N E R O S ■ N A N A
P A K ■ E E L ■ T H O ■ S T N
A R T I E ■ ■ A N T A R C T I C
D O I N G ■ G O O F F L I N E
S L E D S ■ S P I T F I R E S
```

59

```
S E T O S E ■ R E C A P
A S H L A N D ■ T H E G A M E
S T R A N G E G O I N G S O N
S E I N E ■ F I V E T O T E N
I L L ■ R O L F E ■ O B E
E L L A ■ P A S S I N G F A D
R E A R L I T ■ M O O T ■
■ S I M O N E ■ S M I T H S
■ N A V E ■ P U T T O U T
J A M S E S S I O N ■ A U B E
A H A ■ ■ A B N E R ■ S S R
S E N O R I T A S ■ A G A I N
P R I S O N E R O F Z E N D A
E N L A C E D ■ R E O R D E R
R E A S K ■ D R E S S Y
```

60

```
F I S H F A R M ■ B A R D
I N T O O D E E P ■ S O R E R
R E A R O U S A L ■ T A S T E
E P I S T L E ■ A M U S E R S
■ T R E P A N ■ C A P ■ N O S
■ W A T T ■ E D I F I C E
■ A B O D E S ■ S E D U C E R
G L U M ■ ■ L A D S
A F R A M E S ■ F A I L L E
M A N N I S H ■ I N N S
E R S ■ N A E ■ E T H I C S
C O D I C I L ■ S W A S H E R
A M O V E ■ L A T E S T A G E
L E W I S ■ S M A R T E N U P
L O N E ■ A S P E R S E S
```

61

S	P	A	M		P	O	L	K		B	L	U	R	B
T	E	L	E		I	R	O	N		R	E	N	E	E
O	N	T	H	I	N	I	C	E		O	S	C	A	R
W	H	A	T	T	H	E	H	E	C	K		L	I	L
		M	A	S	O	N		S	E	E	H	E	R	E
S	F	O		A	L	T	O		R	N	A			
K	I	N	G	L	E	A	R		F	E	N	D	E	R
A	S	T	R	O		L	A	V		N	O	R	S	E
T	H	E	E	N	D		L	E	G	G	I	E	S	T
		E	G	O		S	H	E	L		W	O	E	
B	E	A	T	S	M	E		E	N	I	A	C		
E	X	T		T	E	X	T	M	E	S	S	A	G	E
E	C	O	N	O		T	E	E	S	H	I	R	T	S
T	I	M	O	R		R	A	N	I		G	E	O	M
S	A	S	S	Y		A	R	T	S		N	Y	S	E

62

T	A	B	L	O	I	D	T	V		A	S	P	E	R
I	F	Y	O	U	D	A	R	E		S	H	O	N	E
R	U	R	I	T	A	N	I	A		L	O	I	N	S
E	S	O	S			I	A	L	S	O		S	U	E
D	E	N		F	E	E	L	S	U	P	T	O	I	T
			F	U	L	L	S	C	R	E	E	N		
U	R	B	A	N	A	R	E	A			S	P	U	D
S	H	O	R		M	A	P	L	E		L	E	N	O
H	O	B	O		D	A	L	L	I	A	N	C	E	
		M	U	S	I	C	R	O	L	L	S			
J	A	C	K	E	T	L	A	P	E	L		S	S	E
E	T	A		I	S	I	T	I			S	W	A	N
N	O	D	O	Z		F	I	N	A	G	L	I	N	G
G	L	O	B	E		F	O	I	L	P	A	P	E	R
A	L	O	E	S		E	N	S	L	A	V	E	R	S

63

A	C	C	O	S	T		C	A	T		O	R	E	
S	H	O	R	T	U		O	L	I	N		S	E	X
F	A	L	C	O	N	C	R	E	S	T		B	A	P
A	S	L		L	A	I	C	A	L		T	O	D	O
O	T	A	D		O	N	A	R	E	D	R	U	M	O
T	E	R	I		A	N	S	A		E	E	R	I	E
		G	A	L	A		N	O	C	E	N	T	S	
	A	B	S	C	A	M		C	N	O	T	E	S	
A	V	O	C	A	D	O		E	E	R	O			
H	A	T	E	R		N	E	S	S		P	A	S	S
B	R	A	N	D	Y	S	N	A	P		S	M	U	T
L	I	N	E		O	T	E	L	L	O		A	R	E
I	C	I		A	D	I	M	E	A	D	O	Z	E	N
S	E	S		S	E	C	Y		C	O	M	E	T	O
S	S	T		E	L	K			E	R	A	S	E	S

64

X	Z	I	B	I	T		D	E	M	O	L	I	S	H
M	A	K	E	M	E		E	V	A	L	U	A	T	E
E	N	E	R	G	Y		C	A	R	D	I	N	A	L
N	E	A	T	O		D	O	N	A	S		F	T	D
			H	O	N	E	Y	S	U	C	K	L	E	
I	N	S		D	A	L	E		D	O	R	E	M	I
H	O	H	O		V	I	D	A		R	U	M	E	N
O	R	A	N	G	E	S		T	I	E	P	I	N	S
P	A	R	E	E		H	I	T	S		A	N	T	E
S	H	E	A	R	S		N	A	P	S		G	S	T
	J	I	M	M	O	R	R	I	S	O	N			
P	O	S		A	N	I	O	N		F	E	R	M	I
E	N	S	E	N	A	D	A		A	T	W	O	O	D
R	E	U	N	I	T	E	D		R	E	T	O	O	L
U	S	E	D	C	A	R	S		K	N	O	T	T	Y

65

H	S	T		S	W	I	S	S	B	A	N	K	S
A	O	R	B		D	I	S	P	E	R	S	I	O	N
S	H	U	E		I	R	R	A	T	I	O	N	A	L
T	I	N	G	E		E	A	S	T	O	N			
Y	O	K	E	M	A	T	E		O	N	E	A	C	T
			N	A	T	A	L	E			L	O	U	
T	H	E	T	I	P	P	I	N	G	P	O	I	N	T
B	E	L	L	L	A	P		G	E	O	R	G	I	E
S	A	L	E	S	R	E	S	I	S	T	A	N	C	E
P	R	E			R	E	N	T	A	L				
S	T	R	A	Y	S		N	E	S	T	E	G	G	S
			G	E	T	F	A	R		O	X	L	I	P
I	N	S	I	N	U	A	T	O	R		A	O	N	E
F	I	R	S	T	F	L	O	O	R		M	A	Z	E
S	T	A	T	E	F	A	R	M	S			T	A	D

66

```
S I M B A   P U F F   T B S P
O N A I R   A T R O P H I E S
U S I N G   N A I L F I L E S
S O N S O F T H E D E S E R T
E L F   S A R A Z E N
S E R B   L I N E R N O T E S
  A R I S E S   I N A L L
R A M O N E S   P A G E B O Y
O M E N S   D O R S A L
D I S C I P L I N E   M E M O
  S E A T I N G   L A B
S W E E T P O T A T O P I E S
M A D D O C T O R   L Y N N E
U N I O N I Z E D   F L E A S
T E E M   D U D S   S E N D S
```

67

```
A S A M I   L E G   J U M P
D I V A N S   A X E   A S T I
A M E R C E   S I N E W A V E
M I S T E R R O G E R S
  I N T E R E S T   A K A
  P I N S A N D N E E D L E S
M A C   E S T A T E S A L E S
O N E S   B U N T
L E S E M A J E S T E   D O S
E L I Z A B E T H A R D E N
S S N   M A R I A N N E
  M E S S E N G E R R N A
N I N E T E E N   O S M I U M
A Q U A   R Y N   S T A T I C
P S S T   S S E   S L A T S
```

68

```
R A I L B I R D   A L B U M S
E D G A R L E E   M A U P I N
C A N T E E N S   O K S A N A
U S O   A N T I Q U E S H O P
S T R O K E S   U N R E E L S
A R E N A S   B I T   D A T A
L A D Y L   M O N T E   D A T
  X E R O X C O P Y
S Y L   G E L E E   S E R F S
T E A M   M I R   B O L E R O
A S P I R I N   S U M P T E R
G O L D E N A G E R S   S E C
G R A C E D   L E G A L I Z E
E N C A S E   O N E L I N E R
R O E P E R   M O R T U A R Y
```

69

```
B U M P S   W H I M W H A M
E T A L I I   H A D A B I T E
A T N O O N   A V E R A G E S
N E E   N F C T E A M   H A H
B R A M   O A S T S   L E S E
A R T O O   N T H   S I R E D
G O E S T O T H E T O P
S T R E T C H E S A C R O S S
  L O S E P A T I E N C E
I D O L S   C R Y   O A T E N
N E U E   G O O S E   D I N T
G M T   T O M B O Y S   P E I
M U S C A T E L   E L S T O N
A R E A C O D E   R E H O N E
R E T R O N Y M   W H E E L
```

70

```
M O S T A C T I V E   O M A R
I S M E L L A R A T   P I L E
S T I C K I T O U T   I S L A
S E T S A   A N N A   U S F L
M A H   G R O T   S M O O T
E L Y S E E   N I L E   U R I
  E L M   S N A P B R I M
E M B R O I L   G R A N I T E
M A R T I N I S   I L A
O S E   S I K H   A S I A N S
T H A N E   E R S T   E E O
I N D O   S W I T   K A R E N
C O B O   P I N A C O L A D A
O T I S   A S K M E L A T E R
N E N E   R E S P O N D E R S
```

71

```
READMYLIPS ROTH
EDDIEMONEY OTHO
SMOKEALARM AHEM
TENET IRIS MERE
DEAD STUD LIB
ASI SEATON ALTO
YESLETS TEACOZY
ORO RAT
BESTBUY DERIDES
ATIT TONEUP EPA
TEL KENS VEIL
CREE TOAT PEPSI
ANNA HOLYPERSON
VATS ONONESSIDE
ELKE NONEWTAXES
```

72

```
SWAP FACTO SLAS
HERS EBOOK AIRP
ORTS RENTS UNDE
RESTIMATE STEER
SIMI GLENNM
ILLER NARY
PAIN SAUNA UPRI
SING AMEND SEAS
ONER LODES ERIE
FARO PREDE
STINED NAPE
PORED INCAPACIT
ATES EVERT RUMI
NANT TAXES CRIN
KLES ANTSY HENS
```

73

```
OFLATE ALMANACS
KLAXON MOONUNIT
LAMENT PUNITIVE
AMPLY QUITS MIR
HERS WELSH PUCE
OWE CODEX LASSO
MAYHAP SITIN
ARSENAL VERTIGO
MOTIF PASSON
MCGEE FLIES ROC
EARN CEASE JADE
XLI HASTO PIETA
IVEHADIT PALLID
CIVILIZE OPTIMA
ONEDOZEN MASSEY
```

74

```
ASPERSE THEURGE
THINKINGOUTLOUD
NICCOLOPAGANINI
OAKY ELATE ASST
CNN CDS
CST OTS POR CAP
HERESTOMANYMORE
INAPERFECTWORLD
DONTBEASTRANGER
ERS AAR SOS ISO
SGT VHS
ARCH MAMIE HEAP
GALAPERFORMANCE
EVENINGRUSHHOUR
DEFACTO SYOSSET
```

75

```
BUDDHA EGGTIMER
ISRAEL SURINAME
SEEMED PEACENIK
TRIPLEWORDSCORE
RIDS ROSIE SWAY
ODE WAN STATE
SLOSHES SOARED
FLED PADS
OPTFOR DELAYED
ERASE CUR MAD
DINE SERIF VANE
ITTAKESALLKINDS
PHASEDIN ONSALE
AERONAUT RIOTER
LEANONME ATREST
```

76

A	L	A	M	O	D	E	■	O	T	T	A	W	A
N	O	N	U	S	E	R	S	■	P	E	A	L	E	D
A	C	I	D	T	E	S	T	■	I	N	R	O	A	D
P	A	M	P	E	R	E	R	■	O	C	T	A	V	E
E	L	A	I	N	E	■	A	S	N	E	E	D	E	D
S	A	T	E	D	■	R	I	P	E	N	S	■
T	R	E	S	■	R	E	G	R	E	T	T	E	R	S
I	E	R	■	S	I	G	H	E	R	S	■	V	E	E
C	A	S	T	I	G	A	T	E	S	■	C	E	C	E
■	E	C	O	L	E	S	■	S	O	R	T	S
A	S	S	A	I	L	E	D	■	S	E	P	S	I	S
R	I	P	P	L	E	■	G	E	T	A	L	I	F	T
A	D	R	O	I	T	■	E	G	O	M	A	N	I	A
B	E	A	T	A	T	■	S	I	L	E	N	C	E	R
S	A	Y	S	N	O	■	S	E	N	D	E	R	S

77

T	O	Y	S	R	U	S	K	I	D	■	M	F	A	S
O	N	E	M	A	N	A	R	M	Y	■	A	L	I	T
A	B	S	O	F	S	T	E	E	L	■	B	U	R	P
S	O	I	R	■	I	M	M	A	D	■	S	W	E
T	A	T	E	■	O	N	L	I	N	E	C	H	A	T
E	R	I	S	■	J	O	I	N	■	P	R	O	V	E
R	D	S	■	B	O	N	N	E	■	O	U	T	E	R
■	M	U	S	■	D	R	X	■
U	L	C	E	R	■	P	I	V	O	T	■	P	S	T
P	E	R	I	L	■	E	D	E	N	■	M	O	M	E
C	H	A	R	A	C	T	E	R	S	■	A	P	I	A
C	A	T	■	P	A	N	A	M	■	L	T	D	S
O	V	I	D	■	B	A	T	O	N	R	O	U	G	E
D	R	O	P	■	A	M	E	N	C	O	R	N	E	R
E	E	N	S	■	L	E	S	T	R	O	Y	E	N	S

78

L	O	S	T	S	T	E	A	M	■	T	R	Y	I	T
A	N	T	I	P	A	S	T	O	■	R	E	U	N	E
Y	O	U	B	E	T	T	E	R	■	A	P	P	L	E
E	N	T	I	C	E	D	■	T	O	P	S	P	I	N
R	E	Z	A	■	B	A	R	S	■	I	N	C
■	S	N	A	R	L	S	■	V	E	E	R
T	H	E	A	T	E	R	O	F	■	B	O	F	F	O
H	A	R	D	A	C	T	T	O	F	O	L	L	O	W
E	I	G	E	R	■	T	H	E	A	B	S	U	R	D
B	R	O	S	■	C	H	E	S	T	S	■
U	S	N	■	F	U	E	L	■	A	C	T	A
S	T	O	N	I	E	R	■	G	U	M	D	R	O	P
H	Y	M	A	N	■	A	M	A	N	A	L	O	N	E
E	L	I	S	E	■	P	O	L	I	C	E	C	A	R
S	E	C	T	S	■	Y	E	A	V	E	R	I	L	Y

79

W	O	R	K	S	H	O	P	■	O	K	A	P	I	S
O	P	E	N	L	I	N	E	■	R	A	M	O	N	E
R	E	B	O	O	T	E	D	■	F	R	A	N	C	E
D	R	A	W	B	R	I	D	G	E	A	H	E	A	D
■	E	L	L	I	O	T	■
S	O	P	H	O	C	L	E	S	■	E	A	G	L	E
A	P	R	O	P	O	S	■	T	A	C	K	L	E	D
D	E	A	V	E	R	■	T	H	R	I	V	E
A	D	D	E	N	D	S	■	S	T	O	O	D	I	N
T	S	A	R	S	■	S	T	E	E	P	N	E	S	S
■	E	N	G	R	A	M	■
S	A	R	A	S	O	T	A	S	P	R	I	N	G	S
P	O	O	R	A	T	■	C	A	T	A	L	I	N	A
I	N	T	I	M	E	■	E	L	E	V	E	N	A	M
N	E	E	D	E	D	■	S	T	R	I	D	E	R	S

80

T	R	I	V	E	T	■	A	S	S	E	S	S	E	D
E	O	S	I	N	E	■	S	T	O	N	E	A	G	E
A	W	O	K	E	N	■	L	E	A	V	I	N	G	S
R	E	G	I	M	E	■	A	R	K	S	■	D	P	S
A	N	O	N	Y	M	■	P	E	I	■	E	R	L	E
T	A	N	G	L	E	S	■	O	N	E	Y	E	A	R
■	I	N	U	I	T	■	T	R	E	N	T
■	I	D	E	N	T	I	T	Y	T	H	E	F	T	■
S	M	I	L	E	■	T	Y	P	E	A	■
P	I	C	K	S	A	T	■	E	N	N	O	B	L	E
E	N	K	E	■	M	O	I	■	T	A	B	L	A	S
C	L	E	■	G	E	A	R	■	A	L	L	O	U	T
T	O	R	E	I	N	T	O	■	C	L	A	U	D	E
E	V	E	A	R	D	E	N	■	L	E	S	S	E	R
R	E	D	R	O	S	E	S	■	E	N	T	E	R	S

81

```
C A P I T A L R   O P P O S E
P R O M I S E E   B R A N C A
A T T E M P T S   O O M P H S
S I T   S E M I T E S   A L I
  S E S   R E D O S   S T E N
  T R O I   J E U   M E R G E
    U N S U N G H E R O E S
A S O L D A S T H E H I L L S
D I D J U S T I C E T O
E N D A S   S A O   A U B E
L I T H   V A L O R   S E D
A S H   K A Y A K E R   S E A
I T I S A N   R I P E N E S S
D E N O T E   E E R I N E S S
E R G O T S   A S O N E M A N
```

82

```
S T E P H E N   C O L B E R T
P O L E A X E   A R A L S E A
I T E R A T E   R I P T O R N
K A I   S O D A P O P   B E L
E S S O   L E T O N   M E D I
T T O P S   D O O   M A S O N
V E N E E R   B L U E N O S E
      N E O N   S A T S
B M X B I K E S   L A M O D E
A I M A T   A T M   L A N E S
F A R R   B R A T S   N A S T
F H A   B A B Y F A T   D O R
L A D A N S E   U L U L A T E
E M I R A T E   J A N E R O E
S M O K I E R   I T S B E S T
```

83

```
C L A S S A C T S   G U L F S
H E R C U L E A N   A T A R I
O N E O R M O R E   U N S E R
P I N U P S   P E L L E T S
S N A R L   W I R E S   P H D
      U S E T A X   F L E E
R E S I S T S   T I J U A N A
E N T R E E   C A N C E L
P R A I S E S   R O C K E R S
L O P S   P O D U N K
Y U L   G L U O N   H A I L S
  T E L L E R S   W A R R E N
S E G U E   S I C K L E A V E
U T U R N   O D O R E A T E R
B O N E S   P O P P Y S E E D
```

84

```
G L U E S T I C K   D E S A C
L A T T E R D A Y   E L E N A
O U T S T A Y E D   B E A N S
O R E   A L L S   A R M L E T
M I K E   A L U M N A   I R A
Y E S N O   R I O   L O I N
    S O N G A N D D A N C E
P E T U N I A   D E E P S E T
O P E R A G L A S S E S
L I R E   H A R   D E L H I
I S R   P O S T I T   D U A D
T O A M A N   D R A M   C U L
I D I O T   V E R S A T I L E
C E N T S   I C E S K A T E R
K I S S Y   D O G O O D E R S
```

85

```
R O E V W A D E   S K E T C H
A N T I E T A M   P I E R C E
C S I M I A M I   A N K A R A
E T C   R R A T I N G   L I D
C A K E   I S T O O   B A D E
A G E N T   K E W   A O L E R
R E T T O N   D A Y S T A R S
    E N N E   S O O T
S T A N G E T Z   S N O C A T
O M I T S   C A L   E M O T E
M O R E   T H R O B   S U L A
E B B   I R A Q W A R   L A P
D I A N N E   A F R A I D S O
A L L U R E   W A N N A B E T
Y E L L E D   I T S A M E S S
```

86

S	Y	M	B	O	L	I	S	T		S	W	A	B	S
Q	U	A	R	T	E	R	T	O		T	H	R	E	E
U	K	R	A	I	N	I	A	N		M	Y	M	A	N
I	F	S		C	A	S	T	E		A	M	E	N	D
R	E	B	A		S	E	E	P		R	E	N	D	S
T	S	A	R	S		S	T	O	G	Y		I	I	I
S	T	R	I	N	G		H	E	R		C	A	P	N
		A	L	L	F	E	M	A	L	E				
J	U	G	S		E	L	O		F	O	R	B	A	D
U	S	O		O	N	E	B	C		N	E	R	D	Y
M	E	T	E	D		E	V	I	E		S	I	R	S
B	A	R	G	E		F	I	E	N	D		N	I	P
O	B	E	Y	S		R	O	N	R	E	A	G	A	N
C	L	A	P	S		O	U	T	O	F	T	U	N	E
D	E	L	T	A		M	S	O	L	Y	M	P	I	A

87

J	A	C	K	W	E	B	B			B	R	I	N	G
I	M	O	N	A	D	I	E	T		L	O	N	E	R
H	I	R	E	L	I	N	G	S		O	Z	A	W	A
A	N	K	L	E	T		S	A	A	B		S	O	D
D	U	E	L	S		C	T	R	L		M	E	R	E
S	S	R	S		R	A	H		A	G	E	N	D	A
				A	I	L	E	D		O	A	S	E	S
	F	I	S	C	A	L	Q	U	A	R	T	E	R	
M	O	D	E	M		S	U	E	M	E				
A	X	E	M	E	N		E	B	B		L	O	R	D
C	H	A	I		E	A	S	Y		M	Y	L	A	I
A	O	L		P	O	U	T		P	Y	R	I	T	E
Q	U	I	T	O		N	I	N	E	L	I	V	E	S
U	N	Z	I	P		T	O	O	N	E	S	I	D	E
E	D	E	N	S		N	B	A	S	T	A	R	S	

88

D	O	O	D	A	D	S		T	O	E	H	O	L	D
I	N	V	A	L	U	E		A	L	L	O	V	E	R
A	D	E	N	I	N	E		R	E	S	T	I	V	E
N	E	R	T	S		S	K	I		A	P	N	E	A
A	P	S	E		S	T	I	F	F		R	E	E	D
R	O	T		S	C	O	T	F	R	E	E			
O	S	A		W	R	I	T		U	L	S	T	E	R
S	I	T	S	O	U	T		M	I	S	S	I	V	E
S	T	E	P	O	N		T	A	T	E		C	I	D
			I	N	C	R	A	T	E	S		T	L	C
C	H	I	T		H	E	X	A	D		L	A	L	A
H	A	S	T	E		A	I	D		D	E	C	O	R
I	D	E	A	T	E	D		O	P	E	N	T	O	P
P	A	R	K	A	V	E		R	O	A	N	O	K	E
S	T	E	E	L	E	R		S	P	R	Y	E	S	T

89

A	K	E	L	A		L	E	S	S	O	N	T	W	O
D	E	T	O	O		O	T	H	E	R	T	H	A	N
U	N	I	O	N		W	H	O	A	T	H	E	R	E
L	O	C	K	E	R	R	O	O	M	S		A	G	E
A	S	K	A		O	A	S	I	S		B	R	A	Y
T	H	E	T	O	P	T	E	N		G	I	M	M	E
E	A	T		H	I	E	S		B	U	O	Y	E	D
			A	Y	E	S		D	A	Y	S			
O	Y	S	T	E	R		W	E	R	E		M	E	L
L	O	U	I	S		A	H	A	R	D	T	I	M	E
D	U	S	T		S	T	A	R	E		O	N	A	N
G	A	S		S	E	T	T	I	N	G	S	U	N	S
O	N	I	M	P	U	L	S	E		A	S	S	A	M
A	D	N	A	U	S	E	A	M		P	E	E	T	E
T	I	G	E	R	S	E	Y	E		E	S	S	E	N

90

A	G	A	P	E		W	A	S	H	A	B	L	E	S
R	O	L	L	O		E	M	A	I	L	L	I	S	T
I	N	P	E	N		B	E	R	T	L	A	N	C	E
D	E	A	D		L	E	N	D	S	A	N	E	A	R
N	F	C		R	E	D	D	I		C	A	P	E	
E	L	I		A	V	I	S		M	A	H	R	E	S
S	A	N	D	P	I	T		N	I	L	E			
S	T	O	O	P	T	O		U	S	E	R	I	D	S
			P	E	E	R		T	R	U	S	T	I	N
R	I	S	E	R	S		S	M	U	T		S	S	E
E	N	O	S			F	E	E	L	S		N	E	E
A	L	L	T	H	E	R	A	G	E		B	O	A	Z
M	O	V	E	A	L	O	N	G		P	A	U	S	E
E	V	E	R	S	I	N	C	E		A	T	S	E	A
R	E	D	S	T	A	T	E	R		C	H	E	S	T

91

```
H O P S   I F F Y   S O N A R
O M I T M A U S   Q U A K E
H A P P Y P I L L   U N T I E
U N E   S E R S   S E C O N D
M I S T E R S O F T E E
  M O R T   M O O G   C A P
T R O T   I C E I C E B A B Y
Y O K O O N O   S K E E T E R
K N E E L E N G T H   A H S O
E A R   E N D O   O G R E
    J A C O B S L A D D E R
S E R E N E   E T D S   R N A
O L O R D   S L E E P M A S K
B L O K E   R O A R   S L U E
S A T Y R   O W L S   U S E D
```

92

```
S I S   E R M A   E B B E T S
I N T E R I O R   P E O R I A
A F R A I D O F T H E D A R K
M O I S T E N   R E V I S E S
    K E R R   G O D E L
S U E D E   C O U R S E P R O
U P S   A G A S S I   S E E M
S T O W   A S P E N   S A G A
H O U R   S T E R E O   R A N
I N T E G R A L S   V A L L I
    C L A N S   R E P O
S P O K A N E   S A R A N A C
C O M I N G T O A M E R I C A
T R A N C E   A V I A T O R S
V E R G E S   R E S T   N E T
```

93

```
S P O T   D A D A S   P L A Y
I O N A   E V I T A   R I C O
R E L I E (F A R M) Y   E T T U
S T O L L E N   S I P H O N
  (O P E N T) R A N S P O R T
I N K I N D   A G O N Y
S O O P A   O V E T T   H A H
A D U E   C A I R O   T A P E
Y E T   T A R O S   C A T E R
    C A M E L   J O K E R S
A H O U S E D I V I D E D
T O P E K A   C H A T T E L
T R E S   W A S (H A S H) O R E
I N R I   A V O I D   A G O G
C Y A N   Y E L P S   T O S S
```

94

```
K O P U N C H   G I G O L O S
I R O N O R E   E V I D E N T
P I T C R E W   T E N D S T O
S N L   D E E J A Y   S A H L
B O O T   D R U G   B E L
A C C R A   S S R S   U R G E
Y O K E L S   T I E O N E O N
    P O W E R P A C K
G O F I G U R E   T H E M G S
A V I D   M I L O   S P A R E
T E X   C A N S   T R E X
E R I N   S I X T U S   T A P
M A N A G E D   A L L R I S E
E G G R O L L   P L A I N E R
N E S C A F E   E A T D I R T
```

95

```
L U G S   F R A N C   S O S A
E L E A   L E V E L   A N A T
A T T N   I N I G O   T C B Y
S R T A   G E A R S   E E R O
H A H N   H E N I E   L I E U
    E T A T   D B L S
C O L O R A D O S P R I N G S
A T A N D T O P E R A T O R S
R O S I E T H E R I V E T E R
    T O N E   M O D E
H A L T   N A F T A   I N C A
I R A E   D R I E R   S O O N
D E U X   A D L A I   H U N G
I N G A   N O L T E   E G G S
N A H S   T R E S S   S H O T
```

96

S	T	R	E	S	S	T	E	S	T	S	■	P	A	L
I	H	A	V	E	N	O	I	D	E	A	■	A	C	E
F	O	R	E	W	A	R	N	I	N	G	■	L	I	S
T	R	I	■	E	G	O	S	■	■	G	O	O	D	S
E	N	T	E	R	■	■	S	P	Y	W	A	R	E	■
D	Y	E	S	■	B	I	W	A	■	E	L	A	N	■
■	■	P	A	G	A	N	I	N	I	■	T	I	S	■
■	C	O	N	C	E	N	T	R	A	T	I	O	N	■
W	O	N	■	H	O	T	E	L	M	A	N	■	■	■
O	M	E	N	■	D	A	L	Y	■	■	G	E	M	S
R	E	Q	U	I	E	M	■	■	D	E	C	O	Y	■
S	O	U	N	D	■	■	I	S	A	O	■	H	U	S
T	V	A	■	E	A	S	T	E	R	N	M	O	S	T
E	E	R	■	S	W	I	S	S	C	H	E	E	S	E
D	R	T	■	T	E	X	A	S	H	O	L	D	E	M

97

R	I	S	O	T	T	O	S	■	R	E	A	T	A	S
O	H	M	E	O	H	M	Y	■	E	C	Z	E	M	A
Y	O	A	D	R	I	A	N	■	P	A	T	E	N	T
G	P	S	■	■	E	N	O	W	■	R	E	B	E	C
B	E	H	A	L	F	■	N	E	E	D	C	A	S	H
I	S	E	R	E	■	S	Y	L	L	■	S	L	I	M
V	O	D	K	A	G	I	M	L	E	T	■	L	A	O
■	■	■	S	P	A	S	■	Y	N	E	Z	■	■	■
M	M	E	■	T	H	E	H	E	A	T	I	S	O	N
R	A	M	S	■	A	N	O	S	■	■	E	T	H	N	O
F	R	A	I	D	N	O	T	■	A	S	S	E	T	S
I	R	I	N	A	■	R	S	V	P	■	■	C	H	I
X	Y	L	E	N	E	■	H	I	N	D	E	R	E	R
I	M	E	A	N	T	■	O	N	E	S	P	A	D	E
T	E	D	D	Y	S	■	T	E	A	T	A	B	L	E

98

L	I	N	C	■	S	P	I	K	E	J	O	N	Z	E
O	N	E	O	■	M	I	N	I	S	E	R	I	E	S
A	D	E	N	■	U	N	I	T	P	R	I	C	E	S
D	I	D	N	T	G	E	T	■	G	E	E	S	E	■
■	S	L	O	W	L	Y	■	W	H	E	N	■	■	■
■	P	E	T	E	Y	■	G	A	U	N	T	L	E	T
D	O	N	E	E	■	Q	U	I	T	S	■	E	X	E
E	S	O	S	■	S	U	I	T	S	■	T	A	P	A
L	E	S	■	F	O	A	L	S	■	W	A	F	E	R
I	D	E	A	L	I	S	T	■	F	I	N	E	R	■
■	■	D	A	L	I	■	B	A	N	Z	A	I	■	■
S	A	G	E	T	■	F	R	I	G	A	T	E	S	■
W	I	N	E	C	O	O	L	E	R	■	N	I	N	E
A	D	A	M	A	N	D	E	V	E	■	I	N	C	A
N	E	W	S	R	E	A	D	E	R	■	A	G	E	S

99

S	Q	U	A	R	E	J	A	W	■	A	B	A	F	T
P	U	N	C	H	L	I	N	E	■	R	E	T	R	O
A	I	R	C	O	O	L	E	D	■	C	A	R	E	S
R	T	E	■	■	P	L	A	G	I	A	R	I	S	T
R	E	S	O	L	E	■	R	E	C	D	■	F	H	A
E	S	T	R	A	D	A	■	H	E	E	L	E	D	■
D	O	S	E	D	■	L	I	M	O	■	X	E	N	A
■	■	■	L	E	M	O	N	D	R	O	P	■	■	■
A	P	E	S	■	Y	E	T	I	■	P	E	A	C	E
L	I	N	E	A	L	■	■	I	B	E	R	I	A	N
A	K	C	■	D	A	L	I	■	A	N	T	R	I	M
B	E	H	A	V	I	O	R	A	L	■	■	T	R	A
A	M	A	T	I	■	P	A	R	T	I	S	A	N	S
M	A	I	M	S	■	E	Q	U	I	N	O	X	E	S
A	N	N	E	E	■	Z	I	N	C	O	X	I	D	E

100

S	M	A	S	H	E	R	O	O	■	D	E	C	O	R
N	O	F	O	O	L	I	N	G	■	A	G	A	P	E
I	N	F	I	E	L	D	E	R	■	D	O	M	E	S
P	R	I	G	■	■	M	E	S	S	T	E	N	T	■
P	O	R	N	O	■	R	O	S	E	■	R	I	T	A
Y	E	M	E	N	■	U	R	S	A	M	I	N	O	R
■	■	■	E	S	S	I	E	■	S	E	P	T	E	T
A	S	S	■	P	A	N	■	E	O	N	■	O	D	S
S	H	O	V	E	L	■	K	E	N	A	N	■	■	■
S	I	L	I	C	A	G	E	L	■	C	U	S	P	S
E	V	I	L	■	M	A	Y	S	■	E	T	H	A	N
M	A	C	L	E	I	S	H	■	■	C	O	R	E	■
B	R	I	A	R	■	B	O	N	A	P	A	R	T	E
L	E	T	G	O	■	A	L	A	B	A	S	T	E	R
Y	E	S	E	S	■	G	E	T	S	R	E	A	D	Y

101

```
T H E P O W E R S T H A T B E
A I R E D A L E T E R R I E R
C H I N E S E C A L E N D A R
H O S T S ■ V A N E ■ I A M S ■
■ ■ ■ D E P ■ ■ C E L S ■ ■ ■
A S L O P E ■ ■ H M O ■ ■ ■ ■
D E A D A S A D O O R N A I L
D E M O L I T I O N D E R B Y
A M E R I C A N T R O T T E R
■ ■ ■ S A D ■ ■ O N S I T E ■
■ R I C H ■ ■ T E E ■ ■ ■ ■ ■
G A P S ■ C L E M ■ C O O T E
I N A P P L E P I E O R D E R
G A S O L I N E L A N T E R N
I T S T O O D E E P F O R M E
```

102

```
■ G A M E ■ ■ D I E T S O D A
B E L I E D ■ O N C E A D A Y
O N E D G E ■ N O O N T I M E
X X X I ■ A T T N ■ N I N E ■
■ ■ ■ S L I P ■ M I N ■ ■ ■ ■
R O A D K I L L ■ A S Y L U M
I D E M A N D A R E ■ ■ E N O
L E I S ■ ■ E Y E ■ ■ O T I S
E T O ■ ■ E S W I T S W I T H
Y O U N M E ■ I N A S E N S E
■ ■ ■ O A R ■ T A B S ■ ■ ■ ■
G U N K ■ A H S O ■ ■ S K I M
P E R F E C T ■ ■ O N E I D A
E L L E R B E E ■ S O T T E D
A S S E S S E S ■ ■ ■ H E A D
```

103

```
C L A I R ■ ■ S P A T U L A S
H O W D O ■ T H A T S L I F E
A R A B Y ■ H I T B O T T O M
F A R R ■ F O R T A S ■ T R A
F L E A M A R K E T ■ G L E N
■ ■ C A S P E R ■ C R E S T ■
■ A V E R T E D ■ M A I T A I
G R I L L E S ■ B E N Z O I C
A G R E E D ■ B R O N Z E D ■
N E T T Y ■ G O A W O L ■ ■ ■
G N U S ■ V A R I E T Y A C T
E T O ■ G A R A N D ■ B R E W
D I S P A R A T E ■ J E T L I
U N O B L I G E D ■ O A S T S
P A S S A G E S ■ ■ T R Y S T
```

104

```
I N F I N I T E ■ N U M B E R
N O R S E M E N ■ O T E L L O
S P A R T A N S ■ H E R O E S
E L I A ■ C E N T I ■ M O V E
C A L E ■ S T A R T ■ A P A R
T C E L L ■ S R A ■ S I E T E
S E R I E S ■ E M B E D D E D
■ ■ ■ E T C ■ S A X ■ ■ ■ ■ ■
I N P E R S O N ■ R E D R A W
N O R M S ■ V I A ■ D E U C E
A T O P ■ B E R M S ■ E N C L
R A V E ■ E N V O I ■ P A R L
U S E R I D ■ A R T I S T E S
S T R O V E ■ N A U S E A T E
H E B R E W ■ A L P H A B E T
```

105

```
J O N S T E W A R T ■ M I Z E
A L O H A T O W E R ■ E N Y A
C D R O M D R I V E ■ D A Z S
K M A R T ■ D R E S S S I Z E
S A N T A S ■ E L S A ■ D Y S
O I D ■ M A J ■ ■ L E O V I
N D A K ■ B I G G E S T F A N
■ ■ ■ E G O M A N I A C ■ ■ ■
B I P A R T I S A N ■ H O P I
A D A N O ■ ■ W E B ■ P E N
R O Y ■ A M C S ■ N A D E R S
W O M E N S L I B ■ D A N S E
A D E N ■ D O N O T E N T E R
R I N D ■ O V E R A N D O U T
E T T E ■ S E X G O D D E S S
```

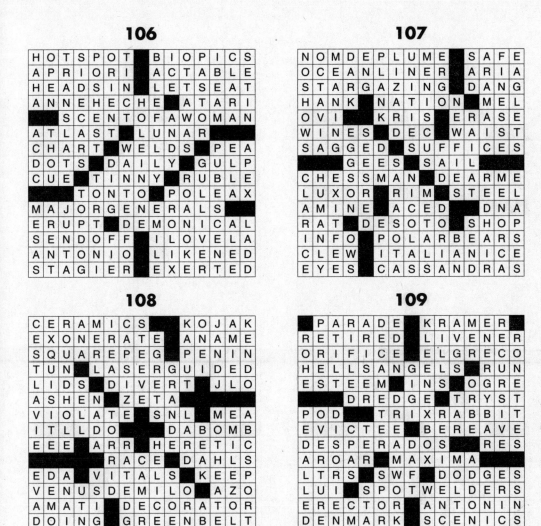

106

H	O	T	S	P	O	T		B	I	O	P	I	C	S
A	P	R	I	O	R	I		A	C	T	A	B	L	E
H	E	A	D	S	I	N		L	E	T	S	E	A	T
A	N	N	E	H	E	C	H	E		A	T	A	R	I
		S	C	E	N	T	O	F	A	W	O	M	A	N
A	T	L	A	S	T		L	U	N	A	R			
C	H	A	R	T		W	E	L	D	S		P	E	A
D	O	T	S		D	A	I	L	Y		G	U	L	P
C	U	E		T	I	N	N	Y		R	U	B	L	E
		T	O	N	T	O		P	O	L	E	A	X	
M	A	J	O	R	G	E	N	E	R	A	L	S		
E	R	U	P	T		D	E	M	O	N	I	C	A	L
S	E	N	D	O	F	F		I	L	O	V	E	L	A
A	N	T	O	N	I	O		L	I	K	E	N	E	D
S	T	A	G	I	E	R		E	X	E	R	T	E	D

107

N	O	M	D	E	P	L	U	M	E		S	A	F	E
O	C	E	A	N	L	I	N	E	R		A	R	I	A
S	T	A	R	G	A	Z	I	N	G		D	A	N	G
H	A	N	K		N	A	T	I	O	N		M	E	L
O	V	I		K	R	I	S		E	R	A	S	E	
W	I	N	E	S		D	E	C		W	A	I	S	T
S	A	G	G	E	D		S	U	F	F	I	C	E	S
		G	E	E	S		S	A	I	L				
C	H	E	S	S	M	A	N		D	E	A	R	M	E
L	U	X	O	R		R	I	M		S	T	E	E	L
A	M	I	N	E		A	C	E	D			D	N	A
R	A	T		D	E	S	O	T	O		S	H	O	P
I	N	F	O		P	O	L	A	R	B	E	A	R	S
C	L	E	W		I	T	A	L	I	A	N	I	C	E
E	Y	E	S		C	A	S	S	A	N	D	R	A	S

108

C	E	R	A	M	I	C	S		K	O	J	A	K
E	X	O	N	E	R	A	T	E		A	N	A	M	E
S	Q	U	A	R	E	P	E	G		P	E	N	I	N
T	U	N		L	A	S	E	R	G	U	I	D	E	D
L	I	D	S		D	I	V	E	R	T		J	L	O
A	S	H	E	N		Z	E	T	A					
V	I	O	L	A	T	E		S	N	L		M	E	A
I	T	L	L	D	O			D	A	B	O	M	B	
E	E	E		A	R	R		H	E	R	E	T	I	C
			R	A	C	E		D	A	H	L	S		
E	D	A		V	I	T	A	L	S		K	E	E	P
V	E	N	U	S	D	E	M	I	L	O		A	Z	O
A	M	A	T	I		D	E	C	O	R	A	T	O	R
D	O	I	N	G		G	R	E	E	N	B	E	L	T
E	S	S	E	N		A	S	S	O	O	N	A	S	

109

	P	A	R	A	D	E		K	R	A	M	E	R	
R	E	T	I	R	E	D		L	I	V	E	N	E	R
O	R	I	F	I	C	E		E	L	G	R	E	C	O
H	E	L	L	S	A	N	G	E	L	S		R	U	N
E	S	T	E	E	M		I	N	S		O	G	R	E
			D	R	E	D	G	E		T	R	Y	S	T
P	O	D		T	R	I	X	R	A	B	B	I	T	
E	V	I	C	T	E	E		B	E	R	E	A	V	E
D	E	S	P	E	R	A	D	O	S			R	E	S
A	R	O	A	R		M	A	X	I	M	A			
L	T	R	S		S	W	F		D	O	D	G	E	S
L	U	I		S	P	O	T	W	E	L	D	E	R	S
E	R	E	C	T	O	R		A	N	T	O	N	I	N
D	E	N	M	A	R	K		S	C	E	N	I	C	S
	S	T	I	N	K	S		P	E	R	S	I	A	

110

S	I	T	A	S	P	E	L	L		A	D	E	L	E
A	P	O	L	L	O	X	I	I		R	E	L	A	X
P	A	R	T	Y	G	I	R	L		M	A	C	Y	S
I	N	T			T	R	I	P	E		A	S	P	
D	A	S	A	N	I	S		S	O	D		P	A	O
		L	O	C		A	T	T		A	I	N	U	
S	T	R	A	T	E	G	I	C	R	O	U	T	E	S
W	H	E	N	I	W	A	S	Y	O	U	R	A	G	E
A	R	B	I	T	R	O	N	R	A	T	I	N	G	S
P	E	E	S		A	L	E		S	I	G			
S	A	L		A	P	B		A	T	E	A	L	O	T
E	D	A		A	S	R	E	D			A	Z	O	
A	K	R	O	N		E	L	D	E	S	T	S	O	N
T	I	M	I	D		A	L	L	S	E	E	I	N	G
S	T	Y	L	E		K	E	E	P	S	A	K	E	S

111

```
G O L D E N P A R A C H U T E
A N T O N I O B A N D E R A S
S O C I A L D E M O C R A T S
E N O S ■ ■ ■ I N S ■ O L E O
S E L ■ S C A D ■ A B S ■ ■ ■
■ ■ B A A ■ ■ I R A ■ A E S
F A M O U S L A S T W O R D S
A L E U T I A N I S L A N D S
K I T T E N O N T H E K E Y S
E T S ■ E O S ■ ■ O R S ■ ■
■ ■ C D S ■ ■ J E W S ■ P O S
C L E O ■ ■ Z I N ■ ■ B A T H
L E A V E S A B A D T A S T E
U N D E R T H E C O U N T E R
E A S T E R N S T A N D A R D
```

112

```
H O M E F R E E ■ D A Y S P A
O N A S L A N T ■ I M O N I T
G E T S A W A Y ■ R I B O S E
W H E A T ■ P I N S ■ W H A
A E R I F Y ■ E N D T I M E S
R A I S E U P ■ A L A M O D E
T R A ■ E N A M I ■ D U B ■
S T L O ■ G R A D S ■ S I G H
■ W S W ■ B L O C K ■ L O I
A G I T A T O ■ F O R C E P S
L E T E R R I P ■ P A R T O N
G O N ■ T E L E ■ M A R S H
O D E D O N ■ A N T E D A T E
R E S O R T ■ L I A R L I A R
E S S E N E ■ S E X S E L L S
```

113

```
J A C K B L A C K ■ E Q U U S
I N H E R I T O R ■ S U P P E
G A R G A N T U A ■ N E G R I
G T O ■ S E A R A C E ■ R I N
L O N G S ■ G A L A ■ E A V E
E M I L ■ B I G S P E N D E R
S Y C A M O R E ■ I C E R S
■ ■ Z E A L ■ R O N A ■ ■
U P P E D ■ F O R E S T E R
S H A R O N T A T E ■ E E R O
T O N S ■ B O S H ■ A D A N A
I N T ■ P A R T I A L ■ L E D
N E L L Y ■ P O R T L I E S T
O N E I L ■ I N A M O R A T A
V O G U E ■ D E S E R T F O X
```

114

```
H U S K E R S ■ A M I D S T
E X H I B I T A ■ M E T E O R
Y O U D A M A N ■ M O E S H A
D R T ■ Y E S D E A R ■ P A L
A I T S ■ S E R I N ■ C A V A
Y A L E U ■ S E E ■ A R I E L
S L E E V E ■ T I A M A R I A
■ ■ H U L K H O G A N ■ ■
W E R E L I V E ■ O H I O A N
O P E R A ■ A G R ■ L A N C E
B I L E ■ O S I E R ■ L E T O
E T A ■ I N S A L E S ■ T U G
G O T O L D ■ N O T A H O P E
O M E N I V ■ T A R R A G O N
N E S T E D ■ D O G G O N E
```

115

```
M O N I C A ■ R A M B L I N G
A N I M A S ■ I C E C A N O E
N I C E S T ■ G R A D U A T E
W O O ■ A I R H O L E ■ D I Z
E N T E ■ N U T S Y ■ T A M E
E D I N A ■ N O S ■ D W Y E R
K I N G S T O N T R I O ■ ■
S P E A K O F T H E D E V I L
■ ■ G U N T H E E N G I N E
S T R E P ■ H E W ■ O G R E S
W O E S ■ R E M A P ■ S T U S
O R A ■ S A M O Y E D ■ U R E
R E D R O B I N ■ S O S O O N
D U T I A B L E ■ T R O U P E
S P O O K I L Y ■ S E N S E D
```

116

```
T H I S J U S T I N   █ G A O L
W I N T E R T I D E   █ O L G A
I D O N T G E T I T   █ I L L S
G E N █ S E M I █ J E N N E T
█ █ S A S S █ L U I G I █
S I C E M █ C E D E █ G A B
I M A N █ S L U G G I S H L Y
G E T A C H A R G E O U T O F
M A S T E R K E Y S █ D E V A
A N C █ L I E D █ B A R E R
█ R A I N S █ M C A N █
A R A W A K █ B A L D █ O B J
C O D A █ A V E R A G E J O E
T A L K █ G O L D M E D A L S
S M E E █ E L L I P S O I D S
```

117

```
B A S K E T C A S E █ D E C O
O T H E R W O M A N █ A R O D
G A R A G E S A L E █ R U D D
A X E █ S E I S M █ W I P E S
R I D S █ D E S I █ I N T W O
T A S E R █ S E N D S █ I O C
█ █ R O Y █ S E A T W O R K
S C R U B U P █ O F F E N D S
C R I M E L A B █ T U B █
R E N █ S E L E S █ L E T B E
A N G L O █ M A M A █ R I L L
B E T O N █ T R E N D █ R A D
B L O G █ A R C A D E G A M E
L E N A █ D E A R R E A D E R
E D E N █ J E T S E T T E R S
```

118

```
R A B B I T S █ G A M E L A W
A Q U A R I A █ I N A P I L E
S U L T A N A █ B A T H T U B
P A R T N E R █ S C A R I N G
E T U I █ D I C O T █ A N S E
R I S E N █ N A N █ H I T E M
S C H R O D E R █ R U M O R S
█ █ M E N A C E R █ █
B A D M A N █ C O O L C A T S
E C R U S █ S A N █ S H I R T
L E S T █ T A S T Y █ A R E O
A R E A R U G █ R E P O M A N
Y O U T U B E █ A C E T A T E
E S S E N E S █ C C R I D E R
D E S S E R T █ T H E C A R S
```

119

```
M I D R I S E █ S S H A P E D
O R I O L E S █ T H E R A P Y
P A R T I A L █ R E F U G E E
S E E S A W █ S O I T G O E S
█ █ C O A C H K █ █
M A S T █ R D A S █ B E B O P
S T I R I T U P █ S O N O R A
D O R A T H E E X P L O R E R
O N E D A Y █ G R I D L O C K
S E D E R █ G O A D █ A N K A
█ █ P R A Y E D █ █
S C O P E O U T █ R E G R E T
L A N O L I N █ U M B R A G E
E R E L O N G █ P A R A G O N
W E B S I T E █ I N A F U N K
```

120

```
B A B A W A W A █ M I S A I M
O R A L E X A M █ O H E N R Y
N O T A B E N E █ S O C C E R
N U T S █ S T R E E P █ H S T
E S L █ █ T I N Y █ B O I L
T E E S █ P O C O █ V E R G E
█ S O N I A █ A L S O R A N S
█ █ F A S C I N A T I N G █
J E T P L A N E █ A D I E U
A S H O E █ G M C S █ E A S T
M I E N █ K O B E █ L S U
P A N █ A N D A L L █ H A T S
A S I A G O █ S I A M E S E S
C O L L E T █ S C H E N K E L
K N E A D S █ Y A R D S A L E
```

121

PASTINA SARALEE
ETHANOL CUTLASS
REAPTHEBENEFITS
MINEO RANT ADIA
STARWITNESS AMY
RIDS MASAI
BRIANENO HABITS
RINSING PERIDOT
ACTIVE CRITTERS
KEEFE AROS
EAR ALBERTVILLE
DRIP ASEA ISEEM
ROOSEVELTISLAND
UNRISEN ENTENTE
MISSORT STAYSON

122

BISHOPS BAPTIST
ANTESUP ALUNSER
THETHRILLISGONE
HOE AEROBES TEM
TULL RANON TYCO
USEAS LGA NEPAL
BEDSHEET MORESO
HASDIBSON
RAMONE MAUNALOA
ANOUK DER STAND
TINT TRACI EMER
AMI OREGANO PDA
TAKEMYWORDFORIT
ATEINTO TRIREME
TORSION SADEYES

123

IRONCHEF ASHARP
MONALISA TOILER
ELEVATOR MUSTDO
ALLAY STEPSONS
NOAII TRIM 3OP
INNO HIDE ABASE
TSE CEMENTMIXER
HMM AID
JOIEDEVIVRE MAR
UNGER ETAT IONE
SAN SSTS LVOV
TRIFECTA BLAME
NOTICE TAPASBAR
OPENON INKWELLS
WERENT EAGLEEYE

124

TAPS SWISSCHARD
HIRT WINECOOLER
AREA ANTARCTICA
LISTON EWOK BOW
INTEL BRAD GIRL
AGOODMANY GUIDO
FLUBS BASKET
STAMINA DUSTERS
TIMING BASTA
TRANE DOIHAVETO
HERD COBS NHLER
ODE BALD SKORTS
MOTHERLODE LORI
AUTODEALER SPAN
STOPSTREET TODO

125

ERAT DAYAN HAMM
NAME AIOLI OMOO
GRAPEFRUITSPOON
RANINTERFERENCE
ADO PERT THY
SEP KOOL AAH
PULLINGAFASTONE
IRAE COCOA MFOR
TONGUEDEPRESSOR
AON OSES UNS
UPC FEAR TAN
PLATINUMBLONDES
SENATORIALSEATS
EBAY LINED RYUN
TELE ACERS ASIS

126

```
C O S E T ■ ■ ■ L I E S T O
A P E X E S ■ E V A N S T O N
P E N P A L ■ M I S S P E L L
E N S U R E ■ E N T I R E L Y
L E O N I D ■ R E P T I L E ■
L A R G E S ■ G R O U T E R ■
A R I E S ■ L E I S ■ ■ ■ ■
■ S A R T R E ■ E T C H E R ■
■ ■ ■ A N D S ■ Y A X E S ■
■ A R C A D I A ■ S C R A P E
■ T E R R I E R ■ O L D M A N
C O L O R A N T ■ N E W I S H
E M I N E N C E ■ I C A N S O
S I N I S T E R ■ C A R E E R
S C E N T S ■ ■ R E E D S
```

127

```
S C A R E T A C T I C ■ L O M
C A M E R A P H O N E ■ A V A
A T A N I M P A S S E ■ K E G
M E L E E ■ E R S T ■ F E R N
P R I E ■ O N M E ■ W I S H I
I S E ■ I N D I S B E L I E F
■ ■ ■ S T E I N ■ O N E D A Y
■ M A T R I X ■ S O T T E D ■
S O L E I L ■ P I T A S ■ ■
T R A V E L L I G H T ■ O C S
A I R E D ■ I N N S ■ L S A T
I B M S ■ K O C H ■ G U A V A
N U I ■ O N T H E D O C K E T
E N S ■ D E T E R I O R A T E
D D T ■ S E A S E R P E N T S
```

128

```
S I L E N T X ■ A S T A R T E
T H E F O R E ■ T H R E E R S
D O G F O O D ■ T I E C L I P
E P I ■ P O O C H E S ■ E O N
N E R F ■ P U R E R ■ Y A L E
I S O L A ■ T A G ■ R E S E W
S O N A T A ■ T Y P E S E T S
■ ■ T E C H ■ M A H I ■ ■
R E N T A C O P ■ C A T N I P
O N E A M ■ K I X ■ B I O M E
S T A X ■ S K E G S ■ S T E R
A R R ■ P H A R A O H ■ U M P
R A P A N U I ■ M R A P R I L
I N A B I N D ■ E T I E N N E
O T R A N T O ■ S A M E S E X
```

129

```
S I M C I T Y ■ Q U I N T S
U N I O N R E P ■ A T N O O N
I T S A D E A L ■ N E X T T O
T H E T O Y ■ A D D ■ S O H O
E A R S ■ ■ O C T A D ■ F E Z
S T Y ■ M I R E S ■ E A T M E
■ ■ ■ T Y P E B ■ B E H E A D
■ S O P H O M O R E J I N X ■
T A N K E D ■ ■ E F L A T ■
W I P E R ■ O F D A Y ■ R O T
O L A ■ O L A F S ■ ■ C E D E
E B R O ■ E K E ■ B O R D E N
G O O D E N ■ C O E X I S T S
G A L O O T ■ T V R E M O T E
S T E R N O ■ A N N E X E D
```

130

```
T R I E D A C A S E ■ V A C A
D A I L Y D O Z E N ■ I D A S
S P I K E D H A I R ■ O A R S
■ ■ ■ O R I E L ■ O I L M E N
C A W ■ S C R E E N T E S T S
O P A H ■ T E A M ■ A T A ■
R I T E A I D ■ U N L I N K S
O P E N T O ■ ■ A I R D R Y
T E R R A N E ■ E M A I L E R
■ ■ C Y R ■ B C D E ■ S E M I
A T O M I C B O M B S ■ R E A
W H O O S H ■ P E R O N ■ ■
A R L O ■ A P P E A L E D T O
S E E R ■ D O E S N T W O R K
H E R E ■ S I D E D I S H E S
```

131

T	R	Y	I	T		E	M	A	G		P	L	O	T
N	O	O	N	E		L	A	T	E		L	O	N	E
U	S	U	A	L		D	I	E	T		A	V	E	R
T	H	A	T	S	S	O	L	A	S	T	Y	E	A	R
		N	I	T	E	R		M	I	R	A	C	L	E
H	I	D	E	A	W	A	Y		T	O	R	O		
E	B	W		R	U	D	E	R		T	E	N	O	N
N	E	H	I		P	O	L	E	S		A	Q	U	A
S	T	O	C	K		S	P	I	E	D		U	R	N
	S	A	I	L		S	T	T	E	R	E	S	A	
A	G	E	N	D	A	S		E	U	L	E	R		
W	H	A	T	S	Y	O	U	R	P	O	I	S	O	N
E	A	R	S		L	A	R	A		U	S	A	G	E
O	N	M	E		O	M	I	T		S	E	L	L	S
F	A	Y	E		W	I	S	E		E	R	L	E	S

132

I	C	K	F	A	C	T	O	R		S	A	H	I	B
C	E	L	L	P	H	O	N	E		E	C	O	N	O
E	Y	E	O	P	E	N	E	R		N	U	T	T	Y
A	L	P	E		R	E	S	U	L	T		H	E	C
G	O	T				D	O	N	E		B	O	R	O
E	N	O	S		D	E	C		F	L	A	U	N	T
			C	L	O	A	K		T	A	B	S	E	T
I	N	B	R	I	E	F		S	O	R	B	E	T	S
T	I	E	I	N	S		E	Q	U	A	L			
S	N	A	P	A	T		R	U	T		E	V	E	S
A	T	M	S		O	T	O	E			E	N	C	
D	E	E			Y	O	U	S	E	E		I	N	R	E
E	N	N	I	S		D	I	Z	Z	Y	D	E	A	N
A	D	D	L	E		O	V	E	R	S	L	E	P	T
L	O	S	E	R		R	E	D	A	L	E	R	T	S

133

S	C	A	M	S		G	L	A	D		C	O	M	A
P	U	R	E	E		R	O	B	E		A	U	L	D
I	T	I	N	A		O	N	L	Y	C	H	I	L	D
K	I	T	T	R	E	D	G	E		R	O	S	E	S
E	T	H	I	O	P	I	A		L	O	O			
	M	O	V	I	N	G	P	I	C	T	U	R	E	
T	H	E	N	E	T		O	A	K		S	N	I	T
R	O	T		R	H	O		D	E	F		A	G	A
E	M	I	T		E	S	P		W	O	M	B	A	T
S	E	C	R	E	T	A	D	M	I	R	E	R		
		A	L	S		J	U	S	T	M	I	S	S	
C	L	A	I	M		C	A	T	E	R	E	D	T	O
C	Y	C	L	O	R	A	M	A		E	N	G	E	L
E	R	T	E		E	V	E	N		S	T	E	N	T
D	E	E	R		F	E	S	T		S	O	D	O	I

134

Q	U	E	E	R	E	Y	E		M	A	R	C	E	L
U	P	I	N	A	R	M	S		A	P	E	R	C	U
A	N	N	E	R	I	C	E		D	O	T	E	L	L
			M	I	C	A		O	E	D	I	P	A	L
C	A	P	I	T	A		H	U	P		T	E	T	
H	A	L	E	Y		M	I	T	R	A	L			
I	R	A	S		M	I	S	S	O	R	E	G	O	N
L	O	N		R	U	N	S	O	U	T		U	N	E
I	N	T	H	E	F	I	E	L	D		G	R	O	W
			U	N	F	O	L	D		M	O	U	N	T
	F	A	R		I	N	F		R	A	I	S	E	S
P	O	L	L	E	N	S		T	E	N	N			
E	N	L	I	S	T		W	I	N	D	G	U	S	T
A	D	O	N	A	I		A	V	E	M	A	R	I	A
R	A	Y	G	U	N		D	O	E	S	T	I	M	E

135

S	P	O	R	T	S	B	R	A		E	L	I	H	U
W	I	N	E	T	H	I	E	F		T	E	N	O	N
O	P	E	N	O	R	D	E	R		S	I	L	L	S
R	E	B		P	E	E	N		B	E	S	I	D	E
E	D	Y	S		D	R	A	M	A	Q	U	E	E	N
T	O	O	L	E		S	C	A	B		R	U	N	T
O	W	N	E	R	S		T	R	I	B	E			
	N	E	E	D	E	D		V	E	R	S	E	S	
			P	E	P	U	P		S	A	U	N	A	S
C	C	V	I		I	N	I	T		T	I	T	L	E
R	A	I	N	M	A	K	E	R	S		T	I	E	S
O	M	E	G	A	S		R	O	A	R		C	S	T
W	E	N	C	H		D	R	I	V	E	T	I	M	E
D	I	N	A	R		P	O	K	E	F	U	N	A	T
S	N	A	R	E		S	T	A	R	S	I	G	N	S

136

```
T H R U █ S I C K A S A D O G
W E E P █ A T A N Y P R I C E
A L A S █ N A T U R A L G A S
S P R I N G L E T █ D E A L T
█ █ █ Z E R O S █ Y E N T A S
A S S I S I █ █ T O R E █ █
S A I N T A L B A N S █ T W O
H U N G █ O I L █ █ M O O N
E L K █ P R I N C E H A R R Y
█ █ █ F A U N █ █ V E R T E X
S P L I N T █ F L E A S █ █
T I A R A █ P A I N T B A L L
O P T I C N E R V E █ A L I A
O P E N H O U S E S █ R O A D
L A R G E P R I N T █ S P R Y
```

137

```
R E N T A C A R █ F L A W E D
O V E R R I C E █ I O D I N E
N O B I G G I E █ G U A R D S
A L B S █ A D D E N D █ E W E
L V I █ A R R I V E █ S T I R
D E S K S █ A N E W █ H A S T
█ S H I N D I G █ T A U P E S
█ █ T E R N █ W O R T █ █
C A S T R O █ C A N D I C E █
R A K E █ P R O S █ E N E R O
I M A N █ S I M I A N █ L A D
C I T █ S H T E T L █ S E S E
K L E P T O █ S Y L L A B U S
E N R O O T █ T O A S T E R S
T E S L A S █ O U T T O S E A
```

138

```
D E T R O I T M I C H I G A N
I T S A F R E E C O U N T R Y
M A K E A M E N T A L N O T E
E L S █ N A S █ U S C █ S E T
█ █ █ █ E S T E S █ █ █ █ █
A S T █ S T A N █ █ H A I M
C H A R L O T T E B R O N T E
T A K E I T O R L E A V E I T
A C E U P O N E S S L E E V E
S K I P █ █ E A S E █ L E D
█ █ S K E D S █ █ █ █ █ █
A M I █ I N E █ B A M █ A S U
S A T E L L I T E S T A T E S
A T E E N A G E R I N L O V E
S T A R S I N O N E S E Y E S
```

139

```
B R U T █ F E T A █ C L I V E
R O P E █ E T O N █ L I T E R
A T T N █ A U C T I O N E E R
G E O D E S I C █ S T E M S █
█ █ N E X T █ A L O H A █ █
A B O R T S █ T O L E R A N T
P A G E R █ B A R D S █ P I A
P R O R A T E █ R E H I R E S
L O O █ V A L S E █ O N I C E
E N D T A B L E █ B R A C E R
█ █ █ A G A I N █ E S T O █
█ B E H A R █ D E S E R T E D
P A L I N D R O M E █ I P S O
F R A N Z █ O F I T █ C I T E
C E L I A █ E F T S █ E T E S
```

140

```
B A N K G U A R D █ A L E R T
O N O N E S W A Y █ A I M E E
B O N E H E A D S █ A B A B A
S N E E R █ Y I P █ C R I E R
█ █ A L I T █ O H R E A L L Y
A N T I G E N █ E E L S █ █
M O A N █ N O R M A L █ M I L
B E L G █ S T O I C █ C E D E
I L L █ H I T E S T █ H M O S
█ █ R O T H █ M E L R O S E
N Y A H N Y A H █ D O O R █
B O G I E █ T O M █ S M A S H
O W E N S █ B U I L T I N T O
M I N O T █ A R T S T U D I O
B E T S Y █ D I T T O M A R K
```

141

J	I	L	L	S	T	J	O	H	N	■	E	D	A	M
O	R	E	O	C	O	O	K	I	E	■	C	O	P	E
C	O	T	T	O	N	E	D	T	O	■	H	O	P	I
K	N	I	T	T	E	D	■	■	S	P	O	R	E	S
E	S	T	■	T	R	I	P	P	■	A	I	M	A	T
Y	O	G	A	■	S	M	A	L	L	S	C	A	L	E
S	N	O	B	S	■	A	N	A	C	T	■	T	S	R
■	■	S	H	A	G	G	Y	D	O	G	■	■	■	■
T	A	E	■	A	L	G	A	E	■	R	E	W	E	T
H	I	G	H	F	L	I	E	R	S	■	E	R	N	E
E	R	G	O	T	■	O	A	S	T	S	■	I	C	E
A	C	R	O	S	S	■	■	C	R	O	P	T	O	P
T	O	O	K	■	P	U	L	L	I	N	H	E	R	E
R	O	L	E	■	A	N	O	U	K	A	I	M	E	E
E	L	L	Y	■	N	U	M	B	E	R	L	E	S	S

142

F	B	I	F	I	L	E	■	T	A	B	A	S	C	O
R	E	C	R	O	O	M	■	O	N	E	S	T	O	P
A	T	E	I	N	T	O	■	P	A	L	E	A	L	E
G	O	B	■	A	T	T	E	S	T	■	A	N	O	N
I	K	E	A	■	S	E	A	T	■	D	R	T		
L	E	E	R	S	■	D	R	O	P	■	A	T	T	O
E	N	R	O	O	T	■	T	R	U	E	L	O	V	E
■	■	■	M	U	R	P	H	Y	B	E	D	■	■	■
O	N	S	A	L	E	A	T	■	S	K	I	B	I	B
L	O	P	S	■	E	N	O	S	■	S	N	I	D	E
D	C	I	■	G	N	U	S	■	E	R	S	T		
P	O	N	D	■	S	L	E	E	P	S	■	D	A	W
R	U	N	U	P	T	O	■	D	E	A	D	E	Y	E
O	N	E	R	O	U	S	■	E	N	D	O	R	S	E
S	T	R	A	I	N	S	■	S	T	E	T	S	O	N

143

C	A	C	T	U	S	■	A	S	K	S	F	O	R
O	N	L	I	N	E	■	C	R	E	A	T	I	V	E
U	G	A	N	D	A	■	L	I	T	T	E	R	E	D
P	L	U	S	E	S	■	A	S	I	T	W	E	R	E
L	E	D	E	R	H	O	S	E	N	■	A	B	L	E
E	D	E	L	W	E	I	S	S	■	P	R	O	A	M
■	■	A	L	L	Y	■	T	O	D	A	Y	S		
■	R	A	T	T	L	Y	■	H	O	I	S	T	S	
M	E	L	E	E	S	■	V	E	I	N	■	■		
A	M	B	E	R	■	T	E	L	L	T	A	L	E	S
F	I	A	T	■	R	E	S	P	E	C	T	I	V	E
I	N	C	I	D	E	N	T	■	T	O	O	L	E	D
O	D	O	M	E	T	E	R	■	T	U	N	I	N	G
S	E	R	E	N	I	T	Y	■	E	N	C	A	S	E
O	R	E	S	T	E	S	■	S	T	E	N	O	S	

144

A	L	P	S	■	J	I	M	I	■	I	T	W	A	S
S	I	R	E	■	A	V	I	S	■	D	W	E	L	T
I	B	I	D	■	V	E	T	O	■	E	E	R	I	E
N	E	V	A	D	A	■	L	E	A	R	N	E	R	
I	R	A	N	I	■	T	A	D	A	■	P	E	N	N
N	A	T	■	S	P	I	N	E	T	S	■	R	E	L
E	L	E	P	H	A	N	T	■	D	O	N	K	E	Y
■	■	P	A	R	T	Y	A	N	I	M	A	L	■	■
M	O	R	T	A	R	■	C	A	R	E	B	E	A	R
A	V	A	■	G	O	T	I	N	T	O	■	M	C	A
C	E	C	E	■	N	A	D	A	■	N	A	P	E	S
A	R	T	L	E	S	S	■	B	E	R	E	T	S	
B	R	I	M	S	■	S	A	V	E	■	O	R	A	L
R	A	C	E	S	■	E	G	A	D	■	M	E	T	E
E	N	E	R	O	■	L	E	N	S	■	A	R	E	S

145

S	A	T	E	■	M	E	N	O	F	S	T	R	A	W
C	L	O	G	■	A	R	E	W	E	T	H	E	R	E
A	G	O	G	■	T	A	B	L	E	L	I	N	E	N
M	A	K	E	L	E	S	S	■	■	O	N	E	A	D
■	■	A	D	O	R	E	■	D	O	U	S	E	R	S
G	A	T	O	R	S	■	C	U	R	I	E	■	■	
O	M	A	N	I	■	R	A	R	E	S	T	E	A	K
B	O	X	■	T	E	N	A	M	■	■	A	C	E	
S	K	I	M	P	E	D	O	N	■	C	A	S	T	E
■	■	A	E	R	I	E	■	C	A	V	E	I	N	
C	O	P	L	A	N	D	■	T	O	N	I	O	■	
A	D	I	O	S	■	■	G	O	M	A	D	F	O	R
P	I	E	D	A	T	E	R	R	E	■	F	U	R	Y
O	U	T	O	N	A	L	I	M	B	■	A	S	E	A
S	M	A	R	T	M	O	N	E	Y	■	N	E	O	N

146

C	H	O	C	O	L	A	T	E	C	O	A	T	E	D
A	E	R	O	B	I	C	E	X	E	R	C	I	S	E
C	A	P	T	I	V	E	A	U	D	I	E	N	C	E
H	R	H		S	E	T	T	L	E	S		C	A	P
E	S	A	S		S	O	R	T	S		T	A	P	E
T	A	N	E	Y		N	O	S		L	I	N	E	N
S	Y	S	T	O	L	E	S		T	E	N	S	E	D
			T	U	B	S		E	E	N	Y			
M	E	T	E	R	S		S	T	R	A	T	E	G	O
A	L	I	E	N		M	I	A		S	I	R	E	N
S	A	L	S		S	I	N	G	S		M	E	T	A
C	P	L		C	O	N	C	E	A	L		M	E	L
A	S	A	N	A	L	T	E	R	N	A	T	I	V	E
R	E	G	I	S	T	E	R	E	D	V	O	T	E	R
A	D	E	L	A	I	D	E	S	L	A	M	E	N	T

147

M	A	N	T	R	A	P	S		S	K	I	M	P	S
I	V	E	H	A	D	I	T		O	N	H	I	R	E
N	O	S	E	C	O	N	E		R	I	O	T	E	D
I	N	T	H	E	R	E	D		E	S	P	O	S	A
O	L	E	O		N	A	M	A	T	H		S	I	T
N	E	R	T	S		L	A	S	H		C	I	D	E
S	A	S	S	E	D		N	E	U	R	O	S	E	S
			E	A	R	S		A	M	O	R			
L	I	S	A	L	O	E	B		B	A	R	C	A	R
U	N	I	T		M	A	L	I		N	E	H	R	U
M	E	L		L	E	M	O	N	S		L	A	M	S
B	R	I	G	I	D		W	H	O	C	A	R	E	S
A	R	C	A	N	A		P	A	L	A	T	I	N	E
G	O	O	V	E	R		O	L	I	V	E	O	I	L
O	R	N	E	R	Y		P	E	D	E	S	T	A	L

148

P	E	R	C	H	E	S		S	T	A	B	L	E	D
O	N	A	L	A	R	K		C	R	A	Y	O	L	A
M	C	G	U	I	R	E		H	A	N	O	V	E	R
E	Y	E	B	R	O	W		O	L	D	B	E	A	N
			C	C	L		S	O	A	P				
M	A	G	O	O		H	E	L	L		N	A	P	S
I	C	O	U	L	D	E	A	T	A	H	O	R	S	E
C	O	R	P	O	R	A	T	E	L	A	D	D	E	R
R	O	G	E	R	O	V	E	R	A	N	D	O	U	T
O	L	E	S		P	E	R	M		G	I	R	D	S
			F	A	N	S		M	O	N				
A	N	N	U	A	L	S		N	O	U	G	A	T	S
B	E	A	S	T	I	E		E	S	T	O	N	I	A
C	A	P	E	A	N	N		S	H	A	F	T	E	D
S	T	A	R	L	E	T		S	E	T	F	I	R	E

149

M	E	C	H		S	H	E	A	F		D	R	U	B
O	L	I	O		H	E	L	G	A		V	E	N	A
M	E	A	T	M	A	R	K	E	T		O	T	I	S
A	V	O	C	A	D	O		R	E	W	R	I	T	E
			H	Y	E	N	A		L	I	A	R		
S	A	H	I	B	S		T	R	I	N	K	E	T	S
A	T	A	L	E		S	T	A	N	D		M	R	I
V	A	N	I	L	L	A	I	C	E	C	R	E	A	M
E	R	G		L	O	I	R	E		H	O	N	D	O
D	I	S	C	I	P	L	E		L	I	S	T	E	N
			H	O	N	E		S	L	I	M	S		
T	H	E	R	E	A	T		O	N	E	E	Y	E	D
H	E	A	T		R	H	I	N	E	S	T	O	N	E
E	A	V	E		E	A	T	E	N		T	U	T	U
O	R	Y	X		D	I	O	R	S		I	D	O	S

150

A	R	C	H		B	A	T	T	E	R		G	A	P
M	A	L	E		U	R	S	U	L	A		A	V	A
A	G	E	D		S	E	A	B	I	S	C	U	I	T
S	T	A	G		H	A	R	M		H	O	G	A	N
S	I	N	E	W	Y		S	A	C		M	U	T	E
E	M	E	R	I	T	I		N	A	P	P	I	E	S
D	E	R		T	A	B	S		T	R	E	N	D	S
			W	H	I	M	S	I	C	A	L			
R	A	C	H	E	L		A	S	H	Y		D	A	S
A	D	H	E	R	E	S		M	A	E	W	E	S	T
D	U	A	L		D	A	H		F	R	A	P	P	E
I	L	I	A	D		T	A	P	E		S	L	I	P
C	A	N	N	E	R	Y	R	O	W		T	O	R	I
A	T	E		L	O	R	E	N	Z		E	R	I	N
L	E	D		L	O	S	S	E	S		D	E	N	S

The New York Times

Crossword Puzzles

The #1 name in crosswords

Available at your local bookstore or online at nytimes.com/nytstore

St. Martin's Griffin